palgrave advances in global governance

Palgrave Advances

Titles include:

Michele M. Betsill, Kathryn Hochstetler and Dimitris Stevis (*editors*)
INTERNATIONAL ENVIRONMENTAL POLITICS

Terrell Carver and James Martin (*editors*)
CONTINENTAL POLITICAL THOUGHT

Michelle Cini and Angela K. Bourne (*editors*)
EUROPEAN UNION STUDIES

Jeffrey Haynes (*editor*)
DEVELOPMENT STUDIES

Jim Whitman (*editor*)
GLOBAL GOVERNANCE

Palgrave Advances
Series Standing Order ISBN 978–1–4039–3512–0 (Hardback)
Series Standing Order ISBN 978–1–4039–3513–7 (Paperback)
(*outside North America only*)

You can receive future titles in this series as they are published by placing a standing order. Please contact your bookseller or, in case of difficulty, write to us at the address below with your name and address, the title of the series and the ISBNs quoted above.

Customer Services Department, Macmillan Distribution Ltd, Houndmills, Basingstoke, Hampshire RG21 6XS, England

palgrave advances in global governance

edited by

jim whitman
department of peace studies
university of bradford, uk

palgrave
macmillan

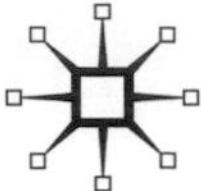

First published 2009 by
PALGRAVE MACMILLAN

Palgrave Macmillan in the UK is an imprint of Macmillan Publishers Limited, registered in England, company number 785998, of Houndmills, Basingstoke, Hampshire RG21 6XS.

Palgrave Macmillan in the US is a division of St Martin's Press LLC, 175 Fifth Avenue, New York, NY 10010.

PALGRAVE MACMILLAN is the global academic imprint of the above companies and has companies and representatives throughout the world.
Palgrave® and Macmillan® are registered trademarks in the United States, the United Kingdom, Europe and other countries.

ISBN: 978–0–230–20165–1 hardback
ISBN: 978–0–230–20166–8 paperback

This book is printed on paper suitable for recycling and made from fully managed and sustained forest sources. Logging, pulping and manufacturing processes are expected to conform to the environmental regulations of the country of origin.

A catalogue record for this book is available from the British Library.
A catalog record for this book is available from the Library of Congress.

10 9 8 7 6 5 4 3 2 1
18 17 16 15 14 13 12 11 10 09

Printed and bound in Great Britain by
CPI Antony Rowe, Chippenham and Eastbourne

contents

preface and acknowledgements

When the report of the Commission on Global Governance appeared in 1995, the term 'global governance' had already been in circulation for a number of years, thanks to the work of forward-looking scholars who were fascinated with the global dimensions of both order and turbulence; with the growing evidence that the principal contours of planetary stability and sustainability were not the preserve of states and the international system; and by the evidence that the global qualities of the human condition suggested a nascent global politics as much as a global arena. In the same year as the Commission's report, James Rosenau published a seminal article, 'Global Governance in the Twenty-first Century,' in the inaugural issue of the journal *Global Governance*. That article not only consolidated much of the disparate work on global governance up to that point, but also set out the themes which have proved to be such a reliable guide to the most pertinent 'who, what, and how?' global governance questions. It has proved rich in primary insights for both theorists and for those with more empirical and issue-specific concerns.

I am very grateful to Professor Rosenau for allowing his original article to be reprinted here as Chapter 1 and for providing the Introduction to this collection. The title of his Introduction, 'Global Governance or Global Governances?' carries a double meaning. The first is a recognition now well-established in the global governance literature: That in its summative form, the term 'global governance' can be employed to depict the overall order of the world – the outcome of innumerable governances of varying degrees of inclusiveness, legitimacy and effectiveness. The second – global governances plural – not only acknowledges our attempts to regulate sector-specific forms of human activity on a global scale (trade, finance) or the regulation of global conditions (the planetary environment, health), but also that the actors, mechanisms, goals and outcomes of global governance are not detached and technocratic, but are intensely political.

This book is thematic, with an emphasis on developed understandings of global governance as a mode of political action – that is, as forms of steering, regulating and controlling. There are no chapter-length sectoral studies; instead, the contributors cite specific structures, actors or instances for illustrative purposes. Chapter 2, 'Actors, Arenas and Issues in Global Governance', by Klaus Dingwerth and Philipp Pattberg, complements and updates James Rosenau's foundational work and provides a particularly clear and well-delineated outline of the scope of current global governance scholarship. The central chapters each present a perspective on global governance as a form of activity in which the actors and structures also have meaning beyond dedicated, functional governance roles. The purpose of the book is to bridge the more theoretical studies of global governance and those devoted to specific issues. My hope is that a wider appreciation of the global dynamics, porous boundaries, rapid reconfigurations of identities and allegiances and the intensification of all forms of human relatedness that are now shaping our world will draw more scholars into work on global governance, whatever their primary disciplinary perspective.

Doubtless there are those who view the field of global governance as a minor tributary of International Relations; and still others who regard it as an interesting but largely abstract approach to world politics and human security. However, as the second year of global financial turbulence threatens to develop from recession to depression, it is difficult to view the concerted actions of states, international organizations and private companies to stave off the worst possibilities as anything other than a form of global governance – albeit belated and rectificatory. Yet there was little in the extensive literature on the global governance of finance before 2008 which suggested that the complexities, electronically mediated risk-taking and tight coupling between financial actors at every level around the world had resulted in a system of systems both unstable and unsustainable. As part of conceiving and enacting forms of global governance that will diminish the present turbulence, we must, of course, confront the deficiencies of what passed as adequate global ordering and regulation in this field. But at the same time, all scholars engaged in the study of global governance, whatever their particular focus, might well consider the implications of the credit crunch and its aftermath for global governance studies. In a world so intensely globalized and on unsustainable environmental trajectories, it is hardly plausible to suppose that recent events require only a wholesale reconsideration of what does or should comprise the effective governance of global finance.

In their particulars at least, the prospects for global governance at the end of the first decade of the twenty-first century are not what we could have discerned at its threshold; and for the immediate future, the challenges will tax more than what James Rosenau described as 'one's appreciation of nuance and one's tolerance of ambiguity' – much as those though will continue to feature. But James Rosenau's willingness to engage with a remarkable range of troubling, disquieting and surprising features of the human drama – fully, imaginatively and with analytical acuity – remain an inspiration to all of us who have joined him in this enterprise.

My sincere thanks to the contributors to this volume, all of whom have many pressing calls on their time and energies, despite which all were enthusiastically committed to this project and greatly reduced the editorial tasks that usually go with such an undertaking. I would also like to acknowledge that Chapter 1, written by James N. Rosenau, first appeared in *Global Governance: A Review of Multilateralism and International Organizations*, Vol. 1, No. 1, Copyright © 1995 by Lynne Rienner Publishers, Inc., used with permission of the publisher.

list of abbreviations

AIDS	Acquired Immunodeficiency Syndrome
APEC	Asia-Pacific Economic Cooperation
BBC	British Broadcasting Corporation
CAS	Court of Arbitration for Sports
CDO	Collateralized Debt Obligation
CEO	Chief Executive Officer
CFA	Chartered Financial Analyst
CHIPS	Clearing House Interbank Payments System
CICC	Coalition for an International Criminal Court
CNN	Cable News Network
CSO	Civil Society Organization
DFID	Department for International Development
DRC	Democratic Republic of the Congo
ECLAC	Economic Commission for Latin America and the Caribbean
ECOMOG	Economic Community of West African States Cease-fire Monitoring Group
ECOWAS	Economic Community of West African States
EEB	European Environmental Bureau
EU	European Union
FAO	Food and Agriculture Organization
FDI	Foreign Direct Investment
FIFA	Federation of International Football Associations
FSC	Forest Stewardship Council
GEF	Global Environmental Facility
GEMS	Global Environmental Monitoring Scheme

GLOBE	Global Legislators Organization for a Balanced Environment
GOARN	Global Outbreak and Alert Response Network
GTZ	Deutsche Gesellschaft für Technische Zusammenarbeit
HIV	Human Immunodeficiency Virus
IBRD	International Bank for Reconstruction and Development
IAEA	International Atomic Energy Agency
ICANN	International Corporation for Assigned Names and Numbers
ICBL	International Campaign to Ban of Landmines
ICCA	International Council of Chemical Associations
ICRC	International Committee of the Red Cross
IFAC	International Federation of Accountants
IFBWW	International Federation of Building and Wood Workers
IGO	International Governmental Organization
IMF	International Monetary Fund
INGO	International Non-Governmental Organization
IO	International Organization
IOC	International Olympic Committee
IPCC	Intergovernmental Panel on Climate Change
IR	International Relations
ISAB	International Accounting Standards Board
ISO	International Organization for Standardization
IUCN	World Conservation Union
MAD	Mutual Assured Destruction
MUNS	Multlateralism and the United Nations System
NAFTA	North American Free Trade Agreement
NATO	North Atlantic Treaty Organization
NGO	Non-Governmental Organization
NPT	Nuclear Non-Proliferation Treaty
NSA	Non-State Organization
OCHA	United Nations Office for the Coordination of Humanitarian Affairs
NTA	New Transatlantic Agenda
ODA	Official Development Aid
OECD	Organization for Economic Cooperation and Development
ONUCA	UN Observer Group in Central America
PPP	Public-Private Partnership
S&P	Standard & Poor
SALW	Small Arms and Light Weapons
SARS	Severe Acute Respiratory Syndrome

SLAPP	Strategic Lawsuit against Public Participation
TCO	Transnational Criminal Organizations
TNC	Transnational Corporation
TRIPS	Trade-Related Aspects of Intellectual Property Rights
TSMO	Transnational Social Movement Organizations
UN	United Nations
UNDP	United Nations Development Program
UNEP	United Nations Environment Program
UNICEF	United Nations Children's Fund
UNIDROIT	International Institute for the Unification of Private Law
UNIFEM	United Nations Development Fund for Women
US	United States
USPTO	United States Patent and Trademark Office
USSR	Union of the Soviet Socialist Republics
WADA	World Anti-Doping Agency
WFP	World Food Program
WHO	World Health Organization
WMD	Weapon of Mass Destruction
WMO	World Meteorological Organization
WTO	World Trade Organization
WWF	World Wildlife Fund

notes on contributors

Klaus Dingwerth is Assistant Professor for International Relations at the University of Bremen, Germany and a Senior Researcher with the international Global Governance Project (glogov.org). For the Global Governance Project, he coordinates the activities of the research group MecGlo – New Mechanisms of Global Governance. His publications include *The New Transnationalism: Transnational Governance and Democratic Legitimacy* (Palgrave Macmillan, 2007).

Jörg Friedrichs is University Lecturer at the University of Oxford. He combines a theoretical interest in global governance, international relations and political sociology with an empirical focus on the transformation of the monopoly of force, international security and the impact of external resource shocks.

Annelies Z. Kamran is a PhD Candidate in Political Science at the City University of New York's Graduate Center. Her dissertation, 'The Structure of Transnational Security Networks,' combines her interests in social network analysis, international security and global governance. Her previous publications include *U.S. Government: An Interactive Approach* (2005) and *Civics: An Interactive Approach* (2008). She is Senior Editor for Content at WorldView Software, in Hicksville, New York.

W. Andy Knight is Professor of International Relations at the University of Alberta and Director of the Peace and Post Conflict Studies Certificate Programme in the Office of Interdisciplinary Studies (OIS). In March 2007, Dr Knight was appointed by the Canadian Foreign Minister to the Board of Governors of the International Development Research Centre (IDRC). He co-edited the international journal, *Global Governance*, from

2000 to 2005, was Vice Chair of the Academic Council on the United Nations System (ACUNS) and is currently a member of the Board of Directors of the John Humphrey Centre for Peace and Human Rights, the Canadian Association for Security and Intelligence Studies (CASIS), the Canadian Consortium for Peace Studies (CCPS) and the Education for Peace Academic and Research Council (EPARC). Professor Knight has written and edited several books, book chapters and journal articles on various aspects of multilateralism, global governance and peace and United Nations reform. His most recent books are *Adapting the United Nations to a Postmodern Era: Lessons Learned* and *Building Sustainable Peace.*

Philipp Pattberg is a Senior Researcher at the Institute for Environmental Studies (IVM), VU Amsterdam, and an Assistant Professor for International Relations at the Department of Political Science, VU Amsterdam. He is also the research coordinator of the international Global Governance Project (glogov.org). His publications include *Private Institutions and Global Governance: The New Politics of Environmental Sustainability* (Edward Elgar, 2007).

Tony Porter is Professor of Political Science at McMaster University in Hamilton, Canada. His research has focused on the regulation and self-regulation of international business. He is the author of *Globalization and Finance* (Polity Press, 2005), *Technology, Governance and Political Conflict in International Industries* (Routledge, 2002) and *States, Markets, and Regimes in Global Finance* (Macmillan, 1993). He is the co-editor, with A. Claire Cutler and Virginia Haufler, of *Private Authority in International Affairs*, (SUNY Press, 1999), and co-editor, with Karsten Ronit, of *The Challenges of Global Business Authority: Democratic Renewal, Stalemate, or Decay?* (SUNY Press, forthcoming).

James N. Rosenau is University Professor of International Affairs, Elliott School of International Affairs, The George Washington University. His extensive writing on global governance includes a number of seminal works, including *Along the Domestic-Foreign Frontier: Exploring Governance in a Turbulent World* (Cambridge University Press, 1997) and *Distant Proximities: Dynamics beyond Globalization* (Princeton University Press, 2003). His most recent book is *People Count! The Networked Individual in World Politics* (Paradigm Publishers, 2007).

Julia Steets is Associate Director of the Global Public Policy Institute (GPPi). Her areas of expertise include global governance, development, networks and partnerships, strategy and evaluation, as well as corporate social responsibility. Julia completed her PhD studies in social science at the University of Erfurt and holds a MSc in History of International Relations from the London School of Economics (LSE) and a Master of Public Administration (MPA) from the Kennedy School of Government, Harvard University, where she was a McCloy Scholar. Prior to joining GPPi as a project manager in 2004, Julia was a program manager at the Körber Foundation's Bergedorf Round Table in Berlin, a consultant with Transparency International's London office as well as an election observer for the OSCE. Julia's publications include *Partnership Accountability: Defining Accountability Standards for Public Policy Partnerships* (forthcoming), *Partnerships for Sustainable Development: On the Road to Implementation* (Berlin, 2006), *Waltz, Jazz or Samba? The Contribution of Locally Driven Partnerships to Sustainable Development* (Berlin, 2005), and *Palästina* (Munich 2001 and 2004, co-authored with Dietmar Herz). Julia has taught at the universities of Bonn and Greifswald and at Berlin's Humboldt University.

Thomas G. Weiss is Presidential Professor of Political Science at The CUNY Graduate Center and Director of the Ralph Bunche Institute for International Studies, where he is co-director of the UN Intellectual History Project. He is President (2008–9) of the International Studies Association, chair (2007–9) of the Academic Council on the UN System (ACUNS) and was awarded the Grand Prix Humanitaire de France 2006. He has been a consultant for foundations and numerous intergovernmental and non- governmental organizations and was editor of Global Governance (2000–5) and research director of the International Commission on Intervention and State Sovereignty (2000–2).

Jim Whitman is a Senior Lecturer in the Department of Peace Studies, University of Bradford, and general editor of the Palgrave *Global Issues* series. His latest books are *The Fundamentals of Global Governance* (Palgrave) and (with Sarah Perrigo, eds), *The Geneva Conventions Under Assault* (Pluto Press).

introduction
global governance or global governances?

james n. rosenau

There is no dearth of governance on a global scale today. Rather, it is structured differently in different parts of the world and in different issue areas, resulting in a plethora of governances. Some analysts argue that there are locales in the world that can be called ungoverned spaces,[1] locales where there is no authority and thus cannot be exercised. This is a misguided line of reasoning. It is more appropriate to contend that there are innumerable centers of authority because the world has moved into an era in which individuals have become paramount and are heeding their own values and impulses, thus serving as their own authority and rendering centralized governance more difficult. More accurately, the emergent era is marked by a wide disaggregation of authority, with networked individuals who think and act in conjunction with others apart from the constraints of formal governmental structures centrally located.

Individuals have become paramount actors mainly because of the Internet and its capacity to link them to others in remote parts of the world. The resulting networks enable individuals to interact and to convey ideas and pictures as well as facts and pictures to places where they have not been before. As a result, people are no longer locked into the circumstances endured by their forefathers. They are now freer to let their minds and families roam widely across long-standing barriers to movement and travel. Among the consequences of their enhanced freedom, people are increasingly inclined to converge, to form organizations, and thereby to pursue their goals collectively.

The jet airplane enables people to move about widely and quickly, to visit family and friends as well as implement tasks associated with their organizations and businesses. It is hardly surprising, therefore, that conflicts have arisen between those who are on the move and governments that want to constrain the flow of people to what are regarded as reasonable levels. A good measure of this flow can be seen in a US State Department estimate that, in 2007, seventeen million people would apply for passport applications.[2] An equally good measure of the efforts of governments to contain the flow is evident in the US plan to build a 28-mile virtual – that is, radar – fence along the US-Mexican and US-Canadian borders designed to catch illegal immigrants who enter the country on foot.[3]

In short, our time can well be characterized as the age of the 'networked individual' – what I like to call the individual revolution – a time that is also marked by another central tendency, the 'organizational explosion'. Taken together, these two dynamics account for an increasing obsolescence of boundaries and an extensive proliferation of centers of authority. The latter process involves groups forming and formalizing such that they have memberships and procedural rules that distinguish them from nonmembers. Their members share the values from which their group derives its existence and coherence as well as setting them apart from other groups or the public in general. However informal their rules may be, such groups are organizations that press for the realization of their goals. In so doing, they advance the goals of the individuals who joined them, thus inextricably linking the individual revolution and the organizational explosion.

Their networking serves as a stimulus to involvement in the course of events. It provides the information as well as the confidence that encourages them to be active in and reflect upon public affairs. Often as small as two people, their networks are flexible, allowing them to share ideas and insights freely and fully. No less important, these networks contribute to the organizational explosion that has swept the world in recent decades. Everywhere, in every country, and every part of the world, new organizations are forming and long-standing ones are growing.

In Pakistan, today, for example, there is an organization of car thieves: it has a publication and convenes annual meetings.[4] One could readily argue that if car thieves can formally organize, then such a development can occur in any realm of human activity. Indeed, that is exactly what marks the global scene today. It is crowded with myriad organizations, each pushing for its own goals, sometimes cooperatively with other organizations and sometimes through conflict with them.

An even more compelling illustration of the emerging era of the individual is provided by the cover of the December 25, 2006/January 1, 2007 issue of *Time* magazine. It offers a shiny rectangular material that serves as a mirror in which one can see an image of oneself. The caption accompanying the picture indicates what one sees when looking in the mirror: 'YOU. Yes, you. You control the Information Age, Welcome to your world.'

It is precisely because of the diverse places in which people are networked that complexity has come to pervade the world scene. With the centers of authority shifting away from governments and toward individuals and other nongovernmental organizations, an ever-greater degree of complexity marks the affairs of communities. What had been coherent patterns of daily life are now less orderly.

In short, with all the independent-minded people and diverse organizations that have climbed onto the global stage, the world is increasingly messy. Yes, a number of global institutions have evolved as a means of controlling and reducing the messiness, but these are by no means sufficient to generate a desirable degree of order. People have become so used to the messiness that it is taken for granted, even ignored.

Given disorderly circumstances, it is hardly surprising that uniform patterns do not mark the ways in which the various centers of authority regulate their affairs and exercise their authority. The multiple governances differ substantially in their goals, methods, and effectiveness. Some seek to achieve compliance exclusively through persuasion; others rely on the threat or use of coercion. Most governance structures employ a combination of, so to speak, the carrot and the stick. In some situations they clash with others, whereas in other situations they cooperate and collectively work on shared problems.

What does the messiness of governance structures, the incoherence of divisive lines of authority, portend for global stability and effectiveness? Is the disarray sufficient to inhibit, even prevent, effective efforts to address problems and resolve differences? Can governance policies circumvent the pitfalls posed by the incoherence of the structures through which they must be implemented? Even though in need of qualification, a positive response to the last question is appropriate. Messiness in governance is not new. On the contrary, it is a condition inherent in any attempt to generate a modicum of order on our disparate and diffuse circumstances. Countries, societies, and communities are composed of diverse groups separated by social and economic distances as well as large physical space. No less important, many groups are at odds with each other and on occasion inclined to resort to physical force.

The more centers of authority proliferate, the less is any one country or group of countries likely to dominate the course of events. A disaggregated global system poses severe problems in terms of its capacity to confront coherently both internal and external challenges. The proliferation highlights the necessity of governance even as it makes governance more difficult. Among other things, proliferating authority centers are likely to lessen the legitimacy and accountability of each center, rendering them more dependent on what unfolds elsewhere in the world.

In short, a system of multiple governances is fragile and vulnerable, ever susceptible to changing circumstances. Such a system can effectively sustain a limited number of significant actors. Beyond that limit, intense reactions may be fostered as different actors converge or contest for scarce resources.

compliance and complexity

Clearly, the concept of compliance is central to any analysis of individuals and their roles in the context of global governance. At a time of protest marches, of pervasive rallies and public upheavals, the question of how and when authority gets exercised and the extent to which its exercise generates compliance on the part of those toward whom it is directed is always problematic. Outcomes of compliance-mobilizing efforts are uncertain because many, perhaps most, individuals are not prepared to submerge their individuality to mass behavior. Their sense of personhood is such that they want to maintain their identity apart from others. Thus their reactions to attempts to mobilize their compliance can be marked by considerable variability.

Furthermore, given a multiplicity of governances, there are bound to be a variety of forms of compliance. The more hierarchical the form of governance, the more are the requests for compliance likely to take the form of demands, whereas the more democratic the form, the greater will be the variability of the ways in which the responding actors comply.

For attempts to achieve compliance, a high degree of complexity must be overcome by the mobilizers. Communities, societies, and the world at large are marked by extensive messiness, by overlapping jurisdictions, by deviant actors, and a host of other factors that intrude to undermine responsiveness to mobilizing efforts. Success in generating desired responses out of such circumstances is bound to be limited, possibly even bordering on failure. As previously noted, people are wary of mobilizers, fearful that hidden agendas are at work that will run counter to their interests. More often than not, in fact, such mobilizing attempts are likely to fall short of their goals and to generate skepticism on the part of their targets, or even outright resistance.

In recent years, the concept of complexity has come to signify more than a vague label attached to situations that are difficult to comprehend. A number of observers have developed elaborate formulations of the concept.[5] At the core of complexity theory is the complex adaptive system – not a cluster of unrelated activities, but a system; not a simple system but a complex one; and not a static, unchanging set of arrangements but a complex adaptive system. Such a system is distinguished by a set of interrelated parts, each one of which is potentially capable of being an autonomous agent that, through acting autonomously, can impact on the others, and all of which either engage in patterned behavior as they sustain day-to-day routines or break with the routines when new challenges require new responses and new patterns. The interrelationships of the agents are what make the system. The capacity of the agents to break with routines and thus initiate unfamiliar feedback processes is what makes the system complex (since in a simple system all the agents consistently act in prescribed ways). The capacity of the agents to cope collectively with the new challenges is what makes the system adaptive.[6]

exercising authority in complex systems

The tasks of governance are, obviously, greater the more complex the system over which authority is exercised. The channels through which compliance is sought are more circuitous and more pervaded with obstacles than is the case for straightforward requests for cooperation. Equally, the same individuals tend to occupy roles in a variety of diverse systems, thus increasing the difficulties of reaching them with mobilization efforts. Or, if they are contacted through several mobilizing efforts, the redundancy may put them off. Their readiness to respond to authority can be fragile if they feel they are merely names on lists used for mass mailings. However, the system's complexity may require seeking to mobilize them through several channels.

Of course, individuals differ in their attitudes toward authority and their readiness to be mobilized. Their collective response may thus be marked by a high degree of variability. Some will be immediately compliant and others will be initially resistant. Mobilizers thus need to be patient and to adjust to the inclinations of those who are the focus of their efforts. Flexibility is a central feature of effective mobilizers. The more open they are to unexpected reactions, the more are they likely to accomplish their goals. If they tend to be rigid and unyielding in their ways, they are likely to give the targets of their efforts an opening to resist and avoid.

Nevertheless, however they respond to authority and attempts to evoke their compliance, individuals are difficult to anticipate. A realm of uncertainty in which their reactions to mobilizing efforts may fluctuate widely, making it impossible to generalize about the potential of any attempt to evoke their responses. Much depends on their affiliations. Those who are members of tightly knit organizations that seek to concert their actions are likely to comply without much prior contemplation or resistance. But those for whom compliance is never a given are likely to be dubious about the intent of mobilizers. Such persons may not respond even if the exercised authority is legitimate and reasonable.

In sum, whatever form global governance may take, it is bound to be pervaded with uncertainties and surprises. It takes two, the governors and the governed, to govern, and they may well have different concerns and goals, thus generating friction in their relationship. Indeed, it is not far-fetched to conclude that successful governance is not easily accomplished and needs continual attention for problems to be addressed and resolved.

notes

1. I recently attended a conference sponsored by the Monterrey Institute of Graduate Studies devoted to the subject of 'Ungoverned Spaces.'
2. Jacqueline Palank, 'State dept. expands staffing to handle passport backlog,' *New York Times*, 20 June 2007, p. A17.
3. Randal C. Archibold, '28-mile virtual fence is rising along the border,' *New York Times*, 26 June 2007, p. A12. See also Ian Austen, 'Quebec and Vermont Towns bond over a sleepy border,' *New York Times*, 18 July 2007, p. A4.
4. *Far Eastern Economic Review*, Vol. 161, 19 March 1998), p. 34.
5. An early and still useful formulation can be found in M. Mitchell Waldrop, *Complexity: The Emerging Science at the Edge of Order and Chaos* (New York: Simon & Schuster, 1992).
6. For an elaboration of the complexity concept, see James N. Rosenau, *Distant Proximities: Dynamics beyond Globalization* (Princeton: Princeton University Press, 2003), chapter, 9.

1
governance in the twenty-first century

james n. rosenau

To anticipate the prospects for global governance in the decades ahead is to discern powerful tensions, profound contradictions, and perplexing paradoxes. It is to search for order in disorder, for coherence in contradiction, and for continuity in change. It is to confront processes that mask both growth and decay. It is to look for authorities that are obscure, boundaries that are in flux, and systems of rule that are emergent. And it is to experience hope embedded in despair.

This is not to imply that the task is impossible. Quite to the contrary, one can discern patterns of governance that are likely to proliferate, others that are likely to attenuate, and still others that are likely to endure as they always have. No, the task is not so much impossible as it is a challenge to one's appreciation of nuance and one's tolerance of ambiguity.

conceptual nuances

To grasp the complexities that pervade world politics, we need to start by drawing a nuanced set of distinctions among the numerous processes and structures that fall within the purview of global governance. Importantly, it is necessary to clarify that global governance refers to more than the formal institutions and organizations through which the management of international affairs is or is not sustained. The United Nations system and national governments are surely central to the conduct of global governance, but they are only part of the full picture. Or at least in this analysis global governance is conceived to include systems of rule at all levels of human activity – from the family to the international organization – in which the pursuit of goals through the exercise of control has transnational repercussions. The reason for this broad formulation is simple: in an evermore interdependent world where what happens in one corner or at one level may have consequences for what occurs at every other corner and level, it seems a mistake to adhere to a narrow definition in which only formal institutions at the national and international levels are considered relevant. In the words of the Council of Rome,

> We use the term governance to denote the command mechanism of a social system and its actions that endeavor to provide security, prosperity, coherence, order and continuity to the system.... Taken broadly, the concept of governance should not be restricted to the national and international systems but should be used in relation to regional, provincial and local governments as well as to other social systems such as education and the military, to private enterprises and even to the microcosm of the family.[1]

Governance, in other words, not only encompasses the activities of governments, but it also includes the many other channels through which 'commands' flow in the form of goals framed, directives issued, and policies pursued.

command and control

But the concept of commands can be misleading. It implies that hierarchy, perhaps even authoritarian rule, characterizes governance systems. Such an implication may be descriptive of many forms of governance, but hierarchy is certainly not a necessary prerequisite to the framing of goals, the issuing of directives, and the pursuit of policies. Indeed, a central theme of this analysis is that often the practices and institutions of governance can and do evolve in such a way as to be minimally dependent on hierarchical, command-based arrangements. Accordingly, while preserving the core of the Council of Rome formulation, here we shall replace the notion of command mechanisms with the concept of control or steering mechanisms, terms that highlight the purposeful nature of governance without presuming the presence of hierarchy. They are terms, moreover, informed by the etymological roots of governance: the term 'derives from the Greek "kybenan" and "kybernetes" which means "to steer" and "pilot or helmsman" respectively (the same Greek root from which 'cybernetics' is derived). The process of governance is the process whereby an organization or society steers itself, and the dynamics of communication and control are central to that process.'[2]

To grasp the concept of control one has to appreciate that it consists of relational phenomena that, taken holistically, constitute systems of rule. Some actors, the controllers, seek to modify the behavior and/or orientations of other actors, the controllees, and the resulting patterns of interaction between the former and the latter can properly be viewed as a system of rule sustained by one or another form of control. It does not matter whether the controllees resist or comply with the efforts of controllers; in either event, attempts at control have been undertaken. But it is not until the attempts become increasingly successful and compliance with them increasingly patterned that a system of rule founded on mechanisms of control can be said to have evolved. Rule systems and control mechanisms, in other words, are founded on a modicum of regularity, a form of recurrent behavior that systematically links the efforts of controllers to the compliance of controllees through either formal or informal channels.[3]

It follows that systems of rule can be maintained and their controls successfully and consistently exerted even in the absence of established legal or political authority. The evolution of intersubjective consensuses based on shared fates and common histories, the possession of information and knowledge, the pressure of active or mobilizable publics, and/or the use of careful planning, good timing, clever manipulation, and hard bargaining can – either separately or in combination – foster control mechanisms that sustain governance without government.[4]

interdependence and proliferation

Implicit in the broad conception of governance as control mechanisms is a premise that interdependence involves not only flows of control, consequence, and causation within systems, but that it also sustains flows across systems. These micro-macro processes – the dynamics whereby values and behaviors at one level get converted into outcomes at more encompassing levels, outcomes that in turn get converted into still other consequences at still more encompassing levels – suggest that global governance knows no boundaries – geographic, social, cultural, economic, or political. If major changes occur in the structure of families, if individual greed proliferates at the expense of social consciences, if people become more analytically skillful, if crime grips neighborhoods, if schools fail to provoke the curiosity of children, if racial or religious prejudices become pervasive, if the drug trade starts distributing its illicit goods through licit channels, if defiance comes to vie with compliance as characteristic responses to authority, if new trading partners are established, if labor and environmental groups in different countries form cross-border coalitions, if cities begin to conduct their own foreign commercial policies – to mention only some of the more conspicuous present-day dynamics – then the consequences of such developments will ripple across and fan out within provincial, regional, national, and international levels as well as across and within local communities. Such is the crazy-quilt nature of modern interdependence. And such is the staggering challenge of global governance.

The challenge continues to intensify as control mechanisms proliferate at a breathtaking rate. For not only has the number of UN members risen from 51 in 1945 to 184 a half-century later, but the density of non-governmental organizations (NGOs) has increased at a comparable pace. More accurately, it has increased at a rate comparable to the continuing growth of the world's population beyond five billion and a projected eight billion in 2025. More and more people, that is, need to concert their actions to cope with the challenges and opportunities of daily life, thus giving rise to more and more organizations to satisfy their needs and wants. Indeed, since the needs and wants of people are most effectively expressed through organized action, the organizational explosion of our time is no less consequential than the population explosion. Hastened by dynamic technologies that have shrunk social, economic, political, and geographic distances and thereby rendered the world evermore interdependent, expanded by the advent of new global challenges such as those posed by a deteriorating environment, an AIDS epidemic, and drug trafficking, and further stimulated by widespread authority crises within existing governance mechanisms, the proliferation of organizations is pervasive at and across all levels of human activity – from neighborhood organizations, community groups, regional networks, national states, and transnational regimes to international systems.

Not only is global life marked by a density of populations but it is also dense with organized activities, thereby complicating and extending the processes of global governance. For while organizations provide decision points through which the steering mechanisms of governance can be carried forward, so may they operate as sources of opposition to any institutions and policies designed to facilitate governance. Put in still another way, if it is the case, as many (including myself) argue, that global life late in the twentieth century is more complex than ever before in history, it is because the world is host to ever greater numbers of organizations in all walks of life and in every corner of every continent. And it is this complexity, along with the competitive impulses that lead some organizations to defy steerage and resort to violence, that makes the tasks of governance at once so difficult and so daunting.

disaggregation and innovation

An obvious but major conceptual premise follows from the foregoing: There is no single organizing principle on which global governance rests, no emergent order around which communities and nations are likely to converge. Global governance is the sum of myriad – literally millions of – control mechanisms driven by different histories, goals, structures, and processes. Perhaps every mechanism shares a history, culture, and structure with a few others, but there are no characteristics or attributes common to all mechanisms. This means that any attempt to assess the dynamics of global governance will perforce have multiple dimensions, that any effort to trace a hierarchical structure of authority that loosely links disparate sources of governance to each other is bound to fail. In terms of governance, the world is too disaggregated for grand logics that postulate a measure of global coherence.

In other words, the continuing disaggregation that has followed the end of the Cold War suggests a further extension of the anarchic structures that have long pervaded world politics. If it was possible to presume that the absence of hierarchy and an ultimate authority signified the presence of anarchy during the era of hegemonic leadership and superpower competition, such a characterization of global governance is all the more pertinent today. Indeed, it might well be observed that a new form of anarchy has evolved in the current period – one that involves not only the absence of a highest authority but that also encompasses such an extensive disaggregation of authority as to allow for much greater flexibility, innovation, and experimentation in the development and application of new control mechanisms.

In sum, while politicians and pundits may speak confidently or longingly about establishing a new world order, such a concept is meaningful only as it relates to the prevention or containment of large-scale violence and war. It is not a concept that can be used synonomously with global governance if by the latter is meant the vast numbers of rule systems that have been caught up in the proliferating networks of an evermore interdependent world.

emergence and evolution

Underlying the growing complexity and continuing disaggregation of modern governance are the obvious but often ignored dynamics of change wherein control mechanisms emerge out of path-dependent conditions and then pass through lengthy processes of either evolution and maturation or decline and demise. To acquire the legitimacy and support they need to endure, successful mechanisms of governance are more likely to evolve out of bottom-up than top-down processes. As such, mechanisms that manage to evoke the consent of the governed are self-organizing systems, steering arrangements that develop through the shared needs of groups and the presence of developments that conduce to the generation and acceptance of shared instruments of control.

But there is no magic in the dynamics of self-organization. Governance does not just suddenly happen. Circumstances have to be suitable, people have to be amenable to collective decisions being made, tendencies toward organization have to develop, habits of cooperation have to evolve, and a readiness not to impede the processes of emergence and evolution has to persist. The proliferation of organizations and their ever greater interdependence may stimulate felt needs for new forms of governance, but the transformation of those needs into established and institutionalized control mechanisms is never automatic and can be marked by a volatility that consumes long stretches of time. Yet at each stage of the transformation, some form of governance can be said to exist, with a preponderance of the control mechanisms at any moment evolving somewhere in the middle of a continuum that runs from nascent to fully institutionalized mechanisms, from informal modes of framing goals, issuing directives, and pursuing policies to formal instruments of decision making, conflict resolution, and resource allocation.

In other words, no matter how institutionalized rule systems may be, governance is not a constant in these turbulent and disaggregated times. It is, rather, in a continuous process of evolution, a becoming that fluctuates between order and disorder as conditions change and emergent properties consolidate and solidify. To analyze governance by freezing it in time is to ensure failure in comprehending its nature and vagaries.

the relocation of authority

Notwithstanding the evolutionary dynamics of control mechanisms and the absence of an overall structural order, it is possible to identify pockets of coherence operating at different levels and in different parts of the world that can serve as bases for assessing the contours of global governance in the future. It may be the case that 'processes of governance at the global level are inherently more fragile, contingent, and unevenly experienced than is the case within most national political systems',[5] but this is not to deny the presence of central tendencies. One such tendency involves an 'upsurge in the collective capacity to govern': despite the rapid pace of ever greater complexity and decentralization – and to some extent because of their exponential dynamics – the world is undergoing 'a remarkable expansion of collective power', an expansion that is highly disaggregated and unfolds unevenly but that nevertheless amounts to a development of rule systems 'that have become (1) more intensive in their permeation of daily life, (2) more permanent over time, (3) more extensive over space, (4) larger in size, (5) wider in functional scope, (6) more constitutionally differentiated, and (7) more bureaucratic'.[6] Global governance in the twenty-first century may not take the form of a single world order, but it will not be lacking in activities designed to bring a measure of coherence to the multitude of jurisdictions that is proliferating on the world stage.

Perhaps even more important, a pervasive tendency can be identified in which major shifts in the location of authority and the site of control mechanisms are under way on every continent and in every country, shifts that are as pronounced in economic and social systems as they are in political systems. Indeed, in some cases the shifts have transferred authority away from the political realm and into the economic and social realms even as in still other instances the shifts occur in the opposite direction.

Partly these shifts have been facilitated by the end of the Cold War and the lifting of the constraints inherent in its bipolar global structure of superpower competition. Partly they have been driven by a search for new, more effective forms of political organization better suited to the turbulent circumstances that have evolved with the shrinking of the world by dynamic technologies. Partly they have been driven by the skill revolution that has enabled citizens to identify more clearly their needs and wants as well as to empower them more thoroughly to engage in collective action. Partly they have been stimulated and sustained by 'subgroupism' – the fragmenting and coalescing of groups into new organizational entities – that has created innumerable new sites from which authority can emerge and to ward which it can gravitate. Partly they have been driven by the continuing globalization of national and local economies that has undermined long-established ways of sustaining commercial and financial relations. And, no less, the shifts have been accelerated by the advent of interdependence is sues – such as environmental pollution, AIDS, monetary crises, and the drug trade – that have fostered new and intensified forms of transnational collaboration as well as new social movements that are serving as transnational voices for change.

In short, the numerous shifts in the loci of governance stem from interactive tensions whereby processes of globalization and localization are simultaneously unfolding on a worldwide scale. In some situations these foregoing dynamics are fostering control mechanisms that extend beyond national boundaries, and in others the need for the psychological comfort of neighborhood or ethnic attachments is leading to the diminution of national entities and the formation or extension of local mechanisms. The combined effect of the simultaneity of these contradictory trends is that of lessening the capacities for governance located at the level of sovereign states and national societies. Much governance will doubtless continue to be sustained by states and their governments initiating and implementing policies in the context of their legal frameworks – and in some instances national governments are likely to work out arrangements for joint governance with rule systems at other levels – but the effectiveness of their policies is likely to be undermined by the proliferation of emergent control mechanisms both within and outside their jurisdictions. In the words of one analyst, 'The very high levels of interdependence and vulnerability stimulated by technological change now necessitate new forms of global political authority and even governance.'[7]

Put more emphatically, perhaps the most significant pattern discernible in the crisscrossing flow of transformed authority involves processes of bifurcation whereby control mechanisms at national levels are, in varying degrees, yielding space to both more encompassing and narrower, less comprehensive forms of governance. For analytic purposes, we shall refer to the former as transnational governance mechanisms and the latter as subnational governance mechanisms, terms that do not preclude institutionalized governmental mechanisms but that allow for the large degree to which our concern is with dynamic and evolving processes rather than with the routinized procedures of national governments.

While transnational and subnational mechanisms differ in the extent of their links across national boundaries – all the former are by definition boundary – spanning forms of control, while some of the latter may not extend beyond the jurisdiction of their states – both types must face the same challenges to governance. Both must deal with a rapidly changing, evermore complex world in which people, information, goods, and ideas are in continuous motion and thus endlessly reconfiguring social, economic, and political horizons. Both are confronted with the instabilities and disorder that derive from resource shortages, budgetary constraints, ethnic rivalries, unemployment, and incipient or real inflation. Both must contend with the ever greater relevance of scientific findings and the epistemic communities that form around those findings. Both are subject to the continuous tensions that spring from the inroads of corrupt practices, organized crime, and restless publics that have little use for politics and politicians. Both must cope with pressures for further fragmentation of subgroups on the one hand and for more extensive transnational links on the other. Both types of mechanisms, in short, have severe adaptive problems and, given the fragility of their legal status and the lack of long-standing habits of support for them, many of both types may fail to maintain their essential structures intact. Global governance, it seems reasonable to anticipate, is likely to consist of proliferating mechanisms that fluctuate between bare survival and increasing institutionalization, between considerable chaos and widening degrees of order.

mechanisms of global governance

Steering mechanisms are spurred into existence through several channels: through the sponsorship of states, through the efforts of actors other than states at the transnational or subnational levels, or through states and other types of actors jointly sponsoring the formation of rule systems. They can also be differentiated by their location on the aforementioned continuum that ranges from full institutionalization on the one hand to nascent processes of rule making and compliance on the other. Although extremes on a continuum, the institutionalized and nascent types of control mechanisms can be causally linked through evolutionary processes. It is possible to trace at least two generic routes that link the degree to which transnational governance mechanisms are institutionalized and the sources that sponsor those developments. One route is the direct, top-down process wherein states create new institutional structures and impose them on the course of events. A second is much more circuitous and involves an indirect, bottom-up process of evolutionary stages wherein nascent dynamics of rule making are sponsored by publics or economies that experience a need for repeated interactions that foster habits and attitudes of cooperation, which in turn generate organizational activities that eventually get transformed into institutionalized control mechanisms. Stated more generally, whatever their sponsorship, the institutionalized mechanisms tend to be marked by explicit hierarchical structures, whereas those at the nascent end of the continuum develop more subtly as a consequence of emergent interaction patterns which, unintentionally, culminate in fledgling control mechanisms for newly formed or transformed systems.

Table 1.1 offers examples of the rule systems derivable from a combination of the several types of sponsors and the two extremes on the continuum, a matrix that suggests the considerable variety and complexity out of which the processes of global governance evolve. In the table, moreover, are hints of the developmental processes whereby nascent mechanisms become institutionalized: as indicated by the arrows, some of the control mechanisms located in the right-hand cells have their origins in the corresponding left-hand cells as interdependence issues that generate pressures from the nongovernmental world for intergovernmental cooperation which, in turn, lead to the formation of issue-based transnational institutions. The history of more than a few control mechanisms charged with addressing

Table 1.1 The sponsorship and institutionalization of control mechanisms

	Nascent		**Institutionalized**
Transnational	* Nongovernmental organizations * Social movements * Epistemic communities * Multinational corporations	Social movements → European Environmental Bureau	* Internet * European Environmental Bureau * credit rating agencies
Not-State sponsored			
Subnational	* Ethnic minorities * Microregions * Cities	Ethnic minorities → American Jewish Lobby; Ethnic minorities → The Greek Lobby	* American Jewish Lobby * The Greek Lobby * Crime Syndicates
State sponsored	* Macroregions * European community * GATT	European community → European Union; GATT → World Trade Organization	* United Nations System * European Union * World Trade Organization
Jointly sponsored	* Cross-Border coalitions * Issue regimes	Issue regimes → Human Rights Regime	* Election Monitoring * Human Rights Regime

environmental problems exemplifies how this subtle evolutionary path can be traversed.

However they originate, and at whatever pace they evolve, transnational governance mechanisms tend to be essentially forward-looking. They may be propelled by dissatisfactions over existing (national or subnational) arrangements, but their evolution is likely to be marked less by despair over the past and present than by hope for the future, by expectations that an expansion beyond existing boundaries will draw upon cooperative impulses that may serve to meet challenges and fill lacunae that would otherwise be left unattended. To be sure, globalizing dynamics tend to create resistance and opposition, since any expansion of governance is bound to be detrimental to those who have a stake in the status quo. Whether they are explicitly and formally designed or subtly and informally constructed; however, transnational systems of governance tend on balance to evolve in a context of hope and progress, a sense of breakthrough, an appreciation that old problems can be circumvented and moved toward either the verge of resolution or the edge of obsolescence. But relatively speaking, subnational mechanisms are usually (though not always) energized by despair, by frustration with existing systems that seems best offset by contracting the scope of governance, by a sense that large-scale cooperation has not worked and that new subgroup arrangements are bound to be more satisfying. That distinction between transnational and subnational governance mechanisms can, of course, be overstated, but it does suggest that the delicacies of global governance at subnational levels may be greater than those at transnational levels.

To highlight the variety of forms transnational governance may take in the twenty-first century, the following discussion focuses on examples listed in Table 1.1. Due to space limitations, only some of the listed examples are subjected to analysis, and even the discussion of those is far from exhaustive. But hopefully both the table and its elaboration convey a sense of the degree to which global governance is likely to become increasingly pervasive and disaggregated in the years ahead.

transnational nascent control mechanisms

private volunteer and profit-making organizations

Irrespective of whether they are volunteer or profit-making organizations, and quite apart from whether their structures are confined to one country or span several, NGOs may serve as the basis for, or actually become, nascent forms of transnational governance. Why? Because in an evermore interdependent world, the need for control mechanisms outstrips the capacity or readiness of national governments to provide them. There are various types of situations in which governments fear involvement will be counterproductive, or where they lack the will or ability to intrude their presence. (And, as noted below, there are numerous circumstances where governments find it expedient to participate in rule systems jointly with organizations from the private sector.)

Put more specifically, just as at the local level 'community associations are taking over more of the functions of municipal governments',[8] and just as in diplomatic situations distinguished individuals from the private sector are called upon when assessments are made that assert, in effect, that 'I don't think any governments wanted to get involved in this,'[9] so are NGOs of all kinds to be found as the central actors in the deliberations of control mechanisms relevant to their spheres of activity. Whether the deliberations involve the generation and allocation of relief supplies in disaster situations around the world or the framing of norms of conduct for trade relationships – to mention only two of the more conspicuous spheres in which transnational governance occurs – volunteer associations or business corporations may make the crucial decisions. In the case of alliances fashioned within and among multinational corporations, for example, it has been found that 'transnational actors, unlike purely domestic ones, have the organizational and informational resources necessary to construct private alternatives to governmental accords'.[10] And even if only a small proportion of NGOs preside over steering mechanisms, their contribution to global governance looms as substantial when it is appreciated that more than 17,000 international nongovernmental organizations (INGOs) in the nonprofit sector were active in the mid-1980s and that in excess of 35,000 transnational corporations with some 150,000 foreign subsidiaries were operating in 1990.[11]

Furthermore, in their activities both volunteer and profit-making organizations are not unmindful of their role in nascent control mechanisms. That can be discerned in the charters of the former and in the public pronouncements of the latter. An especially clear-cut expression along this line was made by the chairman and CEO of the Coca-Cola Company: '[F]our prevailing forces-the preeminence of democratic capitalism, the desire for self-determination, the shift in influence from regulation to investment, and the success of institutions which meet the needs of people-reinforced by today's worldwide communications and dramatic television images, ... all point to a fundamental shift in global power. To be candid, I believe this shift will lead to a future in which the institutions with the most influence by-and-large will be businesses.'[12]

social movements

Much less structured but no less important, social movements have evolved as wellsprings of global governance in recent decades. Indeed, they are perhaps the quintessential case of nascent control mechanisms that have the potential to develop into institutionalized instruments of governance. Their nascency is conspicuous: they have no definite memberships or authority structures; they consist of as many people, as much territory, and as many issues as seem appropriate to the people involved; they have no central headquarters and are spread across numerous locales; and they are all-inclusive, excluding no one and embracing anyone who wishes to be part of the movement. More often than not, social movements are organized around a salient set of issues – like those that highlight the concerns of feminists, environmentalists, or peace activists – and as such, they serve transnational needs that cannot be filled by national governments, organized domestic groups, or private firms. Social movements are thus constituent parts of the globalizing process. They contribute importantly to the noneconomic fabric of ties facilitated by the new communications and transportation technologies. They pick up the pieces, so to speak, that states and businesses leave in their wake by their boundary-crossing activities. Just as the peace movement focuses on the consequences of state interactions, for example, so has the ecological movement become preoccupied with the developmental excesses of transnational corporations. Put even more strongly, 'The point about these antisystemic movements is that they often elude the traditional categories of nation, state, and class. They articulate new ways of experiencing life, a new attitude to time and space, a new sense of history and identity.'[13]

Despite the lack of structural constraints that allow for their growth, however, social movements may not remain permanently inchoate and nascent. At those times when the issues of concern to their members climb high on the global agenda, they may begin to evolve at least temporary organizational arrangements through which to move toward their goals. The International Nestlé Boycott Committee is illustrative in this regard: it organized a seven-year international boycott of Nestlé products and then it was dismantled when the Nestlé Company complied with its demands. In some instances, moreover, the organizational expression of a movement's aspirations can develop enduring features. Fearful that the development of organizational structures might curb their spontaneity, some movement members might be aghast at the prospect of formalized procedures, explicit rules, and specific role assignments, but clearly the march toward goals requires organizational coherence at some point. Thus have transnational social movement organizations (TSMOs) begun to dot the global landscape. Oxfam and Amnesty International are two examples among many that could be cited of movement spin-offs that have evolved toward the institutionalized extreme of the continuum. The European Environmental Bureau (EEB), founded in 1974, has moved less rapidly toward that extreme, but it now has a full-time staff quartered in a Brussels office and shows signs of becoming permanent as the environmental movement matures.[14]

subnational nascent mechanisms: cities and microregions

The concept of regions, both the macro and micro variety, has become increasingly relevant to the processes of global governance. Although originally connotative of territorial space, it is a concept that has evolved as a residual category encompassing those new patterns of interaction that span established political boundaries and at the same time remain within a delimited geographic space. If that space embraces two or more national economies, it can be called a macroregion, whereas a space that spans two or more subnational economies constitutes a microregion.[15] As can be inferred from Table 1.1, both types of regions can emerge out of bottom-up processes and thus evolve out of economic foundations into political institutions. This evolutionary potential makes it 'difficult to work with precise definitions. We cannot define regions because they define themselves by evolving from objective, but dormant, to subjective, active existence'.[16]

Abstract and elusive as it may be, however, the notion of micro and macroregions as residual categories for control mechanisms that span conventional boundaries serves to highlight important features of transnational governance. In the case of microregions, it calls attention to the emergent role of certain cities and 'natural' economic zones as subtle and nascent forms of transnational rule systems that are not sponsored by states and that, instead, emerge out of the activities of other types of actors – which at least initially may foster a relocation of authority from the political to the economic realm. To be sure, some microregions may span conventional boundaries within a single state and thus be more logically treated as instances of subnational control mechanisms, but such a distinction is not drawn here because many such regions are, as noted in the ensuing paragraphs, transnational in scope. Indeed, since they 'are interlinked processes',[17] it is conceivable that the evolution of microregions contributes to the emergence of macroregions, and vice versa.

An insightful example along these lines is provided by the developments that have flowed from the success of a cooperation pact signed in1988 by Lyon, Milan, Stuttgart, and Barcelona, developments that have led one analyst to observe that 'a resurrection of "city states" and regions is quietly transforming Europe's political and economic landscape, diminishing the influence of national governments and redrawing the continental map of power for the 21st century'.[18] All four cities and their surrounding regions have an infrastructure and location that are more suited to the changes at work in Europe. They are attracting huge investments and enjoying a prosperity that has led to new demands for greater autonomy. Some argue that, as a result, the emerging urban centers and economies are fostering 'a new historical dynamism that will ultimately transform the political structure of Europe by creating a new kind of "Hanseatic League" that consists of thriving city-states'.[19] One specialist forecasts that there will be 19 cities with at least 20 million people in the greater metropolitan area by the year 2,000, with the result that 'cities, not nations, will become the principal identity for most people in the world'.[20] Others offer similar interpretations, anticipating that these identity shifts will have profound implications for nationhood and traditional state boundaries.[21]

In addition, what unit is evolving in the place of the nation-state as a natural unit for organizing activity within the economic realm? Again, the data point to the emergence of control mechanisms that are regional in scope. These regional control mechanisms are not governmentally imposed but 'are drawn by the deft but invisible hand of the global market for goods and services'.[22] This is not to say, however, that region states are lacking in structure. On the contrary, since they make 'effective points of entry into the global economy because the very characteristics that define them are shaped by the demands of that economy'.[23] Needless to say, since the borders of regional states are determined by the 'naturalness' of their economic zones and thus rarely coincide with the boundaries of political units, the clash between the incentives induced by markets and the authority of governments is central to the emergence of transnational governance mechanisms. Indeed, it is arguable that a prime change at work in world politics today is a shift in the balance between those two forces, with political authorities finding it increasingly expedient to yield to economic realities. In some instances, moreover, political authorities do not even get to choose to yield, as 'regional economic interdependencies are now more important than political boundaries'.[24] Put differently, 'The implications of region states are not welcome news to established seats of political power, be they politicians or lobbyists. Nation states by definition require a domestic political focus, while region states are ensconced in the global economy.'[25]

This potential clash, however, need not necessarily turn adversarial. Much depends on whether the political authorities welcome and encourage foreign capital investment or whether they insist on protecting their noncompetitive local industries. If they are open to foreign inputs, their economies are more likely to prosper than if they insist on a rigorous maintenance of their political autonomy. But if they do insist on drawing tight lines around their authoritative realms, they are likely to lose out.

It seems clear, in short, that cities and microregions are likely to be major control mechanisms in the world politics of the twenty-first century. Even if the various expectations that they replace states as centers of power prove to be exaggerated, they seem destined to emerge as either partners or adversaries of states as their crucial role becomes more widely recognized and they thereby move from an objective to an intersubjective existence.

state-sponsored mechanisms

Although largely nursed into being through the actions of states, macroregions may be no less nascent than cities and microregions. And like their micro counterparts, the macroregions, which span two or more states, are deeply ensconced in a developmental process that may, in some instances, move steadily toward institutionalization, while in others the evolutionary process may either move slowly or fall short of culminating in formal institutions. Movement toward institutionalization – or in Hettne's felicitous term, 'regionness' – occurs the more a region is marked by 'economic interdependence, communication, cultural homogeneity, coherence, capacity to act and, in particular, capacity to resolve conflicts'.[26]

Whatever their pace or outcome, those processes have come to be known as the 'new' regionalism, which is conceived to be different from the 'old' regionalism in several ways. While the latter was a product of Cold War bipolarity, the former has come into being in the context of present-day multipolarity. In effect, the old regionalism was created on a top-down basis from the outside by the superpowers. The new regionalism, on the other hand, consists of more spontaneous processes from within that unfold largely on a bottom-up basis as the constituent states find common cause in a deepening interdependence. As one observer puts it,

> The process of regionalization from within can be compared with the historical formation of nations states with the important difference that a coercive centre is lacking in processes of regionalization which presuppose a shared intention among the potential members.... The difference between regionalism and the infinite process of spontaneous integration is that there is a politically defined limit to the former process. The limitation, however, is a historical outcome of attempts to find a transnational level of governance which includes certain shared values and minimizes certain shared perceptions of danger. Like the formation of ethnic and national identities, the regional identity is dependent on historical context and shaped by conflicts. And like nations and ethnies, regional formations which have a subjective quality... [are] 'imagined communities'.... Despite enormous historical, structural, and contextual differences, there is an underlying logic behind contemporary processes of regionalization.[27]

Currently, of course, the various new regions of the world are at very different stages of development, with some already having evolved the rudiments of control mechanisms while others are still at earlier stages in the process. As noted below, Europe has advanced the most toward institutionalized steering mechanisms, but the decline of hegemons, the advent of democracies, and the demise of governmentally managed economies throughout the world has fostered the conditions under which the new regionalism can begin to flourish. Pronounced movements in this direction are discernible in the Nordic region, in the Caribbean, in the Andean Group, and in the Southern Cone of South America. Lesser degrees of regionness are evident in the three Asia-Pacific regions – East Asia, South-east Asia, and the European Pacific – and the former Soviet Union, while the regionalization process has yet to become readily recognizable in South Asia, the Middle East, and Africa.

Whatever the degree to which the new regionalism has taken hold in various parts of the world, however, it seems clear that this macrophenomenon is increasingly a central feature of global governance. Indeed, the dynamics of macroregions can be closely linked to those of microregions in the sense that as the former shift authority away from national states, so do they open up space for the latter to evolve their own autonomous control mechanisms. 'This can be seen all over Europe today.'[28] The dynamics of globalization and localization are intimately tied to each other.

Jointly sponsored mechanisms

Issue regimes

Despite a mushrooming of literature around the concept of international regimes – as the rules, norms, principles, and procedures that constitute the control mechanisms through which order and governance in particular issue areas are sustained – there has been little convergence around a precise and shared notion of the essential attributes of regimes. Indeed, 'scholars have fallen into using the term regime so disparately and with such little precision that it ranges from an umbrella for all international relations to little more than a synonym for international organizations'.[29] Notwithstanding this conceptual disarray, however, the conception of governance used here as steering mechanisms that are located on a nascent-to-institutionalized continuum serves to highlight regimes as important sources of global governance. Most notably, since they allow for the evolution of a variety of arrangements whereby nongovernmental as well as governmental actors may frame goals and pursue policies in particular issue areas, regimes meet the need for 'a wider view' that includes not only states, international organizations, and international law 'but also the often implicit understandings between a whole range of actors, some of which [are] not states, which [serve] to structure their cooperation in the face of common problems'.[30] In some instances, the control mechanisms of issue areas may be informal, disorganized, conflictful, and often ineffective in concentrating authority – that is, so rudimentary and nascent that governance is spasmodic and weak. In other cases the control mechanisms may be formalized, well organized, and capable of effectively exercising authority – that is, so fully institutionalized that governance is consistent and strong. But in all regimes, regardless of their stage of development, 'the interaction between the parties is not unconstrained or is not based on independent decision making'.[31] All regimes, that is, have control mechanisms to which their participants feel obliged to accede even if they do not do so repeatedly and systematically.

It is important to stress that whether they are nascent or institutionalized, the control mechanisms of all regimes are sustained by the joint efforts of governmental and nongovernmental actors. This shared responsibility is all too often overlooked in the regime literature. More accurately, although the early work on regimes allowed for the participation of NGOs, subsequent inquiries slipped into treating regimes as if they consisted exclusively of states that were more or less responsive to advice and pressures from the nongovernmental sector. However, from a global governance perspective in which states are only the most formalized control mechanisms, the original conception of regime membership as open to all types of actors again becomes compelling. And viewed in that way, it immediately becomes clear that issue regimes evolve through the joint sponsorship of state and nonstate actors. To be sure, as regimes evolve from the nascent toward the institutionalized extreme of the continuum, the more intergovernmental organizations will acquire the formal authority to make decisions; but movement in that direction is likely to be accompanied by preservation of the joint sponsorship of state and nonstate actors through arrangements that accord formal advisory roles to the relevant NGOs. No issue regime, it seems reasonable to assert, can prosper without control mechanisms that allow for some form of participation by all the interested parties. As one observer puts it with respect to several specific issue regimes,

> Increasingly, this transnationalization of civic participation is redefining the terms of governance in North America, not only in the commercial arena but also on issues such as the environment, human rights, and immigration. Nongovernmental organizations, particularly grassroots groups, located throughout these societies are playing a growing role in setting the parameters of the North American agenda, limiting the ability of public officials to manage their relationship on a strict government-to-government basis, and setting the stage for a much more complete process of interaction.[32]

As indicated in Table 1.1, it follows that not all the steering mechanisms of issue regimes are located at the nascent end of the continuum. Some move persistently toward institutionalization – as was recently the case in the human rights regime when the United Nations created a high commissioner for human rights – while others may be stalemated in an underdeveloped state for considerable periods of time. However, given the ever greater interdependence of global life, it seems doubtful whether any issue area that gains access to the global agenda can avoid evolving at least a rudimentary control mechanism. Once the problems encompassed by an issue area become widely recognized as requiring attention and amelioration, it can hardly remain long without entering at least the first stage of the evolutionary process toward governance. On the other hand, given the disaggregated nature of the global system, it also seems doubtful whether any regime can ever become so fully institutionalized that its rule system evolves a hierarchy through which its top leadership acquires binding legal authority over all its participants. Rather, once a regime acquires a sufficient degree of centralized authority to engage in a modicum of regulatory activities, it undergoes transformation into an international organization, as is suggested in Table 1.1 by the evolution of GATT into the World Trade Organization.

How many issue regimes are there? Endless numbers, if it is recalled that issue areas are essentially a conglomeration of related smaller issues and that each of the latter evolves identifiable mechanisms for governance that are at some variance with other issues in the same area. The global agenda is conceived in terms of large-issue areas only because those are more easily grasped and debated, but it is on the smaller issues that particularistic activities requiring special governance arrangements focus.

cross-border coalitions

Some issue regimes, moreover, are so disaggregated as to encompass what have been called 'cross-border coalitions'.[33] These can be usefully set aside for separate analysis as instances of jointly sponsored, nascent control mechanisms. The emphasis here is on the notion of coalitions, on networks of organizations. As previously noted, INGOs are by definition cross-border organizations, but their spanning of boundaries tends to occur largely through like-minded people from different countries who either share membership in the same transnational organization or belong to national organizations that are brought together under umbrella organizations that are transnational in scope. Cross-border coalitions, on the other hand, consist of organizations that coalesce for common purposes but do not do so under the aegis of an umbrella organization. Some of these may form umbrella INGOs as they move on from the nascent stage of development, but at present most of the new coalitions are still in the earliest stage of formation. They are networks rather than organizations, networks that have been facilitated by the advent of information technologies such as e-mail and electronic conferencing and that thus place their members in continuous touch with each other even though they may only come together in face-to-face meetings on rare occasions. Put more dramatically, 'rather than be represented by a building that people enter, these actors may be located on electronic networks and exist as "virtual communities" that have no precise physical address'.[34]

It is noteworthy that some cross-border coalitions may involve local governments located near national boundaries that find it more expedient on a variety of issues to form coalitions with counterparts across the border than to work with their own provincial or national governments. Such coalitions may even be formed deliberately to avoid drawing 'unnecessary or premature attention from central authorities to local solutions of some local problems by means of informal contacts and "good neighborhood" networks. Often it [is] not a deliberate deception, just an avoidance of unnecessary complications'.[35]

That cross-border coalitions are a nascent form of issue regimes is indicated by the fact that they usually form around problems high on the agendas of their communities. During the 1993 debate over the North American Free Trade Agreement (NAFTA), for example, a number of advocacy groups concerned with environmental, human rights, labor, and immigration issues linked up with their counterparts across the U.S.-Mexican boundary, and in some instances the networks spanned the sectoral issue areas as the implications of NAFTA were discovered to have common consequences for otherwise disparate groups. This is not to say that the advent of cross-border coalitions reduced the degree of conflict over the question of NAFTA's approval. As can be readily expected whenever a control mechanism is at stake, coalitions on one side of the issue generated opposing coalitions.

In short, 'the new local and cross-border NGO movements are a potential wild card. They may be proactive or reactive in a variety of ways, sometimes working with, sometimes against, state and market actors who are not accustomed to regarding civil society as an independent actor'.[36]

transnational institutionalized control mechanisms: credit rating agencies

Turning now to transnational control mechanisms that are located more toward the institutionalized extreme of the governance continuum, the dimension of the global capital markets in which risk is assessed and credit-worthiness legitimated offers examples of both discernible rule systems that came into being through the sponsorship of states and others that evolved historically out of the private sector.[37] The International Monetary Fund (IMF) and the World Bank are illustrative of the former type of mechanism, while Moody's Investors Service and Standard & Poor's Ratings Group (S&P) dominate the ratings market in the private sector. Although the difference between the two types is in some ways considerable – unlike the agencies in the private sector, the IMF and the World Bank derive much of their capacity for governance from the sponsorship and funding by the state system that founded them – they are in one important respect quite similar: in both cases their authority derives at least partially from the specialized knowledge on which their judgments are based and the respect they have earned for adhering to explicit and consistent standards for reaching their conclusions as to the credit-worthiness of enterprises, governments, and countries. And in both cases the judgments they render are authoritative in the sense that the capital markets acquiesce to and conduct themselves on the basis of their ratings. To be sure, fierce debates do break out over the appropriateness of the standards employed to make the risk assessments of debt security, but the credibility of the private rating agencies has not been so effectively challenged as to diminish their status as control mechanisms.

That the private agencies are transnational in scope is indicated by the fact that both Moody's and S&P have branches in London, Paris, Frankfurt, Tokyo, and Sydney. Most of the other agencies in this trillion-dollar market are domestically focused and confine their assessments to the credit-worthiness of borrowers in the countries where they are located, albeit there are signs that a Europewide agency is in the process of evolving.

In sum, the private ratings agencies are a means through which key parts of national and transnational economies are, relatively speaking, insulated from politics. By presiding over that insulation, the agencies have become, in effect, control mechanisms. In other words, 'rating agencies seem to be contributing to a system of rule in which an intersubjective framework is created in which social forces will be self-regulating in accord with the limits of the system'.[38]

subnational institutionalized mechanisms: crime syndicates

It is a measure of the globalization of governance that crime syndicates have evolved institutional forms on a transnational scale, that they can properly be called 'transnational criminal organizations' (TCOs). Their conduct, of course, violates all the norms that are considered to undergird the proper exercise of authority, but their centrality to the course of events is too conspicuous not to note briefly their role among the diverse control mechanisms that now constitute global governance. Indeed, upon reflection it seems clear that, 'with the globalization of trade and growing consumer demands for leisure products, it is only natural that criminal organizations should become increasingly transnational in character,' that they have been 'both contributors to, and beneficiaries of, ... a great increase in transactions across national boundaries that are neither initiated nor controlled by states,'[39] and that,

> not only is transnational activity as open to criminal groups as it is to legitimate multinational corporations, but the character of criminal organizations also makes them particularly suited to exploit these new opportunities. Since criminal groups are used to operating outside the rules, norms and laws of domestic jurisdictions, they have few qualms about crossing national boundaries illegally. In many respects, therefore, TCOs are transnational organizations par excellence. They operate outside the existing structures of authority and power in world politics and have developed sophisticated strategies for circumventing law enforcement in individual states and in the global community of states.[40]

A good measure of how new opportunities have facilitated the explosiveness of TCOs in the present era is provided by the pattern of criminal activities that has evolved in the former Soviet Union since the collapse of the Soviet empire: 'More than 4,000 criminal formations comprising an estimated 100,000 members now operate in Russia alone', and of these, some '150 to 200 ... have international ties'.[41]

While TCOs operate outside the realm of established norms, and while they are marked by considerable diversity in size, structure, goals, and membership, they are nevertheless institutionalized in the sense that they control their affairs in patterned ways that often involve strategic alliances between themselves and national and local criminal organizations, alliances that 'permit them to cooperate with, rather than compete against, indigenously entrenched criminal organizations'.[42] Yet TCOs have not succumbed to excessive bureaucratization. On the contrary, 'they are highly mobile and adaptable and able to operate across national borders with great ease ... partly because of their emphasis on networks rather than formal organizations'.[43] It is interesting and indicative of the dynamics of globalization that legitimate multinational corporations have recently come to resemble TCOs in two ways: first, by developing more fluid and flexible network structures that enable them to take advantage of local conditions and, second, by resorting to strategic alliances that facilitate development on a global scale.

state-sponsored mechanisms

the united nations system

The United Nations is an obvious case of a steering mechanism that was sponsored by states and that took an institutional form from its founding. To be sure, its processes of institutionalization have continued to evolve since 1945 to the point where it is now a complex system of numerous associate agencies and subunits that, collectively, address all the issues on the global agenda and that amount to a vast bureaucracy. The institutional histories of the various agencies differ in a number of respects, but taken as a whole they have become a major center of global governance. They have been a main source of problem identification, information, innovation, and constructive policies in the fields of health, environment, education, agriculture, labor, family, and a number of other issues that are global in scope.

This is not to say that the collective history of the United Nations depicts a straight-line trajectory toward ever greater effectiveness. Quite to the contrary, not only have its many agencies matured enough to be severely and properly criticized for excessive and often misguided bureaucratic practices, but also – and even more important – its primary executive and legislative agencies (the secretary-general, the General Assembly, and the Security Council) have compiled a checkered history with respect to the UN's primary functions of preventive diplomacy, peacekeeping, and peacemaking under chapter VII of its charter. For the first four decades, its record was that of a peripheral player in the Cold War, an era in which it served as a debating arena for major conflicts, especially those that divided the two nuclear superpowers, but accomplished little by way of creating a new world order that provided states security through the aggregation of their collective strength. Then, at the end of the Cold War, the United Nations underwent both a qualitative and quantitative transformation, one that placed it at the very heart of global governance as states turned to the Security Council for action in a number of the major humanitarian and conflict situations that broke out with the end of superpower competition. The inclination to rely on the United Nations, to centralize in it the responsibility for global governance, reached a peak in 1991 with the successful multilateral effort under UN auspices to undo Iraq's conquest of Kuwait.

It is not difficult to demonstrate the quantitative dimensions of the UN's transformation at the end of the Cold War. In 1987, the United Nations had assigned some ten thousand peacekeepers – mostly troops in blue helmets who were supposed to resort to force only if attacked – to five operations around the world on an annual budget of about $233 million. Seven years later the number of troops had risen to 72,000 in 18 different situations at an annual cost of more than $3 billion. Similarly, whereas the Security Council used to meet once a month, by 1994, its schedule involved meeting every day, and often twice a day. In other words, during the first 44 years of its history, the Security Council passed only six resolutions under chapter VII in which 'threats to the peace, breaches of the peace, acts of aggression' were determined to exist. However, between 1990 and 1992, the Security Council adopted 33 such resolutions on Iraq (21), the former Yugoslavia (8), Somalia (2), Liberia (1), and Libya (1).

Even more impressive are the qualitative changes that underlay the UN's transformation: as the Cold War wound down and ended, two remarkable developments became readily discernible. One was the advent of a new consensus among the five permanent members of the Security Council with respect to the desirability of the UN's involvement in peacekeeping activities, and the other was the extension of that consensus to the nonpermanent members, including virtually all of the nonaligned states elected to the council. These changes are evident in the fact that the number of unanimously adopted Security Council resolutions jumped from 61 percent (72 of 119) in 1980–1985 to 84 percent in 1986–1992 (184 of 219). In 1993 alone, the Security Council passed more than 181 resolutions and statements, all of which high-mindedly addressed peacekeeping issues (such as a demand for the end of ethnic cleansing in the former Yugoslavia).

Furthermore, those transformations rendered the United Nations into a control mechanism in the military sense of the term. The organization's operations in both Somalia and Bosnia found the secretary-general conducting himself as commanding general and making the final decisions having to do with the application of air power, the disposition of ground forces, and the dismissal of commanding officers.

Despite those transformations in its role and orientations, in its performances the United Nations has not lived up to the surge of high hopes for it that immediately followed the end of the Cold War. Rather than sustaining movement toward effective global governance, it foundered in Somalia, dawdled in Bosnia, and cumulatively suffered a decline in the esteem with which it is held by both governments and publics. The reasons for this decline are numerous – ranging from a lack of money to a lack of will, from governments that delay paying their dues to publics that resist the commitment of troops to battle – but they add up to a clear-cut inability to carry out and enforce the resolutions of the Security Council. Consensus has evolved on the desirability of the UN's intervening in humanitarian situations, but there is a long distance between agreement on goals and a shared perspective on the provision of the necessary means: the readiness to implement multilateral goals and thereby enhance the UN's authority to achieve effective governance is woefully lacking, leading one analyst to describe the organization's activities in the peacekeeping area as 'faint-hearted multilateralism'.[44]

But the checkered history of the UN's institutionalization suggests that its present limitations may undergo change yet again. The organization continues to occupy a valued and critical position in the complex array of global control mechanisms. The need for collective action in volatile situations is bound to continue, so that it is likely that the world will seek to fill this vacuum by repeatedly turning to the United Nations as the best available means of achieving a modicum of governance. And in the processes of doing so, conceivably, circumstances will arise that swing faint-hearted commitments back in the direction of a more steadfast form of multilateralism.

the european union

Much more so than the United Nations, the history of the European Union (EU) is a record of the evolutionary route to institutionalization. Even a brief account of this history is beyond the scope of this analysis, but it is one macroregion that has passed through various stages of growth to its present status as an elaborately institutionalized instrument of governance for the (increasing number of) countries within its jurisdiction. Sure, it was states that formalized the institutionalization, but they did so as a consequence of transformations that culminated in the member countries holding referenda wherein the establishment of the EU was approved by citizenries. In this sense, the EU offers a paradigmatic example of the dynamics that propel evolutionary processes from nascent to institutionalized steering mechanisms. As one observer puts it, this transformation occurred through 'the gradual blurring of the distinction made between the "Community" and the "nation-states" which agreed to form that community in the first place.... Although the two are by no means linked as tightly as are subnational units to the center in the traditional state, the Community-state entanglement is such that the Community is very far from being a traditional regional organization'.[45] Indeed, such is the evolution of the European Union that it

> is now better conceptualized as a union of states rather than as an organization. The international law doctrine that actors are either states or organizations has become unrealistic.... In [a 1992] decision the Court of Justice established that Community law within its sphere is equal in status to national law. Further, the court has successfully maintained that, because law should be uniform, Community law must take precedence over conflicting national law.[46]

In short, while the EU does not have 'federal law because Community legislation suffers from the defect that its statutes are not legitimized by a democratic legislature',[47] it does have a rule system in the combination of its executive and judicial institutions.

jointly sponsored institutionalized mechanisms

A good illustration of how control mechanisms can evolve toward the institutionalized end of the governance continuum through the sponsorship of both states and NGOs is provided by the emergence of clear-cut patterns wherein it has become established practice for external actors to monitor the conduct of domestic elections in the developing world. Indeed, the monitoring process has become quite elaborate and standardized, with lengthy instructional booklets now available for newcomers to follow when they enter the host country and shoulder their responsibilities as monitors. And no less indicative of the degree of institutionalization is that some of the monitors, such as the United Nations or the National Democratic Institute, send representatives to observe virtually all elections in which outside monitors are present.

Nevertheless, does external monitoring constitute a control mechanism? Most certainly. Whatever hesitations the host countries may have about the presence of outsiders who judge the fairness and propriety of their election procedures, and irrespective of their attempts to circumvent the monitors and load the electoral outcome, now they yield both to the pressure for external monitoring and to the judgments the outsiders make during and after election day. Elections have been postponed because of irregularities in voter lists detected by the external monitors, 'dirty tricks' uncovered during the balloting have been terminated at the insistence of monitors, and the verdict of outsiders that the final tallies were fraudulent has resulted in the holding of new elections. To be sure, a few countries still adamantly refuse admission to outside monitors or do not allow them to be present on a scale sufficient to allow for legitimation of the electoral outcome, but the monitoring process has become so fully institutionalized that normally the host countries overcome their reluctance as they begin to recognize the problems they cause for themselves by refusing to acquiesce to the monitoring process. In other words, the advent of established procedures for the external monitoring of elections demonstrates the large extent to which control mechanisms derive their effectiveness from information and reputation even if their actions are not backed up by constitutional authority. It might even be said that governance in an evermore complex and interdependent world depends less on the issuance of authoritative directives and more on the release of reliable information and the legitimacy inherent in its detail.

As for the presence of both state and NGO actors, the spreading norm that the establishment of democracy justifies the international community's involvement in domestic elections attracts both official and unofficial groups to train and send monitors. Whatever organizations may have led the negotiations that result in the acceptance of outside observers, a number of others (such as the Organization of American States [OAS], the Socialist International, and the Latin American Studies Association in the case of Paraguay's 1993 election) find reasons important to their memberships to be present, and there are few precedents for denying admission to some monitoring teams while accepting others. Although the monitoring process may not be free of friction and competition among the numerous teams, the more procedures have been institutionalized, the greater has been the collaboration among the teams. It is not stretching matters to conclude that not only does the international community turn out in force for domestic elections in distant countries, but also it does so with representatives from many of its diverse segments. In the 1990 Nicaraguan election, for example, 2,578 accredited observers from 278 organizations were present on election day.[48]

continuing and changing forms of governance

The above observations suggest that a full picture of what are likely to be the contours of global governance in the decades ahead requires attention to the dynamics of localization and how they are in part responses to the dynamics of globalization, responses that give rise to what can be called 'distant proximities' that may well become systems of rule with diverse types of control mechanisms. Although some localizing dynamics are initiated by national governments – as when France decided to decentralize its steering apparatus and reduce Paris's control over policy and administrative issues – perhaps the preponderance of them are generated at subnational levels, some with the help and approval of national agencies but many in opposition to national policies, which then extend their scope abroad. The tendencies toward strengthened ethnic subgroups that have surfaced since the end of the Cold War are a case in point. Even though these actors may not have direct ties to supporters in other countries, their activities on the local scene can foster repercussions abroad that thereby transform them into aspects of global governance. The recent struggles in Bosnia, Somalia, and Rwanda are examples. Similarly, since so many of the world's resources, water, and air quality problems originate in subnational communities, and since this level is marked by a proliferation of both governmental and nongovernmental agencies that seek to control these problems within their jurisdiction and to do so through cooperative efforts with transnational counterparts, the environmental area offers another array of local issues that are central to the conduct of global governance.

The emphasis here on transnational and subnational mechanisms is not, of course, to imply that national governments and states are no longer central loci of control in the processes of global governance; they are very central indeed. No account of the global system can ignore them or give them other than a prominent place in the scheme of things. Nevertheless, states have lost some of their earlier dominance of the governance system, as well as their ability to evoke compliance and to govern effectively. This change is in part due to the growing relevance and potential of control mechanisms sustained by transnational and subnational systems of rule.

governance in the twenty-first century

If the analysis were deemed complete here, the reader, like the author, would likely feel let down, as if the final chapter of this story of a disaggregated and fragmenting global system of governance has yet to be written. It is an unfinished story, one's need for closure would assert. It needs a conclusion, a drawing together of the 'big picture', a sweeping assessment that offers some hope that somehow the world can muddle through and evolve techniques of cooperation that will bridge its multitude of disaggregated parts and achieve a measure of coherence that enables future generations to live in peace, achieve sustainable development, and maintain a modicum of creative order. Assessing the overall balance, one's training cries out, show how the various emergent centers of power form a multipolar system of states that will manage to cope with the challenges of war within and among its members. Yes, that's it – depict the overall system as polyarchical and indicate how such an arrangement can generate multilateral institutions of control that effectively address the huge issues that clutter the global agenda. Or, perhaps better, indicate how a hegemon will emerge out of the disaggregation and have enough clout to foster both progress and stability. At the very least, one's analytic impulses demand, suggest how worldwide tendencies toward disaggregation and localization may be offset by no less powerful tendencies toward aggregation and globalization.

Compelling as these alternative interpretations may be, however, they do not quell a sense that it is only a short step from polyarchy to Pollyanna and that one's commitment to responsible analysis must be served by not taking that step. The world is clearly on a path-dependent course, and some of its present outlines can be discerned if, as noted at the outset, allowance is made for nuance and ambiguity. Still, in this time of continuing and profound transformations, too much remains murky to project beyond the immediate present and anticipate long-term trajectories. All one can conclude with confidence is that in the twenty-first century the paths to governance will lead in many directions, some that will emerge into sunlit clearings and others that will descend into dense jungles.

notes

The author is grateful to Walter Truett Anderson and Hongying Wang for their reactions to an early draft of this article.

1. Alexander King and Bertrand Schneider, *The First Global Revolution: A Report of the Council of Rome* (New York: Pantheon Books, 1991), pp. 181–182 (italics added). For other inquiries that support the inclusion of small, seemingly local systems of rule in a broad analytic framework, see John Friedmann, *Empowerment: The Politics of Alternative Development* (Cambridge, Mass.: Blackwell, 1992),

and Robert Huckfeldt, Eric Plutzer, and John Sprague, 'Alternative Contexts of Political Behavior: Churches, Neighborhoods, and Individuals,' *Journal of Politics* 55 (May 1993), pp. 365–381.

2. Steven A. Rosell, *Governing in an Information Society* (Montreal: Institute for Research on Public Policy, 1992), p. 21.
3. Rule systems have much in common with what has come to be called the 'new institutionalism.' See, for example, Robert O. Keohane, 'International Institutions: Two Approaches,' *International Studies Quarterly,* Vol. 32 (December 1988), pp. 379–396; James G. March and Johan P. Olsen, 'The New Institutionalism: Organizational Factors in Political Life,' *American Political Science Review,* Vol. 78 (September 1984), pp. 734–749; and Oran R. Young, 'International Regimes: Toward a New Theory of Institutions,' *World Politics,* Vol. 39 (October 1986), pp. 104–122. For an extended discussion of how the concept of control is especially suited to the analysis of both formal and informal political phenomena, see James N. Rosenau, 'Calculated Control as a Unifying Concept in the Study of International Politics and Foreign Policy,' Research Monograph No. 15 (Princeton: Center of International Studies, Princeton University, 1963).
4. Cf. Rosenau and Ernst-Otto Czempiel (eds), *Governance without Government: Order and Change in World Politics* (Cambridge: Cambridge University Press, 1992). Also see the formulations in Peter Mayer, Volker Rittberger, and Michael Zurn, 'Regime Theory: State of the Art and Perspectives,' in Volker Rittberger (ed.), *Regime Theory and International Relations* (New York: Oxford University Press, 1993), and Timothy J. Sinclair, 'Financial Knowledge as Governance,' a paper presented at the Annual Meeting of the International Studies Association, Acapulco, 23–27 March 1993.
5. Anthony G. McGrew, 'Global Politics in a Transitional Era,' in Anthony G. McGrew and Paul G. Lewis, (eds), *Global Politics: Globalization and the Nation-State* (Cambridge: Polity Press, 1992), p. 318.
6. Martin Hewson, 'The Media of Political Globalization,' a paper presented at the Annual Meeting of the International Studies Association, Washington, D.C., March 1994, p. 2.
7. John Vogler, 'Regimes and the Global Commons: Space, Atmosphere and Oceans,' in McGrew and Lewis, *Global Politics,* p. 118.
8. Diana Jean Schemo, 'Rebuilding of Suburban Dreams,' *New York Times,* 4 May 1994, p. All.
9. Steven Greenhouse, 'Kissinger Will Help Mediate Dispute Over Zulu Homeland,' *New York Times,* 12 April 1994, p. A8.
10. Peter B. Evans, 'Building an Integrative Approach to International and Domestic Politics: Reflections and Projections,' in Peter B. Evans, Harold K. Jacobson, and Robert D. Putnam, (eds), *Double-Edged Diplomacy: International Bargaining and Domestic Politics* (Berkeley: University of California Press, 1993), p. 419. For interesting accounts of how multinational corporations are increasingly inclined to form transnational alliances, see 'The Global Firm: R.I.P.,' *Economist,* 6 February 1993, p. 69, and 'The Fall of Big Business,' *Economist,* 17 April 1993, p. 13.
11. Jan Aart Scholte, *International Relations of Social Change* (Philadelphia: Open University Press, 1993), pp. 44–45.

12. Roberto C. Goizueta, 'The Challenges of Getting What You Wished For,' remarks presented to the Arthur Page Society, Amelia Island, Florida, 21 September 1992.
13. Joseph A. Camilleri, 'Rethinking Sovereignty in a Shrinking, Fragmented World,' in R.B.J. Walker and Saul H. Mendlovitz (eds), *Contending Sovereignties: Redefining Political Community* (Boulder: Lynne Rienner, 1990), p. 35.
14. Janie Leatherman, Ron Pagnucco, and Jackie Smith, 'International Institutions and Transnational Social Movement Organizations: Challenging the State in a Three-Level Game of Global Transformation,' a paper presented at the Annual Meeting of the International Studies Association, Washington, D.C., March 1994, p. 20.
15. Robert W. Cox, 'Global Perestroika,' in Ralph Milband and Leo Panitch, (eds), *Socialist Register* (London: Merlin Press, 1992), p. 34.
16. Björn Hettne, 'The New Regionalism: Implications for Development and Peace,' in Björn Hettne and Andras Inotai (eds), *The New Regionalism: Implications for Global Development and International Security* (Helsinki: UNU World Institute for Development Economics Research, 1994), p. 2.
17. Hettne, 'The New Regionalism,' p. 6.
18. William Drozdiak, 'Revving Up Europe's "Four Motors",' *Washington Post*, 27 March 1994, p. C3.
19. Ibid.
20. Pascal Maragall, quoted in Drozdiak, 'Revving Up Europe's "Four Motors".' For extensive inquiries that posit the transnational roles of cities as increasingly central to the processes of global governance, see Saskia Sassen, *The Global City: New York, London, Tokyo* (Princeton: Princeton University Press, 1991), and Earl H. Fry, Lee H. Radebaugh, and Panayotis Soldatos (eds), *The New International Cities Era: The Global Activities of North American Municipal Governments* (Provo, Utah: Brigham Young University Press, 1989).
21. See, for example, Thomas P. Rohlem, 'Cosmopolitan Cities and Nation States: A "Mediterranean" Model for Asian Regionalism,' a paper presented at the Conference on Asian Regionalism, Maui, 17–19 December 1993; Ricardo Petrilla, as quoted in Drozdiak, 'Revving Up Europe's "Four Motors",' p. C3. For an analysis by the same author that indicates concern over the trend to city-like states, see Petrilla, 'Techno-racism: The City-States of the Global Market Will Create a "New Apartheid",' *Toronto Star*, 9 August 1992; and Kenichi Ohmae, 'The Rise of the Region State,' *Foreign Affairs*, Vol. 72 (Spring 1993), p. 78.
22. Ohmae, 'The Rise of the Region State,' pp. 78–79.
23. Ibid., p. 80.
24. Michael Clough and David Doerge, 'Global Changes and Domestic Transformations: New Possibilities for American Foreign Policy: Report of a Vantage Conference' (Muscatine, Iowa: The Stanley Foundation, 1992), p. 9. For indicators that a similar process is occurring in the Southwest without the approval of Washington, D.C. or Mexico City, see Cathryn L. Thorup, *Redefining Governance in North America: The Impact of Cross-Border Networks and Coalitions on Mexican Immigration into the United States* (Santa Monica: The Rand Corporation, 1993).Although using a different label ('tribes'), a broader discussion of regional states can be found in Joel Kotkin, *Tribes:*

How Race, Religion and Identity Determine Success in the New Global Economy (New York: Random House, 1993).

25. Ohmae, 'The Rise of the Region State,' p. 83.
26. Hettne, 'The New Regionalism,' p. 7.
27. Ibid., pp. 2–3. For another formulation that also differentiates between the old and new regionalism, see Kaisa Lahteenmaki and Jyrki Kakonen, 'Regionalization and Its Impact on the Theory of International Relations,' paper presented at the Annual Meeting of the International Studies Association, Washington, D.C., March 1994, p. 9. For a contrary perspective, see Stephen D. Krasner, 'Regional Economic Blocs and the End of the Cold War,' paper presented at the International Colloqium on Regional Economic Integration, University of Sao Paulo, December 1991.
28. Hettne, 'The New Regionalism,' p. 11.
29. Arthur Stein, 'Coordination and Collaboration: Regimes in an Anarchic World,' in David A. Baldwin (ed.), *Neorealism and Neoliberalism: The Contemporary Debate* (New York: Columbia University Press, 1993), p. 29.
30. Vogler, 'Regimes and the Global Commons,' p. 123.
31. Stein, 'Coordination and Collaboration,' p. 31.
32. Cathryn L. Thorup, 'Redefining Governance in North America: Citizen Diplomacy and Cross-Border Coalitions,' Vol. *Enfoque* (Spring 1993). pp. 1, 12.
33. For a valuable attempt to explore this concept theoretically and empirically, see Thorup, 'The Politics of Free Trade and the Dynamics of Cross-Border Coalitions in U.S-Mexican Relations,' *Columbia Journal of World Business*, Vol. 26 (Summer 1991), pp. 12–26.
34. David Ronfeldt and Cathryn L. Thorup, 'North America in the Era of Cit izen Networks: State, Society, and Security,' (Santa Monica: Rand Corporation, 1993), p. 22.
35. Iyo D. Duchachek, 'The International Dimension of Subnational Government,' *Publius*, Vol. 14 (Fall 1984), p. 25.
36. Ronfeldt and Thorup, 'North America in the Era of Citizen Networks,' p. 24.
37. This brief discussion of the credit rating agencies in the private sector is based on Timothy J. Sinclair, 'The Mobility of Capital and the Dynamics of Global,Governance: Credit Risk Assessment in the Emerging World Order,' a paper presented at the Annual Meeting of the International Studies Association, Washington, D.C., March 1994, and Sinclair, 'Passing Judgment: Credit Rating Processes as Regulatory Mechanisms of Governance in the Emerging World Order,' *Review of International Political Economy*, April 1994.
38. Sinclair, 'The Mobility of Capital and the Dynamics of Global Governance,' p. 16.
39. Phil Williams, 'Transnational Criminal Organizations and International Security,' *Survival*, Vol. 36 (Spring 1994), p. 97. See also Williams, 'International Drug Trafficking: An Industry Analysis,' *Low Intensity Conflict and Law Enforcement*, Vol. 2 (Winter 1993), pp. 397–420. For another dimension of transnational criminality, see Victor T. Levine, 'Transnational Aspects of Political Corruption,' in Arnold J. Heidenheimer, Michael Johnston, and Victor T. LeVine (eds), *Political Corruption: A Handbook* (New Brunswick, N.J.: Transaction, 1989), pp. 685–699.

40. Williams, 'Transnational Criminal Organizations and International Security,' p. 100.
41. Rensselaer W. Lee III, 'Post-Soviet Organized Crime and Western Security Interests,' testimony submitted to the Subcommittee on Terrorism, Narcotics and International Operations, Senate Committee on Foreign Relations, Washington, D.C., 21 April 1994.
42. Williams, 'Transnational Criminal Organizations and International Security,' p. 106.
43. Ibid., p. 105.
44. Thomas Risse-Kappen, 'Faint-Hearted Multilateralism: The Re-Emergence of the United Nations in World Politics,' a paper presented at the Annual Meeting of the International Studies Association, Washington, D.C., March 1994.
45. Alberta Sbragia, 'From "Nation-State" to "Member-State": The Evolution of the European Community,' a paper presented at the Europe After Maastrict Symposium, Washington University, Saint Louis, 1–3 October 1993, pp. 1–2.
46. Christopher Brewin, 'The European Community: A Union of States Without Unity of Government,' in Friedrich Kratochwil and Edward D. Mansfield (eds), *International Organization: A Reader* (New York: HarperCollins, 1994), pp. 301–302.
47. Ibid., p. 302.
48. Of these, 278 organizations were present on election day, with 435 observers fielded by the OAS visiting 3,064 voting sites (some 70 percent of the total) and 237 UN monitors visiting 2,155 sites. In addition, some 1,500 members of the international press corps were on the scene. Cf. Robert A. Pastor, 'Nicaragua's Choice,' in Carl Kaysen, Robert A. Pastor, and Laura W. Reed (eds), *Collective Responses to Regional Problems: The Case of Latin America and the Caribbean* (Cambridge: American Academy of Arts and Sciences, 1994), pp. 18, 21.

2
actors, arenas, and issues in global governance

klaus dingwerth and philipp pattberg

> [Global governance is] the complex of formal and informal institutions, mechanisms, relationships and processes between and among states, markets, citizens and organisations – both intergovernmental and non-governmental – through which collective interests are articulated, rights and obligations established and differences are mediated.[1]

introduction

An Internet search conducted in 1997 revealed 3418 references to 'global governance'. In 2004, the number had risen to almost 200,000 references and by early 2008, the World Wide Web lists well over half-a-million pages that include the term 'global governance'.[2] The figures indicate not only a fast growth of the Internet itself but also an increasing familiarity of the term 'global governance'. Academics and political practitioners are talking about it with ease, universities offer degrees and courses in global governance, and the bookshelves with the 'GG' label are quickly filling.[3] But what is all this 'global governance' talk about? Is global governance a new phenomenon? A novel way of looking at the world? Or is it merely a new label for processes that political scientists have been observing for decades?[4]

We have argued elsewhere that global governance is not merely a label, but indeed best seen as a new perspective that helps us describe, understand, and explain a political world that is itself undergoing profound change.[5] In this chapter, we build on this argument and introduce global governance as the outcome of multiple resource exchanges among various actors. The key distinction between international politics as it used to be and global governance as it currently manifests itself, we argue, is a proliferation of actors that dispose of at least some resources that are necessary to effectively steer the behaviour of individuals and corporate actors across territorial boundaries. This proliferation promotes the multiplication of spheres of authority and it inspires 'new modes of governance' in which governmental and non-governmental organizations join forces in their efforts at governing a particular policy issue.

In what follows, we seek to reconstruct the shift from international politics to global governance in three broad steps. In a first step, we review the global governance literature and seek to identify answers to the question 'What is new about global governance?' (From international politics to global governance: What has changed). In a second step, we zoom in on a particular answer to this question, namely the assumption that a major novelty of global governance lies in the proliferation of actors. We first describe this proliferation (The proliferation of actors in world politics) and then analyse it from a resources dependence perspective (The distribution of governance resources). In a third step, we then ask where, how, and to what end various actors pool and exchange resources and establish governance arrangements beyond the state (Where, how, and to what end? arenas and issues of global governance). In the final section, we discuss the assets and limitations of a resource perspective on global governance.

from international politics to global governance: what has changed?

While theories of global governance are still rare, at least three different accounts of the empirical shift from international politics to global governance are on offer.[6] Probably the best-known version is that of James Rosenau who conceives of global governance as a multiplication of spheres of authority. For Rosenau, this multiplication of spheres of authority beyond the state has several sources. First, the 'skill revolution' has significantly empowered individuals. It has enabled them to process and evaluate information and to create purposeful organizations to articulate and defend their interests. Second, technological change facilitates communication across borders and thus increases the relative share of transnational political relations and activities. Third, the globalization of economic relations strengthens interdependencies among societies and creates a range of powerful new actors such as multinational corporations, transnational professional organizations, or diaspora communities, each of which is capable of creating and maintaining a degree of order within its domain. Taken together, these developments have significantly changed the shape of world politics. As an increasingly wide range of actors control at least some share of cross-border relations, world politics is no longer an exclusive matter of states. Instead, it has become a rather messy arena in which order is created through diverse and often novel mechanisms employed by a multitude of actors.[7]

A second version sees global governance primarily in functionalist terms – that is, as the sum of formal and informal coordination mechanisms that appear because (and wherever) they are beneficial (or 'functional') to the actors who create them, often as a response to cooperation problems induced by economic globalization. Along these lines, Oran Young, for instance, defines global governance as 'the combined efforts of international and transnational regimes'.[8] The form of governance – whether arrangements in particular policy fields are supranational, transgovernmental, or transnational – is seen as primarily determined by the problem structure and the constellation of interests in the policy area of concern.[9]

A third group of authors interpret the move towards global governance as a shift towards a more constitutionalized system of world politics. This shift, they argue, is comprised of essentially two dimensions – a legalization of world politics and a 'societalization' (*Vergesellschaftlichung*) of world politics. In short, world politics is becoming increasingly rule-bound, the rules are increasingly made, implemented, and adjudicated in a law-like manner, and societal actors are increasingly involved in governance beyond the state.[10] A variant of this constitutionalization hypothesis sees the shift from international politics to global governance as a shift from a Westphalian to a post-Westphalian governance norm. In the Westphalian era, this view argues that rules were seen as legitimate as long as they originated from intergovernmental agreements reached without threats or acts of coercion. In the post-Westphalian era, political rules beyond the state are legitimate if representatives of potentially affected interests have agreed upon them in decision-making processes that are inclusive, transparent, accountable, and deliberative.[11]

Leaving aside neo-realist and neo-Marxist approaches that do not identify a major shift in world politics in the first place,[12] we sketch in the following sections a fourth and complementary perspective based on the notion of resource dependent organizations. According to this perspective, effective and efficient governance requires political, financial, cognitive, and moral resources. Political resources refer to control over the behaviour of target actors, not least through the possibility to issue binding regulations and sanction non-compliance. Financial resources include the money that is necessary to implement policies and political projects; for instance, the funds for education programmes, health care, or social policies. Cognitive resources refer to the knowledge and information necessary to make the 'right' decision; they include substantive knowledge about the phenomena to be regulated – for instance about climate change – but also information about the attitudes of target groups towards a particular policy. Finally, moral resources primarily comprise the beliefs of audiences in the legitimacy of a particular policy or political institution.[13] The central argument of this fourth perspective is that while governance resources have been concentrated in the hands of the 'golden-age nation state' in the 1970s and 1980s, they have now become more dispersed.[14] Their dispersion, in turn, has led to the emergence of a system of global governance in which numerous actors and institutions coexist and together create what James Rosenau's has called the 'crazy-quilt' nature of global governance.

the proliferation of actors in world politics

The proliferation of actors is at the centre of much of the global governance literature. Frequently, this literature takes the dramatic rise in the number of international non-governmental organizations as a proof that the nature of world politics has changed. Yet it is not the sheer numbers of INGOs that make the difference. Instead the ability of non-state actors to effectively steer particular aspects of the 'world political system'[15] in certain directions distinguishes global governance from international politics. The political *agency* of a diversity of non-state actors makes the difference. Stated differently, since various types of actors have gained the capacity to form transboundary social institutions to address transnational problems, political agency is increasingly located in sites beyond the state. The following is only a brief list intended to illustrate who these actors are – only some of them are 'new' actors in a strict sense – and in which ways they are agents in contemporary global governance:[16]

- *International organizations.* International organizations are actors in their own right insofar as their decisions can legally bind individual member states even though they have not consented to these decisions. For instance, the United Nations Security Council adopts legally binding resolutions with a majority of 9 of 15 votes. As the 1990 economic sanctions against Iraq illustrate, its decisions are often highly contentious. Nevertheless, all UN members must abide by them. While international organizations rarely govern entire policy fields on their own – even development politics is more than what the World Bank does – they frequently set and implement rules for key areas within these fields.[17]
- *International bureaucracies.* International organizations frequently have secretariats that are responsible for the everyday politics of the organization. In the field of environmental policy, more than two hundred international secretariats administer the many international environmental treaties concluded over the past decades. Like in domestic politics, bureaucracies also matter in international politics. They create, channel and disseminate knowledge, shape powerful discourses, frame problems, and solutions to environmental problems, influence negotiations through their ideas and expertise, and oversee the implementation of projects on the ground.[18] To the extent that knowledge and expertise become increasingly relevant to effectively govern across borders, international bureaucracies can thus be expected to also gain relevance.
- *International non-governmental organizations.* The world political role of nongovernmental lobbying organizations such as Greenpeace, Friends of the Earth, or Amnesty International has been acknowledged and analysed for some decades. Within the larger transformations of world politics, they represent a 'world civic politics' that is reflected in strategies such as agenda-setting, lobbying, participation in international decision-making, campaigning, and occasionally also cooperative rule-making.[19] As witnessed by the success of the International Campaign to Ban of Landmines (ICBL), carefully orchestrated campaigns of environmentalists and human rights activists have proven to be able to change foreign policy decisions of states even in core areas of states' security interests.[20] More recently,

organizations such as the Forest Stewardship Council or the Marine Stewardship Council have established full-fledged transnational regimes that govern particular sub-areas of global environmental governance.[21]

- *Hybrid organizations.* Some organizations that regulate behaviour for entire issue areas of world politics are less easily classified as either private or public – in fact, they are best described as hybrid organizations. For example, the allocation of Internet top-level domains within the World Wide Web is administered by the International Corporation for Assigned Names and Numbers (ICANN). This organization is chartered as a non-profit organization under US law, but is in fact controlled by the US Department of Commerce.[22] Other hybrid organizations include the International Organization for Standardization (ISO), the World Conservation Union (IUCN), or the World Anti-Doping Agency (WADA), all of which fulfil important governance functions and all of which count both governmental and non-governmental organizations as their members.
- *State agencies and local communities.* A growing number of national and sub-national governmental actors including legislatures, regulatory agencies, and courts organize across borders to coordinate their political activities.[23] For instance, over have 800 municipalities – including major US cities like Atlanta, Los Angeles, New Orleans, New York, and San Francisco – commit themselves to reducing their greenhouse gas emissions as a part of the Cities for Climate Protection Campaign.[24]
- *Private foundations* such as the Ford Foundation, the Rockefeller Brothers Fund, or the MacArthur Foundation spend vast sums of money on political projects in countries other than their own. More recent examples include the investment of the Bill and Melissa Gates Foundation in global health governance and the initiation of the United Nations Foundation in 1998. In 2006, the annual budget of the Bill and Melissa Gates Foundation amounted to 1.56 billion US dollars; it thus almost equalled the budget of the World Health Organization of around 2 billion US dollars. In the same year, the United Nations Foundation spent around 233 million US dollars in support of selected UN programs. The figure amounts to approximately 2.5 per cent of the annual budget of the United Nations and exceeds the contributions to the regular UN budget of all individual member states except the United States and Japan.[25]

- *Business actors.* The influence of major companies on international affairs is hardly new. In fact, for some social theories such as Marxism, business actors have long been the key players in global affairs. The old role of the corporate sector in world politics was, however, mainly indirect and limited to lobbying governments 'at home' or influencing the decisions of other governments through foreign direct investment (FDI) and other incentives. Today, many corporations take a more visible, direct role as immediate partners of governments; for example, in the framework of the Global Compact that major corporations have concluded with the United Nations, or in policy partnerships with civil society organizations.[26] Moreover, the relations among industries can also become a driver for political action. This is exemplified by the role the global investment and insurance industries are playing as key drivers of change in business attitudes towards climate change.[27]
- *Epistemic communities.* The recent Nobel Peace Price awarded to the Intergovernmental Panel on Climate Change (IPCC), a network of over 3000 scientists involved in climate change research, is only the latest evidence that knowledge communities are relevant players in global governance. As regulation addresses ever-more complex issues, policy-making inevitably becomes more dependent on expert knowledge, thus enhancing the relevance of epistemic communities.[28] As a result, international networks of scientists and experts emerge, in a mix of self-organization and state-sponsorship, to provide scientific information on both the kind of problems at stake and the options for decision-makers to cope with them.[29]
- *Migrant communities.* A core dimension of globalization is human migration. Yet the role of migrants is not relevant just because migratory flows may threaten national sovereignty or have a potential to instigate political conflict in receiving countries. An equally important feature is the scale of financial flows that go hand in hand with migratory flows. Thus, the overall value of private remittances from industrialized to developing countries is higher than the value of bilateral and multilateral official development aid (ODA) combined and about the same as FDIs in the developing world.[30] This makes migrant communities an important source of financial resources, in particular in development politics.

We could add further actors such as religious communities, professional associations, the media, transnational terrorist networks, or transnational criminal organizations to this list.[31] From a theoretical perspective, it is, however, less interesting to complete the list than to identify what drives the expansion of agency in global governance.[32] As we have argued above, the diversity of agents beyond the state sets global governance apart from international politics. Non-state actors have become relevant agents *to the extent that they command significant levels of governance resources*. Where non-state actors employ their governance resources for political ends or where they create a greater demand for governance resources – for instance, through successfully challenging the legitimacy of the World Trade Organization – global governance becomes more than simply the activity of states. Where individual actors hold *all resources* required to govern across borders, they are likely to do so without the help of other actors. The rules set by the Federation of International Football Associations (FIFA), for instance, effectively govern how football is played, how football clubs and national associations of football clubs are organized, and how national and international competitions are managed. In many cases, however, actors will only control *some resources* and therefore see a need to cooperate with actors who control complementary resources, thereby creating a need for mechanisms and institutions through which they can effectively pool or exchange resources. Before we examine these mechanisms and their outcomes, the following paragraphs sketch how key governance resources are distributed among the various types of actors that populate global governance.

the distribution of governance resources

Table 2.1 provides a rough (and to some extent contestable) overview of how key governance resources are distributed among various actors. As can be seen, only few organizations possess significant political, financial, cognitive, *and* moral resources to govern effectively and efficiently on their own. Nationally, states still control most of these resources; in particular, in the OECD world, they can issue binding regulations, organize distributive policies and gather relevant knowledge for addressing policy problems in an efficient manner, not least through their bureaucracies. Finally, in doing so, democratically elected governments can usually count on their perception as legitimate representatives of their people. Beyond the nation state, such a concentration of resources is rare. Even the European Union, arguably the most advanced organization in this respect, has only limited financial capacities that enable

Table 2.1 Non-state actors and governance resources – Who has what? (brightly shaded = some control; darkly shaded = substantive control)

Type of resource actor	Political (influence)	Financial (money)	Cognitive (information)	Moral (legitimacy)
International organizations				
International bureaucracies				
International NGOs				
Private foundations				
Government agencies				
Hybrid organizations				
Business actors				
Epistemic communities				
Migrant communities				
Religious communities				
Media				

it to govern effectively in some areas like environmental regulation, but prohibit it from pursuing its policies in other areas like social policy. Moreover, the legitimacy of the European Union is regularly challenged by national decision-makers and social groups who then need to be co-opted by the European decision-makers to ensure that governance mechanisms run smoothly.

Political Resources. Only a handful of actors other than states can make decisions that are binding for other actors. These are intergovernmental organizations, hybrid organizations, and a small number of private governance organizations. In human rights politics, the European Court of Human Rights explicitly transcends the interstate system. It grants individuals access to international legal remedies against member states and its judgments are legally binding for member states. In transnational sports governance, the International Olympic Committee (IOC), the World Anti-Doping Agency (WADA), and the Court of Arbitration for Sports (CAS) can all issue transnationally binding decisions about the right of individuals to participate in national and international competitions. In addition, government agencies and local communities can exert political influence to the extent that they coordinate their activities in transgovernmental policy networks and implement joint decisions more or less directly within their own states. Beyond this narrow range, a number of other organizations dispose of some political resources – they are able to control effectively some aspects of the behaviour of some of their members. This includes religious communities and membership associations like the International Federation of Accountants (IFAC) or the International Federation of Building and Wood Workers (IFBWW). All other actors may dispose of *access* to those who make and implement binding decisions, but they do not wield such power themselves.

Financial Resources. Financial resources are required to put political projects into practice. Internationally, only few non-state actors dispose of sizeable funds. They primarily include intergovernmental organizations like the World Bank, the International Monetary Fund (IMF), or the Global Environmental Facility (GEF). In addition, the contributions of private foundations have already been mentioned. In contrast to these organized efforts, the contributions from both business organizations and migrants are less coordinated. Business actors are relevant primarily as the source of FDI flows. Yet although FDI flows may reflect domestic political factors, they are not usually motivated by political ends. The same holds for private remittances from migrant communities. In terms of financial flows from North to South, they reach about the same level as FDI, but they are motivated by personal rather than political ties. Moreover, business investments and private remittances are only weakly organized on a collective scale. As a result, although business organizations and migrant communities invest or transmit large sums abroad, politically motivated actors in global governance have difficulties tapping into these resources.

Cognitive Resources. As can be seen in Table 2.1, knowledge and information are widely dispersed in global governance. Depending on the policy in question, scientists, NGOs, the business community, international bureaucracies, and government agencies may all possess relevant knowledge for addressing a policy problem. For instance, anti-money laundering policies are likely to be inefficient without information and expertise from private banks; environmental policies may fail without expert input; and business regulation may be more efficient if the knowledge of business can be taken into consideration. NGOs are frequently relevant because they employ some of the leading researchers in their fields, because they participate in both national and international policy processes, and because they often have privileged access to information from various societies and governments because of their transnational structures.[33] Intergovernmental organizations and international bureaucracies dispose of expertise in almost all areas of world politics as they pool policy-relevant knowledge of their member states or engage in substantive research of their own. As knowledge brokers in their respective fields, the United Nations Development Programme (UNDP) publishes the annual *Human Development Report*, the United Nations Environment Programme (UNEP) runs the *Global Environmental Monitoring Scheme* (GEMS), and the World Meteorological Organization (WMO), together with the United Nations Environment Program (UNEP), initiated the Intergovernmental Panel on Climate Change (IPCC). Moreover, the secretariats to international conventions collect and disseminate data on member states' compliance with their legal obligations under the respective conventions.

Moral Resources. As a resource that can be exchanged, legitimacy is distinct from money and influence because of its (inter)subjective nature. To have legitimacy means to be considered as legitimate by relevant audiences. Since relevant audiences vary depending on the policy in question and since legitimacy perceptions tend to vary among audiences, it is difficult to make general statements about which actors dispose of legitimacy as a further resource for effective and efficient governance. International bureaucracies derive their legitimacy from their political neutrality.[34] In contrast, NGOs ground their legitimacy on their portrayal as representatives of the voiceless and powerless, and scientists command legitimacy as a result of their expertise in particular areas of policy-making and the general assumption of value-free knowledge. In particular, areas such as environmental governance, where effective governance is virtually impossible without input from the scientific community, policies that openly oppose a scientific consensus may be more difficult to implement. As the representatives of particular regional communities or of the international community at large, intergovernmental organizations equally dispose of significant legitimacy potentials. Yet powerful campaigns by civil society organizations and nationalist movements have challenged these potentials.[35] Finally, campaigns to boost or challenge an actor's legitimacy can be either supported or hindered by the mass media, which thus acts as an important filter for the willingness of public audiences to grant or withhold legitimacy. The media are therefore a further actor to be taken into account in the 'global legitimacy game'.[36]

where, how, and to what end? arenas and issues of global governance

In the preceding sections, we have argued that global governance is more than international politics because it results from the interaction not only of states but also of a plurality of actors. Moreover, we have argued that to achieve their political ends, these actors often need to pool and exchange resources with other actors with either similar or complementary ends. This pooling and exchange can result in formal agreements and institutions or it can occur in informal cooperation; in both cases, it constitutes the nucleus of governance arrangements beyond the state. In this section, we therefore ask where, how, and to what end the various actors pool and exchange their resources to establish global governance.

Where does governance take place? At least at a superficial level, the answer to this first question is relatively straightforward. Actors pool and exchange resources in *intergovernmental, transgovernmental,* and *transnational* arenas. In intergovernmental arenas, states pool their influence, money, knowledge, and legitimacy to realize mutual gains.[37] In transgovernmental arenas, national agencies coordinate their policies to solve policy problems and to extend their own spheres of influence vis-à-vis other actors, including their own central governments.[38] And in transnational arenas, civil society organizations and/or business organizations join forces to effectively govern particular aspects of the behaviour of producers or consumers of economic goods and services.[39] The fourth arena of global governance – supranational governance – is different in this regard since its institutions are often created for the very purpose of governing a particular issue independently of the direct influence of the member states.[40] Political resources are thus pooled to create a new governance level above the existing level; as a result, the supranational arena occasionally seems closer to *government* than *governance.*

Beyond these ideal-type forms of global governance, a number of exchanges occur across as well as within the boundaries that separate these arenas. One form that has received widespread attention is the form of public–private partnerships that have spread in particular in the fields of global sustainability governance and global health governance. For example, in the UN Global Compact, initiated by former UN Secretary General Kofi Annan, the United Nations granted the participating corporations a degree of legitimacy through their association

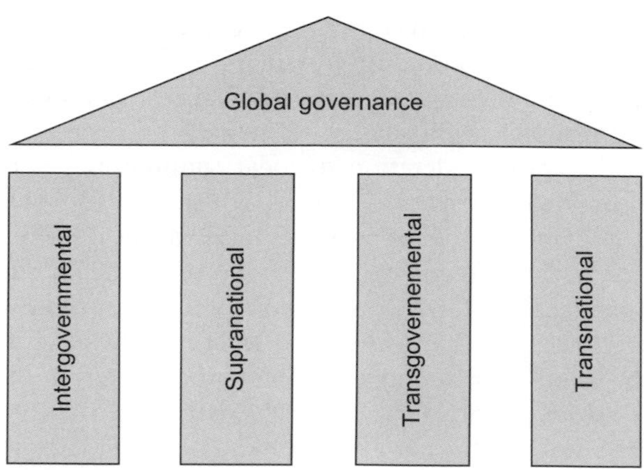

Figure 2.1 **Arenas of global governance**

with the United Nations as a representative of the interests of the international community. In exchange, the UN gains political influence over some aspects of the conduct of large multinational corporations that participate in the Global Compact. The same holds for other cooperative initiatives among business and international or transnational organizations, including agreements between the World Conservation Union and Shell or between the World Wildlife Fund (WWF) and Kodak. In addition, the relations between international organizations and NGOs can also be described in terms of a resource exchange. Kal Raustiala has analysed this process for the environmental domain.[41] On this account, the increased participation of non-governmental environmental actors in intergovernmental decision-making is a result of the broadened scope of international environmental regulation and the resulting complexity of environmental policy-making. These changes have created demand for expert knowledge and information that environmental NGOs possess. However, access to governmental deliberations is not granted to all environmental NGOs, but only to those that command the most relevant resources at the lowest price.

In addition to exchanges across governance arenas, resource exchange can also be observed across levels. A good example is the exchange between transnational advocacy networks that operate at the global level and local NGOs that represent the interests of marginalized stakeholders. Transnational advocacy networks often build their campaigns around the demands of local communities. In this sense, local communities deliver the raw material from which transnational advocacy networks manufacture their global campaigns. As transnational networks are rather scarce and overloaded with work, local concerns are abundant, the price for consideration of local communities is potentially high. Transnational advocacy networks can strategically choose those cases among a large number of concerns raised by local NGOs that meet the demands of their organizational environment, such as donors, the media, or members. Clifford Bob has analysed this intriguing relationship between the global and the local level of civil society in a case study of the Ogoni tribe's struggle against oil exploitation in Nigeria.[42] To sell their story to transnational activist networks, the Ogoni had to reframe their struggle from a predominantly economic conflict about the fair distribution of oil revenues within Nigeria to one about environmental degradation and corporate malpractice.

How does governance take place? In response to this second question, two distinctions can be made. First, resource exchange can be characterized as formal or informal, varying along a continuum of institutionalization. Formal arenas have two distinctive advantages in as much as they allow for centralization and independence. Centralization means that actors can pool their resources to increase both their leverage and efficiency. Independence means that, through creating partially autonomous organizations, actors can make more credible commitments to their cooperating partners.[43] Examples of formal governance arrangements include intergovernmental organizations and private governance organizations such as the Forest Stewardship Council (FSC).[44] The FSC institutionalizes cooperation between social, economic, and environmental interests in the forest sector. To make mutual expectations more stable, the members of the organization have developed detailed procedural rules, including a tripartite decision-making body that gives equal weight to all stakeholders' interests, and accreditation procedures for certification organizations that ensure economic independence from business interests. These rules stabilize actors' expectations about how the other side will act. They ensure that participating civil society organizations will work with, rather than against, participating business organizations and that producers and retailers will not use the FSC-label for purposes other than those stipulated by the organization's regulations.

Yet resource exchanges can also occur on a more informal basis. The public–private partnerships registered with the UN Commission on

Sustainable Development after the 2002 World Summit on Sustainable Development offer a good example. They are often limited in their duration, depend on earmarked funds that leave little room for independent activity, and consequently remain dependent on the individual organizations that constitute the partnership. Further down the continuum, the periodic meetings of the World Economic Forum, a gathering of leading economic, political, and cultural leaders to discuss issues of global importance, or the relation between foundations and their recipient NGOs are also less formalized. In the former example, memberships and the corresponding roles and responsibilities in the World Economic Forum are not clearly defined. In the latter case, cooperation remains informal because the power disparities between a handful donor organizations and the multitude of potential recipients enable foundations to pursue cooperation on their own terms.

The last point hints at a second important distinction, namely between resource exchanges among equals (symmetry) and resource exchanges among unequal partners (asymmetry). While exchanges within the Forest Stewardship Council are, largely, symmetric in terms of power, there are ample illustrations of less symmetric relations. Asymmetric exchange occurs in situations when demand for a certain resource is high but supply is limited or concentrated in the hands of a few. For example, while there are numerous cases of local, social, and environmental degradation, only few actors control the resources to publicize and turn them into a global concern. Similarly, numerous NGOs compete for financial support from private foundations while foundations only rely on a limited number of civil society partners to implement their specific programmes. In sum, the resource dependence perspective thus allows to analyse global governance both with regard to the degree of institutionalization and the symmetry/asymmetry involved. With regard to the latter distinction, the resource dependence perspective explicitly includes power relations in its analysis and is thus largely immune to the common criticism that the global governance literature is power-blind.[45]

What functions does governance serve? After having discussed the arenas of global governance and the specific ways in which resources are exchanged within these arenas, we now turn to the functions that governance arrangements perform. The definition of global governance quoted at the outset of this chapter distinguishes between three such functions – the articulation of collective interests, the establishment of rights and obligations, and the mediation of differences.

As political issues are increasingly discussed at an international level, the *articulation of collective interests* also needs to move up to that level. The central institutions for articulating collective interests at the national level are political parties; in addition, labour unions, employers' associations, and special interest groups are important for aggregating and articulating collective interests. At the international level, political parties have hardly gone global; the Socialist International is still an exception in this regard and the coherence of its members' policies seems questionable. Trade unions and employers' associations are better organized at the transnational level, in particular where institutions like the European Social Dialogue or the tripartite structure of the International Labour Organization create strong incentives to organize across borders. Finally, special interest groups are strongly transnationalized; they include INGOs like the World Wildlife Fund and business associations like the International Council of Chemical Associations (ICCA).

Beyond these single-purpose organizations, new arrangements for interest articulation are emerging on the global political landscape. The Global Legislators Organization for a Balanced Environment (GLOBE) is a prime example. Founded in 1989 as an inter-parliamentary group between the US Congress and European Parliament, GLOBE aims to respond to the challenges of global environmental change. Through dialogues among legislators that 'shadow' international negotiations, the organization has successfully lobbied for a number of environmental legislations since its inception. Examples include the 1992 negotiations of the United Nations Framework Convention on Climate Change and its 1997 Kyoto Protocol as well; and more recently, efforts to establish a stronger international legal regime to stop illegal logging. Yet, as the example of the Ogoni in Nigeria illustrates, the transnational articulation of local interests is not always straight forward, since to be articulated at the international level, collective interests frequently need to be reframed and adapted to resonate with 'global concerns'. The few players that have the capacities to turn a local cause into a global issue thus remain powerful agents in global governance.

A second function of governance arrangements beyond the state is *to establish rights and responsibilities*. This is most clear for international legal instruments concluded in intergovernmental forums and monitored in the transnational or supranational governance arena. Yet rights and responsibilities may also be established in the transnational governance arena where institutions like the Forest Stewardship Council constitute functional equivalents to international regimes. Within the context of an accelerating global forest crisis in the late 1980s and early 1990s, the FSC establishes rights and responsibilities for producers that comply with the Principles and Criteria for Responsible Forest Management. Similarly, the UN Global Compact is not merely a network in which multinational corporations learn to become more responsible 'corporate citizens'.[46] Instead, it is based on legal contracts that establish rights and responsibilities for both the UN and participating firms. Similarly, membership in the FIFA gives a national football association the right to participate in international competitions – for instance, to qualify for the World Cup. At the same time, it obliges the member association to obey the rules and procedures of the international association. In the end, transboundary rights and responsibilities are therefore established wherever interaction is coordinated based on legal or quasi-legal rules. The legalization of world politics thus implies that this second function becomes more relevant across the different arenas of global governance.

Finally, once interests have been articulated and rights and obligations have been established, the *mediation of interests* becomes a third important function of global governance arrangements. Interest mediation is required in various situations. It may be necessary where actors have conflicting views on issues that have not yet been regulated or where the respective regulations are not accepted by at least one of the parties to the dispute. Such a situation, for instance, characterized the international debate over large dams when the actors involved – anti-dam activists, the dams industry, and international financial institutions – agreed to establish the World Commission on Dams and mandated this commission to develop guidelines for future decision-making around large dams.[47] In addition, interest mediation may also be necessary where international or transnational rules exist, but are insufficiently precise to cover all possible cases that may arise under a regulation. Such a situation is characteristic for any legal system. It is the basis on which courts mediate – or, more precisely, adjudicate – between different interpretations of a given rule. Given the increasing density of rule-based cooperation in world politics, it is thus hardly surprising that the number of international and transnational courts (or quasi-courts) has also increased. Institutions like the Dispute Settlement Body of the World Trade Organization or the Court of Arbitration for Sports are thus examples of governance arrangements in which states and non-state actors pool their resources to create effective mechanisms for the mediation of interests.

In terms of resources, not all functions require the same level of influence, money, knowledge, and legitimacy (see also Table 2.2). Thus, the ability to issue binding regulations is primarily required for the establishment of rights and obligations; in addition, it is a defining feature of a particular type of mediating institutions, namely international and transnational courts. For the other purposes – informal mediation or

Table 2.2 Governance functions and key resources – what is needed?

Type of resource actor	Political (influence)	Cognitive (information)	Financial (money)	Moral (legitimacy)	Example
Articulating collective interests	Not required	Knowledge about how to feed in interests and information in the policy process is important	Essential to coordinate interest formation across borders and potentially helpful to raise awareness (e.g. through public campaigns)	Necessary to convince audiences that do not initially share the same interests	International Campaign on the Ban of Landmines (ICBL)
Establishing rights and obligations	Essential to establish effective rights and obligations	Essential to effectively and efficiently address a policy problem (e.g. climate change)	May be required depending on the particular rights or obligations (e.g. distributive policies; monitoring compliance)	Reduces compliance costs since target actors are more likely to comply voluntarily.	UN Security Council decisions about international peacekeeping
Mediating interests	Essential for formal mediating institutions (i.e. courts or quasi-courts); for informal mediators, a 'shadow of hierarchy' may be helpful	Knowledge about underlying causes of different interests and about possible solutions is required to identify common ground	Required to fund the mediating actors and institutions	Legitimacy of mediating institutions facilitates acceptance and thereby enhances prospects for successful settlement (and/or reduces compliance costs)	World Commission on Dams (WCD)

the articulation of interests – this sort of political influence may be helpful, but is not strictly necessary.

In contrast, knowledge is required for all three functions, although to different degrees. To be effective, the articulation of interests may require knowledge about how best to channel these interests into the political arena. Yet it does not presuppose that those who articulate their interests know a great deal about climate change. In contrast, if legal regulations (that is, decisions that establish rights and obligations) are not based on sound knowledge, they will be unable to solve the underlying problem. Similarly, the mediation of interests may not only require that the parties as well as the mediating institutions know (or learn) about their different interests, but also that they know (or learn) the underlying causes of these differences and possible ways of identifying common ground.

Third, money is essential to coordinate the articulation of interests across borders and a powerful resource to increase the awareness of a particular policy problem through public campaigns. Thus, the International Campaign on the Ban of Landmines and the Coalition for an International Criminal Court (CICC) were primarily successful because their concerns were adopted by many citizens around the globe and because they were seen as legitimate by the broader public. Yet they were also among the best-funded civil society campaigns in history – a fact that helped them to gather the support from individuals and to gain substantial moral resources in the first place. For the establishment of rights and obligations, the need for financial resources depends on the policy in question. Thus, for distributive policies, money is by definition essential; for regulatory policies, financial resources are necessary to install mechanisms for effective compliance control. For the mediation of interests, financial resources are mainly necessary to cover the expenses of mediators or mediating institutions.

Finally, legitimacy is usually required for each function – although the precise degree and form may again vary according to the subject area and audience. Thus, obligations will be followed more often if they are accepted as legitimate; interests will be listened to more readily if they are perceived as rightful; and the mediation of interests faces fewer obstacles if mediating institutions are commonly seen as just or fair.

conclusion

Notwithstanding the increased use of the term 'global governance' in both academic and policy circles, a number of authors remain cautious about embracing the concept and argue that world politics has remained more or less the same. Ultimately, they perceive the 'global governance' talk as misleading. For instance, Kenneth Waltz contends that even though globalization may have brought some change, world politics can still be understood in terms of the anarchical nature of the international system, the lack of functional differentiation of the units that compose that system, and the distribution of capabilities among those units.[48] From a more practical point of view, John Bolton has equally disputed the need to 'take global governance seriously' since the major states effectively remain – and should remain – the principal drivers of world politics.[49]

Against this critique, we have argued that global governance is not only a useful concept in analysing world politics, but also a fact. By taking a resource exchange perspective on global governance, we have highlighted that a variety of actors possess agency in world politics, that governance resources are widely distributed and that resource exchanges take place in different arenas and in different ways. In our understanding, the ubiquitous talk about 'global governance' indeed reflects a broader shift in the nature of world politics, and a more explicit resource perspective might help to better understand and explain this shift. However, we also acknowledge shortcomings of the concept of 'global governance,' two of which we will briefly address in the remainder of the conclusions.

The first shortcoming of the current global governance concept is its geographical bias, as the term suggests a level of homogeneity that far transcends contemporary realities. What is usually labelled 'global governance' is rarely global in a literal sense. Beyond the OECD world, in which the dense integration of politics, law, economy, and civil society and the frequent transboundary interlinkages constitutes a post-national system of politics, the 'new second world' of EU enlargement candidates and a few (South) East Asian societies can also be considered as capable of actively and passively participating in global governance. Borrowing from Dieter Senghaas's work, this is very different for the 'third' and 'fourth world'. In the third world, the centres are integrated, if only asymmetrically, in the transnational club of the first and second world, while the periphery is structurally dependent on its own centres and hence incapable of effectively participating in transboundary, let alone global, governance. Finally, in the fourth world, societies no longer dispose of regulatory capacities because the state has either failed or been usurped by private actors. On this account, the necessary preconditions for effective governance through the pooling of complementary resources are virtually absent in large parts of the world, thus making global governance a much less global affair than the label might suggest.[50]

Second, theorizing global governance suffers from an in-built bias towards order. The term global governance not only suggests that governance is actually global, but also that the globe – or a substantial part of it – is effectively governed through processes of resource exchange. However, it can be reasonably questioned whether the concept of governance comes anything but close to the realities of world politics. The field of global governance is commonly divided into specific issue areas such as global economic governance, global environmental governance, or global health governance. Analyses of specific fields of global governance commonly start by establishing an inventory of regulatory mechanisms relevant for the respective field. As an obvious consequence, global governance research primarily sees regulation. In contrast, the absence of regulation – or 'non-governance' – is often overlooked by scholars of global governance.

The resource exchange perspective on global governance introduced in this chapter is at least partially equipped to solve this second problem. Since it departs from the distribution of resources among actors, it shifts the attention from governance arrangements to the resources sustaining them. Moreover, it is generally open to the possibility that individual actors may pursue their political ends not through rule-based coordination (that is, through *governance*) but through other means such as violence, direct action, or ad hoc coalitions that may not count as governance in a more narrow sense. In addition, and in contrast to the global governance label itself, a resource exchange perspective is not necessarily biased towards globality, but capable of highlighting interactions across governance levels. In sum, a resource perspective may provide important insights into the dynamics of global governance, but still falls short of providing a genuine 'theory of global governance'. The challenge cup for establishing such a theory of global governance has yet to be claimed.

notes

1. Ramesh Thakur and Luk Van Langerhove, 'Enhancing Global Governance Through Regional Integration,' Global Governance, Vol. 12, No. 3 (July–September 2006), p. 233.

2. Frank Biermann, 'Global Environmental Governance: Conceptualization and Examples,' *Global Governance Working Paper* No 12. Amsterdam.: The Global Governance Project (glogov.org), p. 5.
3. The British Library catalogue lists 218 titles (as of 25 January 2008) that include 'global governance' in the title, subtitle or series title. The earliest titles date from 1993; for 158 entries (representing 72 per cent of all entries) the year of publication is 2000 or later.
4. Alice Ba and Matthew Hoffmann (2005) 'Introduction: Coherence and Contestation,' in Alice D. Ba and Matthew J. Hoffmann (eds), *Global Governance: Coherence, Contestation, and World Order* (London: Routledge, 2005), pp. 1–14.
5. Klaus Dingwerth and Philipp Pattberg, 'Global Governance as a Perspective on World Politics,' *Global Governance*, Vol. 12, No. 2), 2006, pp. 185–203.
6. Kees van Kersbergen and Frans van Waarden, 'Governance as a Bridge between Disciplines: Cross-Disciplinary Inspiration Regarding Shifts in Governance and Problems of Governability, Accountability and Legitimacy', *European Journal of Political Research*, Vol. 43, 2004, pp. 143–171.
7. See Chapter 1 of this volume. Cf. James N. Rosenau, *Turbulence in World Politics* (Princeton: Princeton University Press, 1990); James N. Rosenau, *Along the Domestic-Foreign Frontier: Exploring Governance in a Turbulent World* (Cambridge: Cambridge University Press, 1997); James N. Rosenau, *Distant Proximities: Dynamics Beyond Globalization* (Princeton: Princeton University Press, 2003) and James N. Rosenau, *The Study of World Politics* (2 volumes) (London: Routledge, 2006). The novelty is contested by some authors; see, for instance, Jörg Friedrichs, 'The Meaning of New Medievalism,' *European Journal of International Relations*, Vol. 7, No. 4, 2001, pp. 475–501 and Thomas Risse and Ursula Lehmkuhl, 'Governance in Areas of Limited Statehood – New Modes of Governance?' Research Program of the Research Centre (SFB) 700, Berlin: Freie Universität, 2006.
8. Oran R. Young, *Governance in World Affairs* (Ithaca: Cornell University Press, 1999), p. 11.
9. In addition to the regime literature, a systems theoretical version of this functionalist argument holds that the shift towards global governance is primarily the move from a segmentary logic of differentiation to a functional logic of differentiation; cf. Mathias Albert and Lena Hilkermeier (eds), *Observing International Relations: Niklas Luhmann and World Politics* (London: Routledge 2004); Helmut Wilke, *Global Governance* (Transcript).
10. Bernhard Zangl and Michael Zürn, 'Make Law, Not War: Internationale und Transnationale Verrechtlichung als Bausteine für Global Governance,' in Bernhard Zangl and Michael Zürn (eds), *Verrechtlichung – Bausteine Für Global* Governance (Bonn: Dietz, 2004), pp. 12–45; Michael Zürn, 'Global Governance as an Emergent Political Order – The Role of Transnational Non-Governmental Organisations,' in Gunnar Folke Schuppert (ed.), *Global Governance and the Role of None-State Actors* (Baden Baden: Nomos, 2006), pp. 31–45.
11. Klaus Dingwerth, Nichtstaatliche Akteure und der Wandel der Governance-Norm (Non-State actors and changing norm of governance), paper presented at the workshop "Macht, Ohnmacht, Gegenmacht – Nichtstaatliche

Akteure im Globalen Regieren", Delmenhorst, Germany, 15–16 June 2007.

12. Cf. Kenneth N Waltz,. 'Globalization and Governance,' *PS Online*, Vol. 32, No. 4, 1999, pp. 693–700; John Bolton, 'Should We Take Global Governance Seriously?' *Chicago Journal of International Law*, Vol. 1, 2000, pp. 205–221; Henk Overbeek, 'Global Governance, Class, Hegemony: A Historical Materialist Perspective,' in Alice D. Ba and Matthew J. Hoffmann (eds), *Global Governance: Coherence, Contestation and World* Order, pp. 39–56.
13. Andreas Nölke, *Transnationale Politiknetzwerke: Eine Analyse grenzüberschreitender politischer Entscheidungsprozesse jenseits des regierungszentrischen Modells* (Leipzig: Universität Leipzig, 2004).
14. Achim Hurrelmann, Stephan Leibfried, Kerstin Martens and Peter Mayer (eds), *Transforming the Golden-Age Nation State* (Basingstoke: Palgrave Macmillan, 2007); Phillip Genschel and Bernhard Zangl, 'Die Zerfaserung von Staatlichkeit und die Zentralität des Staates,' *Aus Politik und Zeitgeschichte*, vol. 20–21, 2007, pp. 10–16.
15. Hedley Bull, *The Anarchical Society: A Study of Order in World Politics* (New York: Columbia University Press, 1977), p. 266.
16. See also Margaret P. Karns and Karen A. Mingst, *International Organizations: The Politics and Processes of Global Governance* (Boulder: Lynne Rienner, 2004), pp. 3–34.
17. Zangl, Bernhard and Volker Rittberger, *International Organisations: Polity, Policy, and Politics* (Basingstoke: Palgrave, 2006).
18. Robert W. Cox and Harold K. Jacobson, *The Anatomy of Influence* (New Haven: Yale University Press, 1973); Michael Barnett and Martha Finnemore, *Rules for the World: International Organizations in Global Politics* (Ithaca and London: Cornell University Press, 2004); Frank Biermann and Bernd Siebenhüner (eds), *Managers of Global Change: The Influence of International Bureaucracies in Environmental Policy* (Cambridge, MA: MIT Press, forthcoming 2009).
19. Paul Wapner, *Environmental Activism and World Civic Politics* (Albany: State University of New York Press, 1996); Stephen Hopgood, *Keepers of the Flame: Understanding Amnesty International* (Ithaca: Cornell University Press, 2006).
20. Richard Price, 'Reversing the Gun Sights: Transnational Civil Society Targets Land Mines,' *International Organization*, Vol. 52, No. 3, 1998, pp. 613–644.
21. Klaus Dingwerth, *The New Transnationalism: Transnational Governance and Democratic Legitimacy* (Basingstoke: Palgrave, 2007); Philipp Pattberg, *Private Institutions and Global Governance: The New Politics of Environmental Sustainability* (Cheltenham: Edward Elgar, 2007).
22. See *Duke Law Journal*, Vol. 50, No. 1, Thirtieth Annual Administrative Law Issue, October 2000, pp. 187–260.
23. Anne-Marie Slaughter, *A New World Order* (Princeton: Princeton University Press, 2005).
24. See International Council of Local Environmental Initiatives, Cities for Climate Protection, available online at URL: http://www.iclei.org/index.php?id=1118
25. For the UN figures, see Sekretariat der Vereinten Nationen, *Konsolidierter Bericht* (New York: United Nations, 2006), p. 6; and United Nations

Secretariat, Assessment of Member States' advances to the Working Capital Fund for the biennium 2006–2007 and contributions to the United Nations regular budget for 2006. UN Document ST/ADM/SER.B/668. For the UN Foundation, see http://www.unfoundation.org/about/financial_info.asp

26. Ruggie, John Gerard, 'Global-Governance Net: The Global Compact as Learning Network,' *Global Governance. A Review of Multilateralism and International Organizations*, Vol. 7, No. 4, 2001, pp. 371–378.
27. David Vogel, *The Market for Virtue. The Potential and Limits of Corporate Social Responsibility* (Washington D.C.: Brookings Institution Press, 2005); see also Robert Falkner (2007) *Business Power and Conflict in International Environmental Politics* (Basingstoke: Palgrave Macmillan); Doris Fuchs, *Understanding Business Power in Global Governance* (Baden-Baden: Nomos, 2007); David L. Levy and Peter J. Newell (eds), *The Business of Global Environmental Governance* (Cambridge, MA: MIT Press, 2005).
28. Peter M. Haas, 'Do regimes matter? Epistemic Communities and Mediterranean Pollution Control,' *International Organization* Vol. 43, No. 3, 1989, pp. 377–403; Clark A. Miller and Paul N. Edwards (eds),. *Changing the Atmosphere: Expert Knowledge and Environmental Governance* (Cambridge, MA: MIT Press, 2001).
29. Frank Biermann, 'Whose Experts? The Role of Geographic Representation in Assessment Institutions,' in Ronald B. Mitchell, William C. Clark, David W. Cash and Nancy Dickson (eds), *Global Environmental Assessments: Information, Institutions and Influence* (Cambridge, Mass.: MIT Press, 2006); S. Jasanoff and M. Long Martello (eds) *Earthly Politics: Local and Global in Environmental Governance*. Cambridge, Mass.: MIT Press, 2004).
30. World Bank, 'Global Economic Prospects: Economic Implications of Remittances and Migration' (Washington, DC: World Bank, 200).
31. Cf. Maryanne Cusimano Love (ed.), *Beyond Sovereignty: Issues for a Global Agenda* (Belmont: Wadsworth Publishing, 2002); Marie-Laure Djélic and Kerstin Sahlin-Andersson (eds), *Transnational Governance: Institutional Dynamics of Regulation* (Cambridge: Cambridge: University Press, 2006); Frank Lechner and John Boli *World Culture: Origins and Consequences* (London: Blackwell, 2005).
32. Since we cannot investigate this question in any great detail in this chapter, it may suffice to say that, in addition to the skill revolution and the technological revolution, the modern idea of sovereign and rational 'actorhood' is a central normative underpinning of the proliferation of formal organizations that is characteristic not only for the conduct of world politics but also for society at large. See Gili S. Drori, John W. Meyer and Hokyu Hwang 'World Society and the Proliferation of Formal Organization,' in Gili S. Drori, John W. Meyer and Hokyu Hwang (eds), *Globalization and Organization: World Society and Organizational Change* (Oxford: Oxford University Press, 2006), pp. 25–49.
33. Kal Raustiala, 'States, NGOs, and International Environmental Institutions,' *International Studies Quarterly*, Vol. 41, No. 4, 1997, pp. 719–740.
34. Ibid.; Per-Olof Busch, 'How to Make a Living in a Straitjacket: Explaining Influences of the Secretariat to the United Nations Framework Convention on Climate Change,' in Frank Biermann and Bernd Siebenhüner (eds),

Managers of Global Change: The Role and Relevance of International Environmental Bureaucracies (Cambridge, MA: MIT Press, forthcoming 2009).

35. Christian Reus-Smit, 'International Crises of Legitimacy,' *International Politics* 44 (2007), pp. 157–174; Michael Zürn, 'Global Governance and Legitimacy Problems', *Government and Opposition*, Vol. 39, 2004, pp. 260–287.
36. Alison van Rooy, *The Global Legitimacy Game: Civil Society, Globalization and Protest* (Basingstoke: Palgrave Macmillan, 2004).
37. Robert O. Keohane, *After Hegemony: Cooperation and Discord in the World Political Economy* (Princeton: Princeton University Press, 1984); Kenneth W. Abbott and Duncan Snidal, 'Why States Act Through Formal International Organizations,' *Journal of Conflict Resolution*, Vol. 42, No. 1, pp. 3–32.
38. Anne-Marie Slaughter, *A New World Order.*
39. A. Claire Cutler, Virginia Haufler and Tony Porter (eds), *Private Authority and International Affairs* (Albany: SUNY Press, 1999); Philipp Pattberg, *Private Institutions and Global Governance: The New Politic of Environmental Sustainability* (Cheltenham: Edward Elgar, 2007).
40. Abbott and Snidal, 'Why States Act Through Formal International Organizations' (supra, note 37); Jonas Tallberg, 'Delegation to Supranational Institutions: Why, How, and with What Consequences?' *West European Politics*, Vol. 25, No. 1, 2002, pp. 23–46.
41. Kal Raustiala, 'States, NGOs, and International Environmental Institutions,' pp. 719–740.
42. Clifford Bob, *The Marketing of Rebellion: Insurgents, Media, and International Activism* (Cambridge: Cambridge University Press, 2005).
43. Abbott and Snidal, 'Why States Act Through Formal International Organizations,' pp. 3–32.
44. Klaus Dingwerth, *The New Transnationalism. Transnational Governance and Democratic Accountability* (Basingstoke: Palgrave Macmillan, 2007); Philipp Pattberg, *Private Institutions and Global Governance: The New Politics of Environmental Sustainability* (Cheltenham: Edward Elgar, 2007).
45. Michael Barnett and Raymond Duvall (eds), *Power in Global Governance* (Cambridge: Cambridge University Press, 2005).
46. John G. Ruggie, 'Global governance.net: The Global Compact as Learning Network,' *Global Governance*, Vol. 7, No. 4, 2001, pp. 371–378.
47. Jennifer M. Brinkerhoff, 'Partnership as a Social Network Mediator for Resolving Global Conflict: The Case of the World Commission on Dams,' *International Journal of Public Administration*, Vol. 25, No. 11, 2002, pp. 1281–1310.
48. Kenneth N. Waltz, 'Globalization and Governance,' *PS Online*, Vol. 32, No. 4, 1999, pp. 693–700.
49. John Bolton, 'Should We Take Global Governance Seriously?' pp. 205–221.
50. Dieter Senghaas, (2003) 'Die Konstitution der Welt: Eine Analyse in friedens-politischer Absicht,' *Leviathan: Berliner Zeitschrift für Sozialwissenschaft*, Vol. 31, No. 1, 2003, pp. 117–152.

3
global governance as international organization

thomas g. weiss and annelies z. kamran

Many readers are perhaps under the mistaken impression that 'international organization' and 'global governance' are synonyms. However, whereas the former concentrates on formal structures, the latter describes a range of formal *and* informal processes that reflect globalization and a growing recognition of problems that defy solutions by a single state. For many analysts, global governance overlaps with the rise of international organizations, which according to Craig Murphy's masterful history of global governance beginning in the nineteenth century are customarily seen as 'what world government we actually have'.[1] However, global governance clearly is not world government – indeed, it is better viewed as the sum of governance processes operating in the *absence* of world government. At the same time, both international organizations (IOs) in general and the United Nations (UN) in particular – the only universal membership and general-purpose international organization – are essential to understanding contemporary global governance.

In addition to interdependence and a burgeoning array of transboundary global problems, the preoccupation with global governance stems from the augmentation in numbers and importance of nonstate actors (civil society and market) and the fact that they are conducting themselves or combining themselves in new ways. The stage for the drama by Inis Claude's two United Nations[2] has, over the past six decades, become increasingly crowded with a diversity of other actors who play more than bit parts. There is substantial evidence that other nonstate actors (NSAs) are increasingly salient. Numerous individuals and institutions that are neither states nor the creation of states (that is, intergovernmental bureaucracies) contribute to and circumscribe virtually every deliberation and decision by the UN and other IOs. In many ways, they could not function without nongovernmental organizations (NGOs), academics, consultants, experts, independent commissions, and other groups of individuals.

'Global Governance as International Organization' permits us to explore Edgar Grande and Louis Pauly's paths to transnational and trans-boundary governance: the establishment of new international organizations at regional and global levels, changes in existing institutions and practices, and the intensification of private transnational activity. These paths of the evolution of cooperation are not completely separate from one another but interact dynamically.[3]

This chapter first examines dominant theories of international relations (IR) and where global governance fits. It then discusses the participation, norms, and dynamics of international organizations in global governance. We use examples from two types of IOs: those with universal membership and those with limited (such as regional) membership.[4] Examples of the former include the UN, as well as the Bretton Woods institutions and the World Trade Organization (WTO), while examples of the latter include the European Union (EU) and the North Atlantic Treaty Organization (NATO), and their growing involvement in issues and processes of global governance. This chapter can only hope to be illustrative; these examples suggest not only the complexity of the topic but also the usefulness of using global governance as the approach to the study of international organization.

dominant theories

Realism was the dominant paradigm in analyzing international politics in the twentieth century. From E. H. Carr's classic *Twenty Years' Crisis, 1919–1939*[5] through Hans Morgenthau's postwar classic *Politics among Nations*,[6] states and their quest for self-interest and power are, in this view, the only subjects worth studying. An updated version is Kenneth Waltz's structural realism,[7] in which the behavior of functionally undifferentiated states is based on the distribution of power.

However, like a stick figure drawing in an anatomy class, Realism and its variants leave out more than they describe. Its parsimony simply ignores much of contemporary affairs. By explaining change at the system level as coming from alterations in the distribution of state power capabilities, the theory says that change comes from within actors, but does not say how or why – which is why the end of the Soviet Union came as such a surprise. Furthermore, it does not explain the contributions by an ever-growing number of nonstate actors – including intergovernmental and nongovernmental organizations and the for-profit sector.

The limitations of Realism have spawned other efforts to capture the behavior within and among states as well as defining, explaining, and predicting NSA behavior. The neoliberal and constructivist schools of IR – exemplified by Robert Keohane and Joseph Nye,[8] and by Alexander Wendt[9] and John Ruggie,[10] respectively – argue that international organizations play an important role in the way that a state's identity and interests are formed. The transmission of ideas, the negotiation of norms, and the provision of information and expertise are significant.

Neither a neoliberal nor a constructivist would deny the importance of material capabilities but would argue that identity and interests are not exclusively determined by them. The two schools differ in that neoliberals assume the primacy of the state. Civil society has a structural effect at the international level through the state. Constructivists, however, see the state and civil society as being socially constituted by each other through ongoing discourse and interaction, and so too are the state and the international system. In particular, they assume that power is held constant while international practices affect state interest, identity, and behavior. In turn, behavior can affect the structure of the system, by changing both the functions of actors and the distribution of capabilities. However, the outcome of the interactions cannot be predicted.

International organizations – both intergovernmental and nongovernmental – produce changes in identities and interests as well, and ultimately, lead to new structures.

Until now, constructivism has had more use as a theory of the formation of state interests and identities (the unit-level) than of structure; however, global governance obliges us to bring structure squarely into the argument. The additional consideration of actors other than states in the processes of global governance leads to a number of unexpected conclusions (at least for Realists and liberal institutionalists) about international politics and international organizations.

definitions of global governance

Global governance is too new a notion to be defined in many political science lexicons, or even in the online edition of *The Oxford English Dictionary*. However, in its inaugural edition in 1995, the journal *Global Governance: A Review Multilateralism and International Organizations* contained definitional attempts by James N. Rosenau and Lawrence S. Finkelstein.

Rosenau writes that governance is concerned with the mechanisms of control (both transnational and subnational practices and institutions) that are essentially related to one another, and when taken together constitute systems of rule. He emphasizes the exponential growth of interdependence as actors proliferate to meet the new needs that are created. The existing world order remains without overarching authority, which does not mean that there is no structure: 'Governance encompasses the activities of governments, but it also includes the many other channels through which "commands" flow in the form of goals framed, directives issued, and policies pursued.'[11] There is no global ordering principle, but global governance is usefully seen as the sum of the formal and informal mechanisms that ensure partial ordering – what Rosenau poetically calls a 'crazy quilt'.

Finkelstein wrote that 'global' denotes a world in which actors other than states play an increasingly important role, and in which decision-making processes are multilevel, connected both within and between states. 'Governance' is an ambiguous term that refers to governing without government, which approaches the title of Rosenau and Ernst Czempiel's earlier set of influential essays, *Governance without Government.*[12] 'Global governance,' for Finkelstein, is 'any purposeful activity intended to "control" or influence someone else that either occurs in the arena occupied by nations or, occurring at other levels, projects influence into that arena.' It is a process of activity, and to differentiate it from other terms, its descriptive rather than normative nature should be emphasized: 'global governance is governing, without sovereign authority, relationships that transcend national frontiers'.[13] Other definitions include the following:

- *Commission on Global Governance 1995*: 'Governance is the sum of the many ways individuals and institutions, public and private, manage their common affairs... At the global level, governance has been viewed primarily as intergovernmental relationships, but it must now be understood as also involving non-governmental organizations (NGOs), citizens' movements, multinational corporations, and the global capital market.'[14]

- *Margaret P. Karns and Karen A. Mingst, 2004:* '[T]he collection of governance-related activities, rules, and mechanisms, formal and informal, existing at a variety of levels in the world today... the cooperative problem-solving arrangements and activities that states and other actors have put into place to deal with various issues and problems.'[15]
- *World Economic Forum 2006*: Governance covers 'the contributions of all the types of actors on the global stage: governments, intergovernmental organizations, the business community and civil society. Governments are the key actors with the lion's share of responsibility for ensuring the achievement of the goals, and the intergovernmental organizations they create are essential tools in that struggle. But governments are unlikely to meet the challenge without the active and large-scale participation of both the private sector and civil society'.[16]

Global governance does not connote good or bad practice but describes cooperative problem-solving arrangements of all types. They may be formal, taking the shape of laws or institutions to manage collective affairs by such actors as state authorities, IGOs, NGOs, private sector entities, other civil society actors, and individuals. But arrangements may also involve such informal mechanisms as practices or guidelines or even temporary units (for example, coalitions). Global governance includes purpose-built regimes as well as market-driven evolutions and adaptations; and as such, it therefore *includes* governments. There is no necessarily anti-state or anti-government bias that emanates from this perspective – too much enthusiasm verges on the worst caricatures of the Ronald Reagan and Margaret Thatcher years, 'anything the state can do the private sector can do better'. We therefore distance ourselves from analysts like B. Guy Peters, who wrote the following about governance without government: 'Society is presumed to be more capable than government of understanding its own affairs and of finding remedies for any problems that are encountered in its functioning.'[17]

We repeat what one of us has written elsewhere, namely that global governance is the complex of formal and informal institutions, mechanisms, relationships, and processes between and among states, markets, citizens, and organizations, both inter and nongovernmental, through which collective interests on the global plane are articulated, rights and obligations are established, and differences are mediated.[18] This definition emphasizes five components that are essential for analyzing contemporary international relations: level of analysis (transnational); issues; nonstate actors; the dynamics of governance; and the interdependent yet loosely-coupled complex international system.

Global governance is about understanding and creating structures through repeated relationships, or patterns of authority, even if they are loose and informal. Important actors are not just states; and interests are partly a result of an actor's attributes and identity, and partly of its structural role and position within the extant world order.

Collectivities of all types are organized to achieve goals, and they draw on different sources of legitimacy. Therefore, for example, a state is organized differently from a corporation, and for different purposes. A state has sovereignty, which requires defending a given territory and exercising authority over its population while acting independently from outside interference. A corporation is organized to make a profit, which requires satisfying certain people (its market). Global governance thus recognizes that people create many kinds of structures – formal and informal, tangible and intangible – that interact with one another and evolve constantly. The potential role of actors depends on an issue is framed, or how it is conceptualized and categorized by actors that are paying attention. A state active in peace and security may not be as engaged on environmental issues, or vice versa – for example, Israel and Japan. Or an NGO can have tremendous impact or rule-making but not on monitoring and enforcement, or vice versa – for instance, the International Campaign to Ban Landmines and Amnesty International.

The notion of 'international community' is a victim of the flux in contemporary world politics. A special section of the journal *Foreign Policy* in Fall 2002 was entitled, 'What Is the International Community?'[19] The lead-in quipped, 'invoking the international community is a lot easier than defining it'. It no longer makes much sense to use the term restrictively because the cast of nonstate characters playing essential roles on the international stage is crucial to addressing virtually every global challenge to human survival and dignity. While international lawyers refer narrowly to the 'peace-loving states', other observers employ the concept more expansively and also include the creations of states in the form of intergovernmental secretariats, while still other commentators also embrace nonstate actors operating internationally.

The furthest stretch is Gareth Evans' inclusion of 'all those actors on the international stage who are capable of influencing for good or for ill the course of events'.[20] As the members of the so-called international community depend on the observer, it is better to avoid the term entirely. The expansion of the term's boundaries for many observers beyond the community of states indicates, however, the importance of a growing number of actors on the global stage. So too does coining the term 'global governance'.

This framing allows us to study outcomes that are normatively suboptimal (that is, less than ideal) and to formulate standardized definitions.[21] Realists study state versus state behavior. Liberal institutionalists scrutinize state interactions with international institutions. Rather than placing constructivism in opposition to either Realism or liberal institutionalism, it is at the other end of a spectrum from both because global governance highlights overall behavior and outcomes.

The advantage of mainstream theories is that their ontology and epistemology are well-known, whereas with global governance both are still being created. However, those who rely exclusively on IR theory to make normative or prescriptive judgments overlook real-world variations. Furthermore, the lens of global governance also permits analysts to consider aspects and impacts of contemporary governance that are undesirable. For example, there should be no reluctance to account for groups with less-than-benign influence, such as the National Rifle Association's transnational role in the Small Arms and Light Weapons trade.[22]

In short, insights from Realism and liberal institutionalism are pertinent to explain actor behavior, but they are misleading or insufficient to understand the ever-changing dynamics of the international system as a whole. That requires the sum of all such relationships, which is the value added of global governance.

IO participation in global governance

International organizations – however weak or inadequate to the task – are integral to global governance. Their participation reflects both formal treaty arrangements by member states as well as ad hoc developments and cooperation among various IOs in the field in the pursuit of shared goals. The United Nations is, of course, the most obvious example of a key IO in global governance, being composed of virtually all states on the planet (192 and counting), with a global mandate in all issue areas – there is nothing that is not on the UN's agenda. For example, the UN's contribution to international peace and security in the area of nuclear weapons has been led by the International Atomic Energy Agency (IAEA) with both its efforts at treaty formulation and operational monitoring, although earlier efforts by the Committee on Disarmament were lackluster. The policy championed by the IAEA has been to control through the idea of openness of information and transparency of operations. Although usually traced back to President Eisenhower's 'Atoms for Peace' speech, the IAEA had its roots even further back in postwar US nuclear policy.

Control of atomic energy was the subject of a heated national debate. But by the spring of 1946, the *de facto* policy of cooperation and sharing of information had been developed by scientists at Los Alamos.[23] In effect, the site leaders made policy to suit themselves without waiting for legislation. And the legislation that was eventually adopted followed their lead; the principles of civilian, democratic control of atomic energy were embedded in the Atomic Energy Act of 1946.[24] This vision was not institutionalized at the international level until Eisenhower made his speech before the General Assembly in December 1953. The norms and principles underpinning the IAEA have evolved, especially concerning weapons and safeguards. Before India's debut as a nuclear power in 1974, only the defeated nations of World War II were required to renounce atomic weapons – afterwards, it has been seen as a condition for all remaining nonnuclear states. Over the years, of course, other countries have 'gone nuclear'. And IAEA safeguards – the measures verifying that nuclear material has not been diverted from peaceful uses – have become conditional on general good behavior and not just limited to, or as a consequence of, a country's declared nuclear capabilities.[25] In effect, it is seeking to *detect* the diversion of nuclear materials. The IAEA thus has become an institutional expression of a double standard on proliferation, leading some to ask whether the Nuclear Non-Proliferation Treaty (NPT) regime is virtually dead.

Contrary to Eisenhower's original vision, there is no technical fix to a political problem; and so the Achilles heel of the IAEA has always been setting policy, which cannot be formulated without a consensus on criteria for the possession of nuclear power. There are no agreed standards for a country to develop nuclear capabilities, and no consistent punishments for those that operate outside the regime. When the IAEA has been allowed to operate, it has been remarkably successful. But the decision to 'aim' the IAEA at a particular state is taken by other states, as illustrated by the case of Iraq.

There are also regional international organizations integral to global processes, politics, and governance. The North Atlantic Treaty Organization (NATO) is an example of a regional IO that has been intimately part of contemporary global governance processes. Essential to European governance since 1949, it has become a participant 'outside of area' after the end of the Cold War with its expansion into various forms of peace operations, subcontracted from the United Nations in the Balkans and Afghanistan. This evolution has been somewhat ad hoc, but NATO is a crucial piece of the global governance security puzzle. Originally created to 'keep the Americans in, the Russians out, and the Germans down'[26] in Europe, NATO's peace operations in Bosnia, Kosovo, and Afghanistan have addressed peace and security well outside its traditional area of operations. In the course of deployment in Afghanistan, NATO members have had to negotiate what their national troops would and would not do for NATO. The organization also has had to decide on the modalities of associating such other major powers as Japan.[27] These consensus-building exercises are likely to set a precedent for future operations.

Nevertheless, European efforts are not unusual, and regional operations have been monitored across Africa by a host of the continent's regional and subregional organizations.[28] These cases provide interesting parallels in global governance, as the type of lead actor in each situation differs markedly but the felt need and institutional response were similar.

The search for peace in Central America in the 1980s demonstrates the weaknesses as well as the strength that IOs' flexibility can provide.[29] The civil wars of the Central American region began in the 1970s and were the result of endemic inequality in the distribution of power and wealth,[30] made worse by outside support and Cold War rivalry.

The weakness of IOs is that, as in the case of the Organization of American States (OAS), they can be held hostage by the political weight of a regional hegemon like the United States. Washington's foreign policy in the region was guided by the dread of communist control of strategic assets such as the Panama Canal.[31] As such, American Cold War fears prevented the OAS from taking effective action. The end of the Cold War allowed a new summit environment to be created by the ad hoc Contadora Group of regional leaders led by President Oscar Arias Sánchez of Costa Rica. These regional summits produced agreements on everything from elections to national reconciliation and became known as the Esquipulas II process.

The OAS was conspicuous by its absence – in Nicaragua, the important institutions diplomatically were the ad hoc regional groups, which were complemented by operations directed by the United Nations such as the UN Observer Group in Central America (ONUCA). In El Salvador, the important institution both militarily and politically was the UN, which conducted processes such as the discussions in Mexico City. Furthermore, there was harmonization of NGO activities with those of IOs, addressing the needs of El Salvadorans and Nicaraguans for human security. These private engagements and operations facilitated state and international diplomatic and military processes – in fact, the process would not have proceeded as effectively without IOs and NGOs.[32]

In contrast to the leadership role taken by the ad hoc Contadora Group in Central America, the civil war in Liberia prompted a response from the Economic Community of West African States (ECOWAS) that was dominated by a regional hegemon – in this case, Nigeria. When it became clear that help from outside the region, especially from the United States, would not be forthcoming, ECOWAS created the Economic Community of West African States Cease-fire Monitoring Group (ECOMOG) in 1990. Nigeria, which supplied the bulk of the troops, material, and financial backing, also dominated the strategy and tactics of ECOMOG.

ECOMOG's record was mixed. In theory, ECOWAS deserved praise for acting to secure the region; in practice, the force was beset with problems. Herbert Howe argued that the experience was contrary to what had been anticipated by those who expected regional organizations to understand the conflict and terrain better than outsiders, be more accepted by combatants, and have a stronger commitment and to deploy more appropriate equipment and personnel. ECOMOG demonstrated that regional peacekeeping might be inadequate and actually prolong war.[33] ECOMOG had insufficient intelligence resources in the area, inadequate equipment, and too many corrupt personnel; and more than once, it used and was used by differing armed factions in the civil war. The purpose for which it was formed – securing the region's peace – failed, and neighboring Sierra Leone also became embroiled in the widening conflict. ECOMOG wound down operations in Liberia in 1998 after the election of Charles Taylor, at the same time it had to ramp them up in Sierra Leone.[34] However, ECOMOG's recapture of Freetown in 1999 helped pave the way for a peace agreement and the introduction of UN peacekeepers. That war was officially declared over in 2002.[35]

These cases illustrate that some conditions are necessary without being sufficient for IO participation in the global governance of international peace and security. When most IOs were created by member states, it was not foreseen that they would be interacting with so many different kinds of actors at so many levels in so many essential ways – so, oftentimes, there is only the vaguest of provisions in many of their charters and statutes for the range of interactions that global governance implies. The discovery of shared goals and the flexibility of new interactions both within and among IOs are a step in the right direction and usually sufficient for problem solving even if statutes lag behind the reality of global governance.

norms and IOs in global governance

A relatively recent effort at norm-building by international organizations was the Global Compact at the 2000 Millennium Summit. The Global Compact is the concrete manifestation of Kofi Annan's vision for the United Nations to more adequately incorporate into its own work the energy and resources of the private sector – both the for-profit and the non-profit variety. The result was the agreement that business, labor, and civil society incorporate ten principles into practice through a learning network hosted by the UN. This approach represents a dramatic departure from the far more rigid state regulatory notions of the past toward a more far-reaching and flexible system of global governance that takes advantage of a host of actors and of learning rather than regulation.[36]

Principles 1 and 2 are businesses should support and respect the protection of internationally proclaimed human rights; and make sure that they are not complicit in human rights abuses.[37] Principles 3–6 are businesses should uphold the freedom of association and the effective recognition of the right to collective bargaining; the elimination of all forms of forced and compulsory labor; the effective abolition of child labor; and the elimination of discrimination in respect of employment and occupation. Principles 7–9 are businesses should support a precautionary approach to environmental challenges; undertake initiatives to promote greater environmental responsibility; and encourage the development and diffusion of environmentally friendly technologies.

Norm creation by IOs for global governance involves both navigating the troubled waters between evaluation and ethics, on the one hand,

and supporting the status quo, on the other hand. The UN's role in the shift to more private-sector-friendly norms was slow in coming; for decades, the world organization was quite hostile to the idea of free markets and partial to state regulation and action. The Global Compact essentially aims to determine whether companies can be shamed into doing business in a way that respects human rights, even in countries where the government does not. The practices of corporations are monitored by NGOs and then put forward more generally as examples of best practices for others to emulate.

Furthermore, the consensus about the Global Compact shows that norm creation in global governance involves more than one type of actor – here, leaving aside NSAs would obviously be shortsighted, even counterproductive, in ensuring analytical and practical accountability. For instance, both Calvert Investments, a socially responsible mutual-bond fund provider, and UNIFEM's 'Women's Principles' focus specifically on gendered employment issues such as sexual harassment, discrimination, and danger to reproductive health.[38] The Global Compact embraces the for-profit and not just not-for-profit worlds, which is quite distinct from the earlier almost total aversion by developing countries to Transnational Corporations (TNCs) beginning in mid-1970s, and the top-down regulation proposed as a solution over several decades by the Centre on TNCs.[39] Principle 10 (businesses should work against all forms of corruption, including extortion and bribery) represents a clear break with the government-regulation model of the past and instead emphasizes better corporate practices spreading as their success and profitability becomes known.

According to Anne-Marie Slaughter, trans-governmental networks of regulators, judges, and legislators extend norms by expanding the reach of states, building trust and creating relationships and reputations, exchanging information about best practices and different approaches to common issues, and offering both technical assistance and professional socialization to those coming from less-developed countries. For example, the Asia-Pacific Economic Cooperation (APEC) is a regional organization made up of 21 member economies and it is designed to promote economic cooperation and growth as well as the liberalization and facilitation of trade and investment within the Asia-Pacific region. It has 'pioneered a mode of governance that consists primarily in assessing current practices of member-states, benchmarking them, and adopting individualized national plans'[40] for trade and investment liberalization.

Furthermore, APEC does so without a governing document – it is not an international organization in a strictly legal sense. Slaughter argues that by disaggregating the duties of the state in this way, these networks can exchange information horizontally among government officials across various arenas and enforcement vertically – in Europe, from supranational to national governments. However, such a vision leaves unanswered questions of sovereignty: where does final political authority rest?[41] In other words, how could the actions of such networks be held accountable, and to whom?

While the Global Compact indicates experimentation at the world level and APEC at the regional level between member states with other actors, the treatment of human rights in Europe suggests how in that region states are relating not simply to NGOs and IGOs but even to individuals. This departure for global governance within Europe holds lessons for global governance elsewhere because the basis for complaints in international law has traditionally been states.[42]

The European Convention on Human Rights and Fundamental Freedoms defined a set of civil and political rights. The European Commission on Human Rights served for a time as a collective conciliator, responding to state or private complaints to seek out-of-court settlements. The European Court of Human Rights existed to give binding judgments about the legality of state policies under the convention. All states in the Council of Europe bound themselves to abide by the convention. In a profoundly far-reaching precedent, all governments allowed their citizens to have the right of individual petition to the commission, a body that could then – failing a negotiated agreement – take the petition to the European Court of Human Rights. And all states eventually accepted the supranational authority of the court. Its judgments holding state policies illegal were voluntarily respected by member states. This regional international regime for human rights functions through international agencies made up of independent individuals rather than state officials – although there is a Committee of Ministers made up of state representatives.

In the mid-1990s, the Council of Europe's members progressively accorded individuals standing to sue in the European Court of Human Rights without having the commission to represent them. Thus, an individual would have almost the same legal 'personality' – or in legal jargon, status – in the court as a state. The international protection of civil and political rights under the European Convention generated such a large number of cases that the commission was eliminated to streamline procedures. Individuals were allowed to proceed directly to a lower chamber of the International Court for an initial review of the admissibility of their complaints. If they meet procedural requirements, individuals can move on to the substantive phase, basically on an equal footing with state representatives; the details of the European situation show that 'muscular' protection of human rights is possible when there is sufficient political will and a willingness to move beyond the fixed boundaries of states and the intergovernmental bodies that they have created. For the time being, the European situation is anomalous. There are fledgling regional human rights regimes, in the Western Hemisphere and Africa, but they do not equal the West European record in successfully protecting human rights.

The previous discussion shows the extent to which the expansion of issues and actors on the stage of global governance has been accompanied by the expansion of norms formulated, agreed, and disseminated by IOs. In short, it is impossible to have a discussion of contemporary international relations – be the topic peace and security, human rights, or sustainable development – without using the perspective of global governance.

dynamics of global governance and IOs

The next frontier in global governance theory concerns the need to foresee kinds of changes and general patterns of change within the international system. Kalevi J. Holsti makes clear that we need to be very specific about what we label as 'change'. It is easy to say something has changed, but it is far more useful to say how it has changed and by how much. He defines markers of change as trends (preferably measured over long periods), and great events that interrupt typical patterns, a category that includes significant social and technological innovations. He also identifies different concepts of change: 'novelty or replacement, change as addition or subtraction, increased complexity, transformation, reversion, and obsolescence'.[43]

Holsti uses international institutions as his marker of change. He defines them as patterned practices, based on a coherent set of ideas or beliefs that reflect norms. Holsti looks at the foundational institutions (those that constitute the system) of sovereignty, territoriality, and international law as well as the procedural institutions (those that regulate the system) of diplomacy, trade, colonialism, and war. By juxtaposing the beginnings of sovereignty with current conditions, he finds that the practices, ideas, and norms have indeed changed. States are now vastly more complex entities than even a few decades, let alone a few centuries, ago. The range of government activities has continually expanded and proliferated. However, the 'core ideas of the constitutive aspects of sovereignty, including constitutional independence, exclusive legal jurisdiction within a defined territory, and legal equality, have remained essentially the same throughout the ages.... The only critical change ... is the obsolescence of the right of conquest'.[44]

While states have therefore not changed much, the core message of Holsti's work for international organizations in global governance is that states have indeed seen change. The foundational institutions were new in the late seventeenth century, but they have become more complex or been transformed by technology. Moreover, the procedural institutions of the international system have become more complicated in practice (for example, diplomacy), have increased so much that they are not comparable (for example, communications and trade), and in some cases have become obsolete (colonialism), or have reverted to previous operating methods (war in some regions).

An example of universal change in international organizations' interactions is the response to the December 2004 tsunami in the Indian Ocean. A quick glance through the databases of the United Nations Office for the Coordination of Humanitarian Affairs (OCHA) will show that most humanitarian and complex emergencies are responded to by a constellation of familiar actors: major humanitarian donor states, intergovernmental organizations, and transnational nongovernmental organizations. The network structure for many disasters contains actors who have probably established routine patterns of interaction.

However, the massive global response to the tsunami required a transformative change in this network. The influx of many new actors appears at first to be simply an additive change, which was accommodated using hubs. New actors linked to existing actors, and the better known and more established the existing actor, the more likely it was to become a hub. This created a phenomenon known in network analysis as the scale-free network: some hubs gain an apparently unlimited number of links and no one actor is typical of the others.[45] As a result, the most important actors in terms of number of links (and therefore amount of money) received from others were the International Federation of the Red Cross/Red Crescent, the International Organization for Migration, OCHA, and the World Health Organization.[46] This created a network that not only had more actors, but that also had a different structure than the typical humanitarian response.

The same network analysis framework can also be applied to regionalism to categorize change. Louise Fawcett traces the resurgence of regional activity (what she calls the 'new regionalism') to the end of the Cold War and economic change.[47] The end of the Cold War brought new attitudes toward international cooperation, first and foremost being the change of heart by the former Soviet Union, but also including the increased activity of the UN Security Council, and the increase in both the number and activity of regional organizations especially in burden-sharing with the UN. The expansion of actors and problems along with the increased pace of communications and decisions has led to increased complexity. It also brought decentralization of the international system, which demonstrated the robustness of existing regional organizations such as the EU and NATO, as well as the new independence and vulnerability of regional associations of developing countries from the old East-West alliances, an example of transformation.

An example of dramatic change in a regional institution is ECLAC, the Economic Commission for Latin America and the Caribbean (formerly, simply ECLA). Here, the change was not so much in the ideas that the organization fostered and promoted, but in the time frame through which the institution viewed its work. From the beginning, it focused on the seminal ideas such as the deterioration in Latin American economies, the asymmetrical relations between the core and periphery in the global economy, and the impact of this on domestic economies.[48] However, in the 1970s, the growing influence of actors such as the World Bank, the increasingly hostile climate created by the overthrow of Salvador Allende, and the new focus on emerging issues of poverty all led to economic depression and a focus during the 1980s on crisis management. According to Gert Rosenthal, this situation lasted until the return of less doctrinaire approaches at the end of the Cold War and economic recovery.[49] This change in environment allowed ECLAC to revert to its former long-term, holistic focus.

Such analyses of change in international politics not only illustrate the importance of a global governance perspective but also have direct policy implications. For example, a structural analysis could show which states are becoming weaker relative to other actors. Their situations could then be investigated more closely to uncover the possible reasons, which could be compared to actors with similar structural patterns elsewhere in the system. As one group of analysts writes, 'Finding local fluidity and global stability ... suggests that change moves through structurally equivalent actors.'[50]

conclusion

It may be most useful to think of global governance as the capacity of the international system to provide government-like services in the absence of a world government. Global governance has been so difficult to grasp because its manifestations sometimes seem inconsistent. Imploding states and the European Union are part of contemporary reality, which reflect James Rosenau's awkward but accurate coining, 'fragmegration'.[51] Keeping in mind simultaneously what seem like inconsistencies is a perceptual problem, not an indicator that global governance cannot be understood or made to work better. Without adequate depictions of what is going on, policy prescriptions are elusive – hence, we see simultaneous calls for both world government and for stronger states, for stronger civil society and controls on the abuses by uncivil members of civil society.

Global governance does not imply that a world government will inevitably evolve, but that enhanced international cooperation is certainly a prerogative. Ironically, sovereignty's shortcomings can only be overcome by sovereigns because 'successful governance *beyond* the state depends essentially on the state *itself*'.[52] In any case, far more robust international organizations are bound to be part of the mix, whereas many contemporary analyses seem to hope that a combination of markets and civil society can compensate for the absence of central authority. Quite simply, Amnesty International and Toyota will not halt genocide in Darfur and reverse climate change.

At this time, it is impossible to use global governance theory to predict global system change or system-wide conflict, but that does not distinguish it from other bodies of theory. We suspect that as global governance theory develops and knowledge improves, we will use it to investigate structural constraints and opportunities, and therefore the dynamic patterns of world politics. It is an analytical device to understand what is happening even if it lacks predictive or prescriptive power. In spite of what appears random at present, global governance is about numerous actors' self-organizing through formal and informal means to meet worldwide challenges, to provide more order than would occur naturally.

The study of structure, or the paths and processes of interactions, is essential to the study of agency, which is crucial for policy formulation and action. Dynamic structures and institutions are produced, reproduced, and transformed by human agency.[53] The stage for the drama by international society has become increasingly crowded with a diversity of actors who play more than bit parts. States are still on the stage, national interests have not receded as an important basis for decision making and international secretariats still largely serve these state masters. However, there is substantial evidence that nonstate actors are increasingly salient for every sector and problem. Our task then is to create a qualitative model of global governance that can identify the most important processes by which human beings can regain better control over the globe's destiny.

notes

1. Craig N. Murphy, 'Global Governance: Poorly Done and Poorly Understood,' *International Affairs*, Vol. 76, No. 4, 2000, p. 789.
2. Inis L. Claude, Jr., *Swords Into Plowshares: The Problems and Prospects of International Organization* (New York: Random House, 1956) and 'Peace and Security: Prospective Roles for the Two United Nations,' *Global Governance*, Vol. 2, No. 3, 1996, pp. 289–298.
3. Edgar Grande and Louis W. Pauly, 'Complex Sovereignty and the Emergence of Transnational Authority,' in Edgar Grande and Louis W. Pauly (eds), *Complex Sovereignty: Reconstituting Political Authority in the Twenty-first Century* (Toronto: University of Toronto Press, 2005), p. 290.
4. Margaret P. Karns and Karen A. Mingst, *International Organizations: The Politics and Processes of Global Governance* (Boulder, CO: Lynne Rienner Publishers, 2004).
5. Edward Hallett Carr, *Twenty Years' Crisis, 1919–1939: An Introduction to the Study of International Relations*, 2nd edn (New York: St. Martin's Press, 1946).
6. Hans J. Morgenthau, *Politics among Nations: The Struggle for Power and Peace* (New York: Alfred A. Knopf, 1948).
7. Kenneth Waltz, *Theory of International Politics* (Boston: McGraw-Hill, 1979).
8. Robert O. Keohane and Joseph S. Nye, *Power and Interdependence*, 3rd edn (New York: Longman, 2001).
9. Alexander Wendt, 'Anarchy is What States Make of It: The Social Construction of Power Politics,' *International Organization*, Vol. 46, No. 2, 1992, pp. 391–425.
10. John G. Ruggie, *Constructing the World Polity* (London: Routledge, 1998).
11. James N. Rosenau, 'Governance in the Twenty-First Century,' *Global Governance*, Vol. 1, No. 1, 1995, p. 14.
12. James N. Rosenau and Ernst-Otto Czempiel (eds), *Governance without Government: Order and Change in World Politics* (Cambridge: Cambridge University Press, 1992).

13. Lawrence S. Finkelstein, 'What is Global Governance?' *Global Governance*, Vol. 1, No. 1, 1995, pp. 368–369.
14. Commission on Global Governance, *Our Global Neighborhood* (New York: Oxford University Press, 1995), pp. 2–3.
15. Margaret P. Karns and Karen A. Mingst, *International Organizations: The Politics and Processes of Global Governance* (Boulder, CO: Lynne Rienner Publishers, 2004), p. 4.
16. World Economic Forum, *Global Governance Initiative Annual Report 2006* (Washington, D.C.: Communications Development Incorporated, 2006), p. ix.
17. B. Guy Peters, 'Governance: A Garbage Can Perspective,' in *Complex Sovereignty* (Toronto: University of Toronto Press, 2005), p. 72.
18. Ramesh Thakur and Thomas G Weiss, *The UN and Global Governance: An Unfinished History* (Bloomington: Indiana University Press, forthcoming).
19. Gareth Evans, 'True Believer,' *Foreign Policy*, September/October 2002 (132), pp. 28–46.
20. Evans, *Foreign Policy*, March/April 2001, p. 28. A subsequent special section of the same journal was titled '"Where Is the International Community?" and "What Is the International Community?"' with ten contradictory essays. See *Foreign Policy*, September/October 2002, pp. 28–46.
21. Jeffrey T. Checkel, 'The Constructivist Turn in International Relations Theory,' *World Politics*, Vol. 50, No. 2, 1998, p. 339.
22. Clifford Bob, 'Gunning for the Globe: Movement and Countermovement in the Small Arms Control Process,' paper presented at the annual meeting of the International Studies Association 48th Annual Convention, 28 February 2007.
23. For example, see the following papers from the National Archives and Records Administration: Dr. Richard C. Tolman, letters to Captain Parsons requesting memo on postwar policy dated 30 September 1944 and 29 September 1944; and W.S. Parsons' *Memo on Post War Policy for Governmental Research Toward Nuclear Weapons*, addressed to Dr. Tolman (via Dr. J. Robert Oppenheimer), dated 5 October 1944. For an overview, see 'Civilian Control of Atomic Energy, 1945–1946,' http://www.mbe.doe.gov/me70/manhattan/civilian_control.htm
24. Atomic Energy Act of 1946, Public Law 585, 79th Congress.
25. Joseph F. Pilat (ed.), *Atoms for Peace After Thirty Years* (Boulder, CO: Westview Press, 1984), p. 25.
26. Susanne Koelbl, 'Germany's Bundeswehr Steps out on the Global Stage,' *Spiegel Online International*, 17 June 2005, http://www.spiegel.de/international/spiegel/0,1518,360869,00.html accessed 1 August 2007.
27. Paul Reynolds, 'NATO looks for global role,' *BBC News*, 27 November 2006, http://news.bbc.co.uk/2/hi/europe/6185738.stm accessed 31 July 2007.
28. Jeremy Levitt, *Africa: Selected Documents on Constitutive, Conflict and Security, Humanitarian, and Judicial Issues* (Ardsley, NY: Transaction Publishers, 2003).
29. S. Neil MacFarlane and Thomas G. Weiss, 'The United Nations, Regional Organizations and Human Security: Building Theory in Central America,' *Third World Quarterly*, Vol. 15, No. 2, 1994, pp. 277–295.

30. John A. Booth and Thomas W. Walker, *Understanding Central America* (Boulder, CO: Westview Press, 1999), p. 150.
31. Ibid., p. 171.
32. MacFarlane and Weiss, 'The United Nations, Regional Organizations and Human Security,' pp. 288–289.
33. Herbert Howe, 'Lessons of Liberia: ECOMOG and Regional Peacekeeping,' *International Security*, Vol. 21, No. 3, 1996–1997, pp. 145–176.
34. BBC News, 'Profile: Ecomog,' http://news.bbc.co.uk/2/hi/africa/country_profiles/2364029.stm, accessed 9/11/07.
35. BBC News, 'Timeline: Sierra Leone: A chronology of key events,' http://news.bbc.co.uk/2/hi/africa/country_profiles/1065898.stm, accessed 9/18/07.
36. John G. Ruggie, 'global_governance.net: The Global Compact as Learning Network,' *Global Governance*, Vol. 7, No. 4, 2001, pp. 371–378.
37. UN Global Compact, http://www.unglobalcompact.org/Portal/Default.asp
38. Stacy A. Teicher, 'If Cultures Subdue, Work Can Liberate,' *The Christian Science Monitor*, 1 July 2004.
39. See Tagi Sagafi-Nejad, in collaboration with John Dunning, *The UN and Transnationals, from Code to Compact* (Bloomington: Indiana University Press, 2008).
40. Anne-Marie Slaughter, *A New World Order* (Princeton, NJ: Princeton University Press, 2004), p. 142.
41. Christopher Bickerton, Philip Cunliffe and Alexander Gourevitch (eds), *Politics Without Sovereignty : A Critique of Contemporary International Relations* (London: University College London Press, 2007).
42. This discussion is based on Thomas G. Weiss, David P. Forsythe, Roger A. Coate and Kelly-Kate Pease, *The United Nations and Changing World Politics*, 5th edn (Boulder, CO: Westview, 2007), chapter 5.
43. K. J. Holsti, *Taming the Sovereigns: Institutional Change in International Politics* (Cambridge: Cambridge University Press, 2004), pp. 12–13.
44. Ibid., 141.
45. Albert-László Barabási, *Linked: The New Science of Networks* (New York: Perseus Publishing, 2002).
46. Annelies Z. Kamran, 'Structure of a Transnational Human Security Network: The Response to the Indian Ocean Tsunami of 26 December 2004,' *Proceedings of The Institute of Mathematics and its Applications and ONCE-CS conference on Mathematics in the Science of Complex Systems*, 18–21 September 2006, University of Warwick, UK, http://phoenixweb.open.ac.uk/complexity/MITSOCS%2706b.pdf
47. Louise Fawcett, 'Regionalism in Historical Perspective,' in Louise Fawcett and Andrew Hurrell (eds), *Regionalism in World Politics: Regional Organization and International Order* (Oxford: Oxford University Press, 1995).
48. Gert Rosenthal, 'ECLAC: A Commitment to a Latin American Way Toward Development,' in Yves Berthelot (ed.), *Unity and Diversity in Development Ideas: Perspectives from the UN Regional Commissions* (Bloomington: Indiana University Press, 2004), p. 169.
49. Ibid., 178–179.
50. Moody, McFarland and Bender-deMoll, 'Dynamic Network Visualization,' *American Journal of Sociology*, Vol. 110, 2005, p. 1227.

became ascendant, seemed to support this idea. The sharp delineation and careful control of territorial borders were evident worldwide. Governments also actively sought to build their capacities to control their economies and to shape their societies. In domestic politics pluralist theories in which states had been seen as responding to societal influences were increasingly displaced by theories emphasizing the autonomy of states.[1]

Even as state-centric theories were becoming ascendant the empirical signs of a growing penetration of state territorial and institutional boundaries were beginning to be recognized.[2] Today, as the chapters in this book show, traditional realist theories that treat states as the only significant actor are challenged by a great many approaches that recognize the widely varied and important roles played by non-state actors in global governance. Nevertheless, both theories that focus on the power of states and theories that focus on the power of non-state actors often continue to see these two categories of state and non-state actors as relatively distinct, bounded and autonomous.

For instance, one response to growing interdependence on the part of state-centric theories has been the development of principal–agent theories in which it is acknowledged that sometimes non-state actors can be significant.[3] However, this significance is seen as arising because states (principals) rationally choose to delegate certain functions to these non-state actors (their agents). States do this because it is cost effective to do so, perhaps because there are economies of scale in having a non-state organization carry out certain activities on behalf of all states or because states will trust information that is produced by a relatively autonomous non-governmental organization more than information that is produced by other states. Monitoring of agents by principals is always costly so, in general, states will only choose to delegate when the benefits from delegation outweigh the costs. While there are a great many useful insights that can be obtained from the principal–agent approach it tends to treat the state as a rational unitary and autonomous actor that can choose to delegate or not. The non-state actors are treated as having almost the same type of independence as would a lawyer that an individual might hire.

A quite different response to growing interdependence has been to emphasize the independent initiatives of non-state actors through concepts such as global civil society[4] or private authority.[5] Considering the intense criticism that has been articulated by global civil society of states, on issues like human rights or the environment, it is not surprising that global civil society has often been counterposed to the state system and its independence from states has been emphasized. The literature on private authority has highlighted the ability of international business actors to create and elicit compliance with rules in ways that complement or substitute for the rules produced by states. This literature has also tended to focus on relatively independent instances of non-governmental power. Overall, it is quite tempting to see state power and the power of non-governmental actors as competing tendencies and then to make assessments of which is likely to fare better in the years to come. For instance, those who see globalization as an unstoppable trend are likely to see state power as being eroded by the growth of the power of non-governmental actors while realists will predict that states will retain their power. Although trying to measure the relative power of state and non-state actors is useful, this approach tends to obscure more complex relations among the different types of actors.

conceptualizing the complex relationship between state and non-state actors

A starting point in analysing the relationship between state and non-state actors is to examine the ontology we use in thinking about these actors. How do we think about the fundamental character of actors – their primary constitutive features? One ontology is to see each actor as unified, bounded and self-directed, and to see everything else as an environment for that actor. A second ontology is to see the world as made up of shared institutions, meanings or practices that give rise to actors, including ones that appear as independent. In international relations theory the metaphors of billiard balls and webs have been used to illustrate the differences between these two ontologies.[6] Although the metaphor of a web is useful in highlighting interconnectedness, a concept that is better at capturing the discontinuities and instances of partial autonomy is the *assemblage*. Originally used in art, an assemblage is created out of disparate elements, each of which has meanings or purposes that might be quite unrelated to the other elements, but which together are brought into a new relationship with one another to create an arrangement with its own distinctive meaning or purpose.[7]

Sassen[8] and others[9] have begun developing the notion of global assemblages in which elements of nation states can be plugged into new global arrangements while retaining linkages to their previous national functions. This concept can be applied to the relationship between public and private actors and institutions as well, such as when a private-sector risk management practice, originally developed for business reasons, is incorporated into public sector regulatory arrangements. This type of ontology is useful in helping reveal relationships that might otherwise be obscured by an ontology that incorrectly assumes that key actors and institutions, including states and firms, must essentially be either public or private.

While the notion of an assemblage can be applied in many different settings and historical periods, there are numerous signs that the major actors and institutions that had been seen as unified and bounded in previous historical periods are becoming less so, and that the assemblage metaphor reflects these changes well. The corporation, which in the mid-twentieth century was often portrayed as a hierarchical bureaucratic monolith, is now seen as closely linked to transnational networks or value chains[10] in which the boundaries between suppliers, contractors, marketers and even customers[11] have become increasingly complex. Similarly the Internet and cell phone technology, combined with the mobility and new competences of activists, has contributed to more complex and amorphous new social movements and coalitions in which hierarchical political organizations, like traditional parties, are not needed to coordinate actions. Slaughter[12] has analysed the *disaggregated state*, in which functions previously carried out by officials within the boundaries of particular states are now carried out in far-flung transnational policy networks, with a wide mix of public and private elements (note that here and for the rest of this chapter 'private' includes all actors that are not public sector – both business actors and civil society organizations).

The state has become more disaggregated not only in its policy-making but also in how it seeks to shape the conduct of the targets of its policies and the implementation of its rules. Rather than 'command and control' regulation that is centralized at the top of the state there is an increasing tendency to set benchmarks or rules, sometimes with the assistance of non-state actors, and then to allow decentralized implementation or even self-regulation.[13] These arrangements often rely on various external mechanisms, including peer review, private-sector auditing or market pressures for monitoring and encouraging compliance with the benchmarks or rules.

There are numerous labels and concepts that scholars and policy-makers have developed to analyse this shift in governance. Levi-Faur and Jordana[14] have identified the emergence of the *regulatory state*.

Foucault's concept of *governmentality* has been used to highlight the shift from centralized control of conduct to the creation of the decentralized conditions for a form of self-regulation that brings practices into conformity with the imperatives of power – a process that he also labels 'control at a distance' and the 'conduct of conduct'.[15] Börzel and Risse[16] explore varieties of transnational governance arrangements using the 'public–private partnership' label. Many official studies and reports have noted the hybrid and varied character of the public/private mixes that can occur in regulatory arrangements (*Lex Fori*).[17] The Organization for Economic Cooperation and Development (OECD) has noted that 'effective regulation must interact with pre-existing "indigenous" normative orderings in the target population, including management systems and cultures within organizations, self-regulatory capacities by the public and civil society, and gatekeeper roles played by third parties including professionals, insurance companies, and rating agencies'.[18]

In addition to this change in regulation and related to it, the state's role in the delivery of services has also been changing. Services or functions that previously would have been seen as central responsibilities of states have been privatized, contracted out, or devolved to public–private partnerships, including education, financial regulation, prisons, military activities, and border control.[19] There are many reasons that have been identified for this shift, including the capturing and dismantling of the state by private-sector interests; the search for efficiency in government, and the difficulty of states in coping with the fast pace and complexity of globalization. The increased competence of citizens and business, concerns about the excessive power of state bureaucracies and advances in telecommunications, have all contributed to the desire and ability of non-state actors to carry out functions that previously were the responsibility of states.

varieties of entanglements

Taken together the above changes suggest that there will be a great number and variety of ways in which the public and private can be entangled at the international level. States, firms and civil society organizations have all become more disaggregated, with their boundaries becoming fuzzier. The state has increasingly drawn on non-governmental actors and institutions in carrying out its functions. With the globalization of business and civil society organizations any individual state may interact with transnational non-governmental actors in new ways. States too

asymmetric information, but such licensing can be harnessed to state regulatory goals if the state requires it as a condition for authorizing activities linked to its territory.

The International Accounting Standards Board (ISAB) is one of the strongest transnational private-sector rule makers. It is organized as a corporation but it has a relatively autonomous board of standard setters that create rules that accounts use in preparing financial reports. These in turn are used by investors in assessing the value of firms, and as financial markets have become more globalized there are more market incentives for firms and investors to use a single set of international standards. The power of the standards come not just from the market, or the highly concentrated structure of the accounting industry, dominated by four big firms but also from the decisions of governments about whether to accept accounts prepared with these standards in their jurisdictions. Today most jurisdictions, significantly the European Union, have accepted the IASB's standards or are working towards using them. Earlier on in the history of international accounting standards the endorsement of public sector securities regulators at the International Organization of Securities Commissions was also very important in creating momentum for the standards.

Responsible care is another well developed self-regulatory initiative in the chemical industry. It was created as public concern about the damage created by chemicals to the environment and hazards associated with chemical weapons escalated. The arrangement, managed by the International Council of Chemical Associations, has eight 'Fundamental Features' that national chemical associations are expected to implement, including procedures for verification. Critics have contended that because the programme is voluntary, it mainly functions to prevent meaningful regulation. In response the programme has begun strengthening mechanisms of accountability, including, for instance, a requirement by the US association that all members must be certified by independent accredited auditing firms.[26]

the entanglement of market pressures and public institutions

While the impact of globalized markets on states has been widely recognized as substantial the many varied ways in which this impact is mobilized is often underestimated. Considerable attention has been devoted to the problem of the 'race to the bottom', where multinational firms play one jurisdiction off another and thereby obtain policies, such as low taxes or lax regulation, which benefit them at the expense of a government and its citizens. Although there are opposing market tendencies that encourage a 'race to the top', such as the desire of some firms to operate in well-regulated jurisdictions, or to bring all jurisdictions up to the standards of their home jurisdiction,[27] it is certainly agreed that governments are competing more aggressively for foreign investment than in the past. The impact of international financial markets on states is amplified by ratings agencies which measure the performance of indebted states against criteria of concern to investors, and since a bad rating will raise the cost of borrowing significantly the agencies can wield a power over governments which rivals that of the government's citizens, even in democracies.[28] There are countless examples of governments of wealthy countries working unilaterally or in international organizations to respond to the interests of firms or investors headquartered in their jurisdictions, including by creating rules to reduce power of competing states in the developing world, as with the US role in the International Monetary Fund, or in pushing for strengthened intellectual property rules in the World Trade Organization.[29] This can complement and amplify market pressures for the states at which they are targeted.

Global markets can also be used to strengthen states and to control business. Braithwaite and Drahos[30] argue that competition policy can be creatively used by non-governmental actors to counter the power of large multinational firms that may seek to control markets. Ethical investing or micro-financing can promote social purposes that deviate from strictly commercial considerations and that can complement the goals of governments. Concerns about reputation in markets can stimulate voluntary programmes that complement public-policy goals,[31] although many critics have expressed a high degree of scepticism about voluntary corporate social responsibility programmes. Financial regulators have sought to have international standards, codes and other rules formulated in such a way that market actors will incorporate them in their decision-making and thereby create pressures for compliance.[32] A more complex example is government-mandated requirements for car owners to insure their vehicles, which in turn has made insurers key advocates of strong vehicle safety standards, which has helped the transnational tendency of these standards to harmonize upwards rather than downwards. Insurers have also lent their weight to efforts to address global warming,[33] and the risk-mitigation preferences of insurers can induce prudent behaviour on firms that they insure. Some of this prudence may complement public-policy goals of states. States, coordinating through the Financial Action Task Force housed at the OECD, have conscripted firms in the fight against terrorist financing and money laundering by requiring them to engage in detailed monitoring and reporting of questionable financial transactions.

public and private entanglements in private international law

Traditionally almost all international law has been public law that is concerned with the relations among states. Private law, which regulates relations among firms, families, individuals and other non-state actors, has primarily been domestic, and private international law mainly concerned itself with determining which domestic law should apply in transnational disputes. However, in recent years there has been an upswing in interest in the harmonization of private law. The central locus of this has been the Hague Conference[34] although many other international organizations, such as the International Institute for the Unification of Private Law (UNIDROIT)[35] have also been involved. As well as being the subjects of private international law, non-governmental actors also have been actively involved in harmonization efforts at the international level. International institutions such as the World Bank have also increasingly recognized the importance of private law, such as contract law, for economic development.

While private law has been important in resolving transnational commercial disputes and family issues such as transnational abductions of children, it has also been seen as an instrument for promoting human rights. In the United States, the Alien Tort Claims Act has been used to put pressure in US courts on multinational corporations which are alleged to have engaged in human rights abuses abroad.[36] Tort law is a branch of private law that is concerned with personal harms, such as product liability, medical malpractice or assault. Although the use of tort law for social purposes seemed promising to some activists it is dependent on its strength in particular jurisdictions. The United States has been the jurisdiction most amenable to this type of litigation, but the G. W. Bush administration and the US Supreme Court had taken strong and successful initiatives to restrict the use of Tort law.[37] The use of tort law for social purposes also depends on the initiative of strong civil society organizations, which are not present in all jurisdictions. Nevertheless, in the United States tort law continues to be an important way to hold firms accountable and some other jurisdictions have permitted the use of private law to promote human rights.[38] There are many less direct ways in which tort law also can influence global governance.

For instance, compliance with US product safety regulation depends on the threat of private litigation and although this threat has been significantly weakened by the Bush administration and the Supreme Court it continues to have an impact on product safety standards, which then are carried to the global level either through the export of those products abroad, through the requirements imposed on foreign multinationals through their US operations, and by the spread of such legal practices by policy mimesis or the diffusion effects of multinational law firms.

transnational service delivery in public/private partnerships

Domestically a striking feature of public administration over the past two decades has been the shifting of services previously performed by the public sector to the private sector. The relationship between the public and private in these arrangements can vary greatly, from the complete privatization of a government service so that it is provided by a private firm just like other commercialized products and services, through joint ventures in which public and private actors are both involved in the delivery of a single service, to the contracting out of small parts of a service that otherwise continues to be delivered by the public sector. The degree of transnationalization of these arrangements can vary greatly as well, with either the public or private side of the provider of the service, along with the clientele, all having the potential to be less or more global.

In the security area the growth of private military companies and other types of war-related contractors is an example of this phenomenon.[39] Similarly, border control and airline security involves extensive entanglement of public and private actors.[40] In development assistance the World Bank has long sought to involve the private sector, for instance by creating in 1956 the International Finance Corporation to finance private-sector projects, but the role of non-governmental actors has escalated rapidly since then. For instance, the only regional development bank to be created since the 1970s, the European Bank for Reconstruction, established in 1991, very explicitly privileges the private sector in its efforts.[41] The voluntary sector has also greatly increased its role in development assistance. For instance, in 2005, US official development assistance totalled $27.6 billion while private assistance from the United States to developing countries totalled $95.2 billion, of which $61.7 was individual remittances.[42] In 2007, the Gates Foundation alone disbursed $2 billion in grants.[43] About 6 percent of all reported official aid to developing countries has been provided through non-governmental organizations and public–private partnerships.[44]

the creation of new public/private spaces

Historically the boundary between public and private has always had a great deal of political significance even if the content and meanings of the two realms that it demarcates are ambiguous and contested. In one meaning the public is where power is legitimately and explicitly constructed and exercised – especially the state – and the private remains outside this, whether private is taken to mean the personal and individual, the family or private-sector business. As feminist scholars and other critics have argued, this way of casting the dualism is itself political since it can obscure the power relations on the private side of the divide, and it can exclude activities and actors located on the private side from the legitimate contestation and exercise of power on the public side. A second meaning of public distinguishes it from both the state and the private. The growth of democracy was accompanied by the growth of public deliberative spaces in coffee houses and elsewhere.[45] Like the concept of civil society, this space was seen as mediating between the state and the private, and as a mechanism for constituting the citizenry's identity and holding the state accountable.

Through most of the twentieth century in both of the above conceptions the public was seen as sharply bounded not only from the private but also from the world outside the state's borders. More recently these boundaries are becoming less clear-cut. As Ong comments, 'The confluence of processes of territorialization and deterritorialization is re-configuring connections between political space, entitlements, and political action.'[46] The growth of global civil society and the development of technologies for sustaining an emergent global public sphere, most notably the Internet, are well-recognized ways in which this reconfiguration of public space is occurring. In the practical logistics of these there are numerous ways in which the public and private are entangled, including financial support from states for some civil society organizations, and the public investments and legal infrastructures that enable the new technologies. Just as important, however, are the more abstract political complementarities between these reconfigured publics and the public sector, with the new publics provoking change and providing legitimacy for the public sector, while depending on it as a focal point, a mechanism on which to project and implement political aspirations. However, the new public/private spaces also can be exclusive, and therefore more damaging for democracy, as with the cosmopolitan spaces associated with airports, elite policy networks, gated expatriate communities, luxury malls, premium brand identities or intranets.

conclusion: public and private entanglements in global governance

The above areas in which public and private are entangled illustrate the complexity of the relationships between these two, and why we should not just see them as two autonomous and bounded spheres in competition with each other. If we underestimate the public tendrils and surfaces that are present in the spheres we think of as private, or vice versa, we cannot fully understand global governance. Public and private actors continue to compete and struggle with one another, but increasingly this is mediated through their mutual entanglements, and these entanglements make them increasingly dependent on one another.

Elements of these entanglements have always been present in the relationship between public and private, but in recent decades the number, variety and complexity of these have escalated. Multiple hybrid public/private institutions and practices have emerged at the domestic level and this hybridity has intersected with an equally complex national/global hybridity. These relationships cut across all the areas identified in the previous section. For instance, the Clearing House Interbank Payments System (CHIPS), responsible for mediating 95 percent of global dollar transactions among banks, is located in New York, administered by a New York-based consortium of banks. It regulates the conduct of the banks that use it through real-time computer algorithms that detect excessively risky activities; it also draws on New York State law and only accepts members that are regulated by the US Federal Reserve. By stabilizing this set of transactions CHIPS complements the prudential regulatory initiatives of states at the national and transnational levels.[47]

The assemblage metaphor set out earlier in this chapter captures this complexity well. The previous section revealed a great number of arrangements that contribute to global governance by drawing together practices, institutions and rules that also have other less global meanings and entanglements. These arrangements in turn exist in a complementary relationship to one another, constituting a global assemblage. At times these various assemblages are deliberately brought together by rational strategic actors, but at other times they are brought into proximity by other relatively autonomous flows of action that are not

with democracy if the state retains enough influence to ensure that the public interest prevails.

In sum, it is important, both for our ability to understand the development of global governance and for our ability to help design new global institutions that enhance citizens' well-being, for us to be able to discern the increasingly wide variety of public–private entanglements that are part of global governance. It is increasingly inadequate to treat key actors, including states, firms and citizens groups, as autonomous and bounded institutions that compete strategically with one another in ways that do not involve complex entanglements. These entanglements are only likely to increase in number and significance, as will the need to shape them to support rather than undermine our ability in conditions of globalization to construct a world that can enhance human well-being.

notes

1. Eric A. Nordlinger, *On the Autonomy of the Democratic State* (Cambridge: Harvard University Press, 1981); Nicos Poulantzas, *Political Power and Social Classes* (London: New Left Books, 1974).
2. Robert O. Keohane and Joseph S. Nye Jr. (eds), *Transnational Relations and World Politics* (Cambridge: Harvard University Press, 1972).
3. Darren G. Hawkins, David A. Lake, Daniel L. Nielson and Michael J. Tierney (eds), *Delegation and Agency in International Organizations* (Cambridge: Cambridge University Press, 2006).
4. Mary Kaldor, *Global Civil Society: An Answer to War* (Cambridge: Polity Press, 2003).
5. A. Claire Cutler, Tony Porter and Virginia Haufler (eds), *Private Authority and International Affairs.* New York, NY: SUNY Press, 1999); R. B. Hall and T. J. Biersteker (eds), *The Emergence of Private Authority in the International System* (Cambridge: Cambridge University Press, 2002).
6. J. Martin Rochester, *Between Two Epochs: What's Ahead for America, the World, and Global Politics in the 21st Century?* (Upper Saddle River, NJ.: Prentice-Hall, 2001), Chapter 3, 'Billiard Balls and Cobwebs,' pp. 31–97.
7. Manuel DeLanda, *A New Philosophy of Society: Assemblage Theory and Social Complexity* (London: Continuum, 2006).
8. Saskia Sassen, *Territory, Authority, Rights: From Medieval to Global Assemblages* (Princeton: Princeton University Press, 2006).
9. Aihwa Ong and Stephen J. Collier, *Global Assemblages: Technology, Politics and Ethics as Anthropological Problems* (Malden: Blackwell, 2005).
10. Peter Dicken, Philip F. Kelly, Kris Olds and Henry Wai-Chung Yeung, 'Chains and Networks, Territories and Scales: Towards a Relational Framework for Analyzing the Global Economy,' *Global Networks*, Vol. 1, No. 2, 2001, pp. 19–112.

11. Don Tapscott and Anthony D. Williams. *Wikinomics: How Mass Collaboration Changes Everything* (New York: Portfolio, 2006).
12. Anne-Maire Slaughter, *A New World Order* (Princeton: Princeton University Press, 2004); see also Hans Krause Hansen and Dorte Salskov-Iversen (eds), *Critical Perspectives on Private Authority in Global Politics* (Basingstoke: Palgrave, 2008).
13. Peter N. Grabosky, 'Using Non-Governmental Resources to Foster Regulatory Compliance,' *Governance*, Vol. 8, No. 4, 1995, pp. 527–550; Darren Sinclair, 'Self-Regulation Versus Command and Control? Beyond False Dichotomies,' *Law and Policy*, Vol. 19, No. 4, 1997, p. 529.
14. David Levi-Faur and Jacint Jordana (eds), 'The Rise of Regulatory Capitalism: The Global Diffusion of a New Order,' *The Annals of the American Academy of Political and Social Science*, Vol. 598, March 1005.
15. Graham Burchell, Colin Gordon and Peter Miller (eds),*The Foucault Effect: Studies in Governmentality* (Chicago: University of Chicago Press, 1991).
16. Tanja A Börzel and Thomas Risse, 'Public-Private Partnerships: Effective and Legitimate Tools of Transnational Governance?' in Edgar Grande and Louis W. Pauly (eds), *Complex Sovereignty: Reconstituting Political Authority in the Twenty-First Century* (Toronto: University of Toronto Press, 2007), pp. 195–216.
17. 'La Meilleure Pratique dans le Recours à des Normes Juridiques "douces" et son Application aux Consommateurs au sein de l'Union Européen,' Étude réalisée à la demande de la Commission européenne. Brussels: DG SANCO.
18. Organization for Economic Cooperation and Development, 'Reducing the Risk of Policy Failure: Challenges for Regulatory Compliance', 2000, p. 77. Available at: www.oecd.org/puma/pubs/index.htm
19. Pauline Rosenau Vaillancourt, *Public-Private Policy Partnerships* (Cambridge: MIT Press, 1999).
20. For a different development of the concept of entanglements see Michel Callon (ed.), *The Laws of the Markets* (London: Blackwell, 1998).
21. George Stigler, *The Citizen and the State: Essays on Regulation* (Chicago: University of Chicago Press, 1975).
22. Rawi Abdelal, *Capital Rules: The Construction of Global Finance* (Cambridge: Harvard University Press, 2007).
23. Wolfgang Reinicke and Francis Deng, *Critical Choices: The United Nations, Networks, and the Future of Global Governance* (Ottawa: IRDC, 2000).
24. http://www.semiconductorcouncil.org/about/history.html
25. http://www.tabd.com/about
26. http://www.americanchemistry.com/s_responsiblecare/sec_members.asp?CID=1322&DID=4865
27. David Vogel, *Trading Up: Consumer and Environmental Regulation in a Global Economy* (Cambridge: Harvard University Press, 1995).
28. Timothy Sinclair, *New Masters of Capital: American Bond Rating Agencies and the Politics of Creditworthiness* (Ithaca: Cornell University Press, 2005).
29. Susan K. Sell, *Private Power, Public* Law: The *Globalization of Intellectual Property Rights* (Cambridge: Cambridge University Press, 2003).
30. John Braithwaite and Peter Drahos, *Global Business Regulation* (Cambridge: Cambridge University Press, 2000).

31. Aseem Prakash and Matthew Potoski, 'Collective Action Through Voluntary Environmental Programs: A Club Theory Perspective,' *Policy Studies Journal*, Vol. 35, No. 4, 2007, pp. 773–792.
32. Tony Porter, *Globalization and Finance* (Cambridge: Polity, 2005).
33. Ron Scherer, 'New Combatant Against Global Warming: Insurance Industry,' *Christian Science Monitor*, 13October 2006, online edition.
34. www.hcch.net
35. www.unidroit.org
36. Ronen Shamir, 'Between Self-Regulation and the Alien Tort Claims Act: On the Contested Concept of Corporate Social Responsibility,' *Law and Society Review*, Vol. 38, No. 4, 2004, pp. 635–663.
37. Jeffrey Rosen, 'Supreme Court Inc.,' *New York Times Magazine*, 16 March 2008, Online edition.
38. Trevor C.W. Farrow, 'Globalization, International Human Rights, and Civil Procedure,' *Alberta Law Review*, Vol. 41, December 2003, p. 671.
39. Deborah Avant, *The Market for Force: The Consequences of Privatizing Security* (Cambridge: Cambridge University Press, 2005).
40. Tony Porter, 'Disaggregating Authority in Global Governance,' in Hans Krause Hansen and Dorte Salskov-Iversen (eds), *Critical Perspectives on Private Authority in Global Politics (*Basingstoke: Palgrave Macmillan, 2008), pp. 27–50.
41. As it says on its website, 'despite its public sector shareholders, it invests mainly in private enterprises, usually together with commercial partners.' (www.ebrd.com/about/index.htm)
42. Hudson Institute, *Index of Global Philanthropy*. Available at gpr.hudson.org/files/publications/IndexGlobalPhilanthropy2007.pdf
43. www.gatesfoundation.org/MediaCenter/FactSheet/default.htm
44. International Development Association, 'Aid Architecture: An Overview of the Main Trends in Official Development Assistance Flows,' February 2007, p. 16. Available at siteresources.worldbank.org/IDA/Resources/Seminar%20 PDFs/73449-1172525976405/3492866-1172527584498/Aidarchitecture.pdf
45. Jürgen Habermas, *The Structural Transformation of the Public Sphere: An Inquiry into a Category of Bourgeois Society* (Cambridge, Mass.: MIT Press, 1989).
46. Aihwa Ong, *Global Assemblages*, p. 796.
47. Porter, *Globalization and Finance* pp. 114–115.
48. For an account of public-private interactions with some similarities to the one set out here see Braithwaite and Drahos, *Global Business Regulation*.
49. David Held, *Democracy and the Global Order: From the Modern State to Cosmopolitan Governance* (Cambridge: Polity, 2005).

5
global governance as liberal hegemony

jörg friedrichs

In early 2000, South African women huckstering fruit on the highway from Johannesburg to Maputo were driven away from their customary activity because the street they used to work on had become the emblem of an infrastructural trans-border region, called the Maputo Development Corridor. By 2004, Turkish Marxists had learnt an important lesson: to get international funding for the activities of their NGOs, they had to use the language of human rights rather than slogans about class struggle and social emancipation. In an attempt at pre-emptive apologetics, the White House stated in December 2008 that the foreign policy of the outgoing President George W. Bush had promoted a freedom agenda for democracy and liberty.

Are these disparate occurrences related? Believe it or not, from the perspective of some people there is a common denominator. Thus, the eviction of the South African hawkers can be seen as just one episode in the construction of a micro-region linking the local to the global under the auspices of neoliberal ideology.[1] Similarly, it is possible to argue that the 'conversion' of Turkish Marxists from economic and social to civil and political rights shows how 'the issues and priorities of global governance have become domesticated'.[2] Finally, the attribution of a freedom agenda to George W. Bush arguably tells us less about the true motives behind his foreign policy than about the indispensability of liberal values as a veneer of legitimacy to mantle the less-appealing aspects of military power.[3] The unifying theme is the assumption that events in the global polity are shaped by the hegemony of liberal values.

Opponents of this view will argue that this takes it too far. The South African police was simply enforcing the law of the land which stipulates that peddling on streets is an illegal activity. Turkish Marxists followed the same rent-seeking logic as other aid recipients. And by 2008, the credibility of the outgoing Bush administration had worn rather thin. These are reasonable objections, and we should be careful not to accept the assumption of liberal hegemony without having critically assessed its pros and its cons. Nevertheless, the hypothesis of global governance as liberal hegemony is worthy of critical evaluation. And this is precisely what I do in this chapter.

After a brief explication of my own presuppositions, I elaborate on the social philosophy of Antonio Gramsci to enunciate the notion of hegemony. I then reflect upon the notion of hegemonic liberalism and reject hyperbolic views of global governance as outright liberal hegemony. Instead, I suggest a more balanced view that takes liberalism seriously while at the same time being sceptical about the prospects of actually establishing its hegemony. I argue that global governance is best understood not as liberal hegemony *per se* but as the hegemonic project of the liberal part of global civil society. It is easy to see that the anti-globalization movement is even weaker than its liberal sparring partner. A discussion of the same issue complex in terms of Karl Polanyi's double movement leads to similar results. I therefore propose an understanding of global governance not so much as liberal hegemony but rather as a stage for haphazard moves to establish liberal hegemony and quixotic counter-moves to prevent this from happening.

presuppositions

This chapter reviews the scholarship of those authors who subscribe to some narrative about liberal hegemony lurking behind global governance. Such narratives are often combined with the notion of alternative, counter-hegemonic forms of global governance. Most of the authors under review are radicals – some in the tradition of Marx, others in the tradition of Gramsci, and still others in the tradition of Polanyi.

I am not personally committed to any of these views. But I do believe that they offer an interesting normative and analytical alternative to the mainstream literature on global governance. In the mainstream literature, the term 'global governance' is often used as a cover for the weary recognition that the world has become exceedingly complex and almost ungovernable. Authors such as James Rosenau state that the planet has entered an era of turbulence and unpredictability, which they call global governance. While one may celebrate this from a post-modernist viewpoint, from a social, scientific perspective it is an oath of disclosure.

In antithesis to such analytical defeatism, the authors under review in this chapter share the fascinating and somewhat staggering claim that global governance can be part of a story on 'how it all hangs together'. They seem to suggest that it is still possible to provide a sort of grand, historical narrative. If this claim is warranted, either entirely or in part, this is bound to have a rejuvenating effect on political science. It may also have important implications for political practice.

Given the prevailing sense of normative and analytical agnosticism, the burden of proof is clearly with those who claim that a master-narrative is still possible. Nevertheless, their views should be examined with genuine intellectual curiosity. If they are right, their contribution is more valuable than the defeatism of those who use terms like global governance as a shortcut for saying that the world is increasingly complex. After all, grand theorizing is about making bold and well-argued statements.

Of course this does not imply that one has to share the normative convictions and political biases of the authors under review. It simply means that we should be willing to review their scholarship without premature mental closure. Before we start our conceptual exploration on global governance as liberal hegemony, one disclaimer is in order. 'Hegemony' is understood here not primarily as military preponderance, as is often the case in the International Relations literature. Instead, it is understood in terms of the unorthodox Marxism of Gramsci. Following this tradition, hegemony can be defined as a specific constellation of social order where in the absence of coercion, consent is to a large extent negotiated.[4]

from marx to gramsci

As a wayward Hegelian, Karl Marx saw dialectics at work almost everywhere. Most notably, he understood the history of all mankind as a sequence of dialectical struggles. Surprisingly, however, Marx mostly failed to recognize any dialectics between the material and non-material conditions of social life. He saw society as determined by relations of production. 'The totality of these relations of production constitutes the economic structure of society, the real foundation, on which arises a legal and political superstructure and to which correspond definite forms of social consciousness. The mode of production of material life conditions the general process of social, political and intellectual life.'[5]

The Italian Marxist Antonio Gramsci was deeply unsatisfied with such economic determinism. He therefore introduced dialectics into the relations between base and superstructure.[6] To Gramsci, social relations at the level of the superstructure can both reinforce and undermine the material basis. Under normal circumstances, the dominant class controlling the means of production will make sure that the superstructure reflects its fundamental needs. This implies a certain control of the formal apparatus of coercion embodied by the state. At the same time, the dominant class will try to make sure it controls the realm of civil society where consent is negotiated in the absence of coercion. If this is successful, hegemony is firmly in place. If not, the dominant class is likely to be challenged by a counter-movement.

Where Marx failed to see any dialectics, Gramsci saw two forms of dialectics at work simultaneously. To the dialectics between economic structure and superstructure he added other dialectics at the level of the superstructure itself – namely, the dialectics between state ('political society') on the one hand and civil society on the other.[7] When the system is in a condition of stability, the elements of this 'trialectic' are mutually reinforcing. Civil society and political society support one another, while they also support and are in turn supported by the economic basis upon which they rest. Gramsci calls such a synergetic constellation an 'historical bloc'. Under such circumstances, the economic structure and the coalitions at the level of social and political superstructure constitute a sustainable ('organic') order. The custodian of this order is a dominant class controlling the economy, permeating the state and holding the hegemony over civil society. Gramsci suggests that the hegemony of the dominant class over the rest of civil society is a crucial part of such sustainable order.

When a historical bloc falls into crisis, its elements enter into conflict. However, this does not necessarily mean that a revolutionary 'war of movement' is imminent. It takes more than a minor crisis to bring a homeostatic system down. In a protracted 'war of position', revolutionaries will try to lay the ground for an alternative historical bloc. They will strategically operate on both the state and civil society to undermine the dominant configuration of order. It is not enough for them to sabotage the capitalist economy and to attack the capitalist state head-on. They also need to make it impossible for the dominant class to negotiate consent in the absence of coercion. Only when the dominant class has lost its hegemony over civil society is the time ripe for an upheaval in which eventually the old historical bloc is overthrown and replaced by a new historical bloc spearheaded by the revolutionaries. When the new historical bloc is successful and becomes hegemonic, economic structure and socio-political superstructure enter into a new equilibrium.

In the original formulation of the theory by Gramsci, historical blocs are forged at the level of the nation state. More recently, however, scholars such as Robert Cox have pointed out that historical blocs can spillover into the international sphere.[8] The historical blocs in the dominant countries will have certain 'milieu goals' which they will try to implement at the international level. For example, liberal hegemony in the dominant country makes a liberal international economic order far more likely. Capitalist markets and liberal civil society have an inherent tendency to transcend national boundaries, and this can be expected to lead to an internationalized historical bloc. The *Pax Britannica* of the nineteenth century and the *Pax Americana* of the twentieth century come to mind here. Cox argued that, in addition to their military ascendancy, Great Britain and the United States as the countries hosting the most advanced and productive economies of these periods had a profound influence on the economic, social and political order of other countries and of the international system at large.[9]

If one adopts such a neo-Gramscian view, the crucial question is whether economic globalization can be said to constitute the basis, and liberal global governance the superstructure, of an embryonic historical bloc at the planetary level.

hegemonic neoliberalism

Most of the authors under review share a view that liberal values constitute the normative content enshrined in the dominant form of global governance. In most cases they do not talk about liberalism as such but prefer the term 'neoliberalism'. Either way, the main point is that liberal values are seen as hegemonic.

Despite occasional attempts to provide a lexical definition of hegemonic neoliberalism, the phenomenon is best understood in the context of a grand historical narrative, with the sequence of classical liberalism; embedded liberalism; neoliberalism. According to the authoritative version of that narrative, neoliberalism is an avatar of nineteenth-century classical liberalism, after an interlude of embedded liberalism in the post-war era. As it were, classical market liberalism entered a crisis in the first half of the twentieth century. After serious turmoil and two world wars, this led to the embedded liberalism compromise under the Breton Woods System. Keynesianism entered a crisis in the early 1970s, however. As a result of this crisis, the 'tamed capitalism' of the early post-war years became increasingly untenable and market liberalism was reborn in the shape of neoliberalism. Since then, as the story goes, neoliberalism has reached the status of uncontested hegemony.[10]

A stark representative of this view is Susanne Soederberg.[11] She argues that the tenets of neoliberalism have become part of a 'new commonsense'. As any other form of commonsense, neoliberalism relies on a wide consensus and is taken so much for granted that it does not have to be justified any more. Instead, it has become possible to talk about economic globalization and global governance as secular trends to which there is no alternative. From the viewpoint of this neoliberal commonsense, global governance provides the socio-political superstructure to economic globalization. Nevertheless, Soederberg argues that the assumed inevitability of neoliberalism rests on false consciousness. The falsity of neoliberal commonsense becomes apparent when confronted with the reality of capitalist crises and exploitation in the South. In typical Marxist fashion, Soederberg proposes historical materialism as a method with which to 'critique' global governance and to uncover the inherent contradictions and relations of domination hidden in neoliberal commonsense. She asserts that, after the demise of the Breton Woods System, neoliberal hegemony has been in a permanent crisis. Soederberg does not deny that there have been certain gambits in response to the crisis. For example, the Washington consensus of the 1990s has been modified in response to its apparent failure. The Clinton and the Bush administrations have, each in its own way, attempted to restructure the political superstructure of global capitalism. Nevertheless, she is adamant in emphasizing that such attempts can only provide limited temporal and spatial fixes to prevent the system from collapsing. Global governance is at best an idle attempt to conceal the crisis.

Such positions are paradoxical. On the one hand, neoliberalism is seen as so powerful that it constitutes a universal commonsense that displaces all conceivable alternatives. On the other hand, it is a house of cards that will collapse under the weight of its own contradictions.

It is easy to see that both of these assertions can hardly be true at the same time. On the one hand, one should be careful not to commit the error of reifying liberal hegemony as inexorable historical necessity. On the other hand, neoliberalism should be taken more seriously because markets are endowed with a discursive authority that stabilizes widely shared beliefs in the legitimacy of liberal economics.[12]

hyperbolic views

The inherent contradictions in Susanne Soederberg's views are not an isolated case. Most authors under review in this chapter are leftist radicals. This is not to disqualify them or to deny that some of them are striving for a balanced view. But many are carried by their extreme political convictions towards hyperbolic views. They have a tendency to strangely oscillate between hope and despair. In one moment they rage against liberal hegemony as an odious machine from which there is no escape. In the next moment they call for a relentless fight against this all-powerful machine. Radical mood swings are characteristic of leftist radicals, both in scholarship and in practice.

The bottom-line in most of such radical scholarship is anti-capitalism. Leftists habitually denounce market fundamentalism and the managerialism of the World Bank and other International Financial Institutions. In 2000, one scholar went as far as calling the World Bank the 'mother of all governments', endowed with a dehumanizing 'matrix for global governance'.[13] Journalist Naomi Klein sees a global conspiracy of ultraliberal 'Chicago boys' thriving on disaster and applying sadistic shock therapies that will benefit exploitative business interests.[14] The upshot is that global capitalism and liberal hegemony are extremely powerful and mean. If liberal hegemony is really so powerful and mean, it would seem that the odds for counter-hegemonic movements are bad. However, this does not dissuade authors in this genre from calling for eschatological struggles. They are in awe of liberal capitalism's iron fist while at the same time sneering at the giant's feet of clay.[15]

Suffice it to quote the fervent appeal at the end of Hardt and Negri's *Empire*. After depicting empire in the most inescapable terms on more than 400 pages, resistance seems either pointless or paradoxical. 'Today, after so many capitalist victories, after socialist hopes have withered in disillusionment, and after capitalist violence against labour has been solidified under the name of ultraliberalism, why is it that instances of militancy still arise?' But then, only one page later, the whole scenery has completely changed. 'This is a revolution that no power will control – because biopower and communism, cooperation and revolution remain together, in love, simplicity, and also innocence. This is the irrepressible lightness and joy of being communist.'[16]

To be sure, hyperbole is not the exclusive domain of leftist radicals. While leftist radicals tend to demonize liberal hegemony as a capitalist plot, radical liberals and even neo-conservatives take the opposite route and embrace hegemonic liberalism as the harbinger of freedom and democracy. They take a crusading attitude towards liberal values and celebrate the virtues of 'liberal imperialism'. From their viewpoint, US military unilateralism endows liberal values such as democracy and open markets with the necessary clout. In its use of imperialist means to liberal ends, even the Bush administration could be seen as promoting the cause of liberal hegemony.[17]

towards a balanced view

Hyperbolic views may be appealing to sectarian believers, both to the left and to the right of the spectrum, but they are seriously out of balance. Another imbalance consists in the fact that even mainstream policy-oriented scholarship switches between talk about 'empire' and 'decline' every ten years or so. For example, after less than a decade of talk about American unilateralism and neoliberal empire, pundits are now reverting to the discourse of multilateralism and hegemonic decline.[18]

This fails to consider a fundamentally important fact that is obvious to anybody working from a genuine Gramscian perspective: Market fundamentalism and militarism attest to the weakness and not to the strength of liberal hegemony. Market fundamentalism undermines the existence of a vibrant societal sphere and thus liberal hegemony. As we have seen, the whole point about hegemony is that it relies on the non-coercive negotiation of consent. In a hyper-liberal scenario where everything is transformed into a marketable commodity, there is little or no space left for society to negotiate consent and determine its purpose. As Polanyi has forcefully shown (and as will be discussed in greater depth towards the end of this chapter), commodification cannot be complete lest society destroys itself. Liberal hegemony presupposes a vibrant societal sphere, which however is undermined by market fundamentalism; market fundamentalism is therefore corrosive of liberal hegemony.[19]

Something similar goes for militarism. To the extent that liberal values are really hegemonic, they do not grow out of the barrel of a gun. Already under Ronald Reagan, the repeated recourse to military unilateralism attested to a difficulty to negotiate consent in the absence of coercion, that is a weakness of liberal hegemony.[20] For the same reason, liberal scholars are now claiming that the United States needs to climb down from the imperial ambitions of the Bush administration and focus more on the production and reproduction of liberal international order if it wants to preserve (or restore) the normative consensus on which American power ultimately rests.[21]

The corrosive effects of market fundamentalism and military unilateralism have jeopardized the vigour and sustainability of liberal governance, despite the fact that the policies of the late Bush administration were not so much a radical departure from Clintonian liberalism but rather the continuation of neoliberalism by military means.[22] A few years ago, there were hopes that global governance might be harnessed to deal with the pernicious problems of new wars and underdevelopment.[23] Such optimism has been frustrated in the wake of the War on Terror and the World Financial Crisis. But there is no need to go into the other extreme and declare the bankruptcy of liberal governance. A balanced view will recognize that, on the one hand, the uncontested hegemony of global civil society is not in the cards. On the other hand, the hegemonic quest of liberalism goes on. From a balanced viewpoint, it is appropriate to talk about liberal hegemony not so much as political reality but rather as a political project.

liberal hegemony as a project

So far the history of mankind has not seen uncontested hegemony. Uncontested hegemony would mean that a society is fully able to negotiate consent in the absence of coercion (except maybe for criminal deviance and pathological madness). Political society could then be absorbed into civil society, and the state could be allowed to die off. While this would be germane to the classless utopias of Karl Marx and other eschatological thinkers, no human society has ever reached that point.

Although there has not been a single case of uncontested hegemony, there have been approximations. There have been cases in time and space where a certain degree of hegemony was achieved by the dominant class. Nineteenth-century England is the classical example of liberal hegemony – despite the rise of trade unions and other forms of contestation around the same time. Under *Pax Britannica*, liberal hegemony at the domestic level was also extended to the international sphere. Thus, the era of free trade before World War I was the international extension of the domestic liberal hegemony in the British homeland.[24] Embedded liberalism and the international order based on *Pax Americana* after World War II constitute another case in point.

Although *Pax Britannica* and *Pax Americana* were approximations to liberal hegemony, in neither of these cases was liberal hegemony uncontested. *Pax Britannica* coincided with working-class contestation, and *Pax Americana* with the Cold War. This should somewhat lower expectations about global governance, which is weaker than either *Pax Britannica* or *Pax Americana*. Global governance is not liberal hegemony but at best a liberal hegemonic project. Not even in the mid-1990s, during the heydays of enthusiasm about global governance, was there any reason to believe that neoliberalism would be strong enough to become truly hegemonic and contribute to a full-blown historical bloc. Susan Strange rightly emphasized the problem that, while the old formula of political regulation based on the nation state (aka embedded liberalism) was withering away under the impact of globalization, there was no regulatory alternative available to fill the vacuum. This was aggravated by the fact that globalization was leading to additional regulatory needs that hadn't even existed under national enclosure. As a result, there was a widening gap between decreasing regulatory capacities and increasing regulatory needs.[25]

The 2000s have painfully borne out this scepticism. On the one hand, neoliberalism is the name of the game in the absence of more powerful alternatives. The conventional understanding of global governance is conceptually inseparable from an intuitive notion of liberal hegemony. On the other hand, liberal global governance is unable to 're-embed' economic globalization. It is therefore impossible to equate global governance with liberal hegemony. Global governance represents the aspiration of liberalism for hegemonic status, but given the shortage of social and political regulation at the global level this aspiration is not borne out by reality.

This is not to deny that liberal global governance holds some promise in the absence of other regulatory options. It offers a welcome venue where consent can sometimes be negotiated in the absence of coercion. Liberal global governance is the only conceivable option to solve important problems. However, the potentialities of this are limited.

Global governance can at best offer a partial surrogate for some of those regulatory functions that the state is not able or willing to fulfil any more.[26] There is a shortage of political governance at the level of the nation state, and there is clearly no government worthy of that name at the global level. Against this dramatic dearth of regulatory options, governance can offer at best partial remedy. Moreover, liberal values such as freedom, democracy and free enterprise are far from being universal. They are spread too unevenly over the planet to be the bedrock for a normative consensus throughout global society (a cursory glance over the newspaper is enough to confirm that there is periodical recourse to fiscal intervention and military force when liberal values are too weak to provide a modicum of stability and order).

In short, liberal global governance does not constitute an 'organic' civil superstructure to economic globalization. It is therefore best understood not as liberal hegemony, but as the hegemonic project of the liberal part of global civil society.

counter-hegemonic projects

While there is a danger of overestimating the hegemonic power of liberalism, we should be even more cautious not to overestimate counter-hegemonic projects. There is not even the shade of a unified counter-project to hegemonic liberalism. At best there is a variety of counter-projects, in the plural. There is a quest for radical alternatives to liberal global governance under the banner of the so-called anti- or alter-globalization movement, but the disparate social forces represented in that movement have never crystallized into a unified political project. From an ideological and organizational point of view, the weaknesses and contradictions in the movement against economic globalization and liberal global governance are obvious.[27]

To the dismay of anti-globalization activists, events have made abundantly clear that the weakness of liberal hegemony does not equal to the strength of their counter-hegemonic projects. The transnational protest movement igniting the riots in Seattle and Genoa, as well as the World Social Forum meetings in Porto Alegre and elsewhere, have been working under the assumption that, whenever there is a crisis in economic globalization and neoliberal global governance, such as the 1997 Asian Crisis or the Argentine Crisis between 1999 and 2002, the time is ripe for alternative forms of globalization and global governance. But this has not materialized. The latest wave of the transnational movement ebbed away after the rallies against the Iraq War in 2003. In 2007, the World Social Forum in Nairobi decided that in the following year there would be no global summit. And it remains to be seen to what extent anti-globalization activists will be able to exploit the World Financial Crisis of 2008/2009.

In the face of exuberant aspirations that 'a better world is possible', a reincarnate Karl Marx would be the first to emphasize that in the present conjuncture there are no socio-economic reasons to take the anti-globalization movement seriously. Where are the tensions between relations of property and relations of production which might empower the downtrodden? Where is the bourgeoisie from which hegemony might be wrested? Where is the proletariat that might become the subject of historical change?

Even less than uncontested liberal hegemony, are we witnessing the advent of an alternative counter-hegemonic bloc? If liberal global governance is not hegemony as such but only the hegemonic project of liberal civil society, then the anti-globalization movement is not even a coherent counter-hegemonic project but at best the stage for a polyphony (or, as critics would say: cacophony) of voluntaristic projects.

double movement?

As an alternative to the Gramscian perspective adopted so far, it is possible to follow the perspective of Karl Polanyi in adopting the notion of a double movement. In this view, economic globalization is a secular movement, and the various attempts to establish global governance amount to a counter-movement. To explore this eventuality, let us briefly spell out what such a double movement would entail.[28]

Polanyi's fundamental insight was that markets defy and need regulation at the same time. Markets have a tendency to expand into and encroach upon the rest of human relations. Thus, slaves have been replaced by workers competing on the labour market; feudal land has become real estate; caring mothers have been replaced by waged nurses; and ingenious inventions have become intellectual property. For good and for ill, there seems to be a secular trend towards commodification.

However, there is a problem with this trend. Insofar as the purpose of market exchanges is the fulfilment of human needs in a social context, and insofar as that social context rests upon conditions that cannot be produced by the market itself, commodification risks destroying the human fabric upon which the market itself rests. No market can exist in the long run without society being able to reproduce itself in a sustainable way. Markets need a certain degree of social peace, an entrepreneurial class that subscribes to values such as integrity and workers endowed with an adequate work ethic. These economic preconditions cannot be produced by the market alone. On the contrary, an ever-expanding market has a tendency of undermining the social preconditions of its own existence. Against this tendency, Polanyi invoked non-commodified forms of social and political regulation which would contain the destructive tendencies of the market. A market without limits would be utterly self-defeating, and this is why Polanyi is correct that markets defy and need social and political regulation at the same time.

Polanyi saw a remedy to the destructive potential of the market in the self-healing mechanism of the 'double movement'. The double movement is a patterned sequence where expansionary moves on the part of the market are held in check by social and political counter-movements.

Under the banner of economic globalization, the market has expanded once more. Today as well as in earlier epochs, the clash between the so-called free market and the need for social and political regulation is inescapable and can only be solved creatively. To offset the destructive potential inherent in the expansion of the capitalist market, society needs to reassert itself in a counter-movement. This makes it tempting to assume that the movement of economic globalization and the counter-movement of global governance (both liberal and otherwise) are two sides of the same coin. In fact, while Polanyi was thinking in terms of national economies, it is possible to strip his thought of methodological nationalism.[29] In such a view, economic globalization can be understood as a market-liberal movement 'dis-embedding' the economy from its regulatory framework in the nation state of old, while global governance is a social-liberal counter-movement to re-regulate the globalized economy in a new transnational framework.

However, there is no guarantee that every movement will lead to an appropriate counter-movement. Even assuming that economic globalization can be seen as a coherent historical movement, the decisive question is can the various social networks sailing under the flag of global governance converge into a counter-movement to tame the movement of economic globalization?

From a Polanyian perspective, there is a variety of attempts to tame globalization through global governance. However, the various currents in this would-be counter-movement are highly incongruent: hegemonic and counter-hegemonic, progressive and reactionary, left-wing and right-wing, cosmopolitan and communitarian, secular and religious, moderate and fundamentalist.

At first glance, this is fully in line with what Polanyi would have predicted. Whenever there is a double movement, economic deregulation comes first and social and political re-regulation comes second. The fragmented nature of the counter-movement is hardly surprising given the fact that the social forces representing the movement do not only have the first-mover advantage but also many opportunities to co-opt parts of the counter-movement, while the reverse is simply not the case.

Nevertheless, it would be too confident to assume that every movement will arouse an adequate counter-movement. In the case of nineteenth-century liberalism the double movement was ultimately completed, but this was a relatively close thing. The world had to go though atrocious turmoil between 1914 and 1945 to reach a temporary equilibrium in the embedded liberalism compromise. After the demise of that equilibrium in only one generation, who guarantees that economic globalization will again usher in an adequate counter-movement to provide a new equilibrium?

How can we be so sure that the historical movement known as globalization will unleash an appropriate counter-movement? And even if this should happen, who tells us that this counter-movement will not be accompanied by atrocious turmoil? Why should the social forces behind global markets voluntarily consent into their 'taming'? Why should they not triumph over all attempts to limit their leeway, burying under their own success the social foundations upon which they ultimately rest?

Polanyi is certainly right that, in the absence of an appropriate counter-movement, the market undermines its own foundations. If unchecked, the expansion of the market will destroy the foundations on which the social fabric rests, including the market itself. Nevertheless, the reconstitution of equitable foundations is not a matter of historical necessity. On methodological grounds, it is impossible for the social scientist to predict that something will happen because it should (or must) happen.

conclusion

There are two important lessons to be drawn. First, while the notion of liberal hegemony offers an interesting lens to understand global governance, we should avoid the hyperbolic views that are often associated with it. Second, we should also avoid wishful thinking and seriously contemplate the possibility that global governance (liberal or otherwise) may be insufficient to counter-balance economic globalization.

There is no need to fall prey to conspiratorial thinking and assume, with Robert Cox, that there is a global 'nébuleuse' orchestrating what we experience as globalization and global governance.[30] Similarly, deterministic views of liberal hegemony as a product of the inexorable advance of global capitalism are misplaced. We are not in an eschatological 'war of position' between hegemonic and counter-hegemonic forces, and the world is not experiencing a process of historic bloc formation.[31] Nor is it appropriate to assume that economic globalization can be easily 'tamed' by global civil society. Even though John Ruggie seems still to believe that the UN-sponsored learning network of the *Global Compact* can unite transnational business with international labour and NGOs in an effort to restore embedded liberalism at the global level, hegemonic order is unlikely to emerge as the peaceful outcome of deliberative forums offered by enlightened international bureaucrats.[32]

Instead of going down any of these roads, we can use the Gramscian notion of hegemony and counter-hegemony (as well as the Polanyian notion of movements and counter-movements) as a source of analytical insight, while keeping critical distance from inadequate applications – whether conspiratorial, deterministic or simply naïve. From our analytical perspective, liberal global governance is best understood not as a reality but as a political project, namely as the political project of liberal civil society.

At this point, the time has come to debunk another myth related to liberal global governance. It is not true that 'transnational civil society' equals 'global civil society'. Transnational civil society has a Western bias, and that bias is not decreasing.[33] It is therefore better to talk about transatlantic civil society, which is predominantly liberal.[34] Under the auspices of economic globalization, primarily Western NGOs try to instil liberal values such as respect for democracy and human rights to economic and political actors. The assumption is that global governance is in a position to fill the regulative gap created by economic globalization and the concomitant retreat of the state. 'Governance' as opposed to 'government' transports the very optimistic and typically liberal belief that things can happily work out as the result of polycentric interaction, rather than necessarily and always being the result of power relationships.

This is the hopeful viewpoint of liberal-minded people. It is noble, ingenuous and exceedingly optimistic. Nevertheless, it constitutes a significant social reality insofar as it is the presumption under which these people operate. It helps them to go about their work if they can see themselves as part of global civil society and as contributing to the noble cause of liberal global governance. While such hegemonic liberalism is presently the most powerful transnational political project, it is only a default position in the absence of a credible challenge. Counter-hegemonic projects such as the anti-globalization movement do not offer such a credible challenge, insofar as they are even more remote from attaining hegemonic status than liberalism. But this does not keep anti-globalization activists from nourishing hegemonic ambitions.

Whether attainable or not, the imagery of hegemony is the presumption under which ideological and political battles between a variety of orientations are taking place. As social scientists, we should always take the 'working assumptions' of acting people seriously. At the same time, however, we need to keep critical distance from their presuppositions. This is possible if we understand global governance as the space where a variety of political projects compete for hegemonic status – no matter if they are ever going to attain it. Upon reflection it would therefore seem that global governance is not the sphere where eschatological struggles for world supremacy are staged. Instead, global governance is a political arena for haphazard moves to establish liberal hegemony and quixotic counter-moves trying to prevent liberal hegemony from being established and proposing radical alternatives.

notes

Thanks are due to Barbara Harriss-White, Rodney Bruce Hall and my students for their valuable comments.

1. Ian Taylor, 'Globalization and Regionalization in Africa: Reactions to Attempts at Neo-Liberal Regionalism,' *Review of International Political Economy*, Vol. 10, No. 2, 2003, pp. 310–330, at p. 324.
2. Başak Çali and Ayça Ergun, 'Global Governance and Domestic Politics: Fragmented Visions,' in Markus Lederer and Philipp S. Müller (eds), *Criticizing Global Governance* (Basingstoke: Palgrave Macmillan, 2005), pp. 161–176, at p. 164.
3. The White House, *Highlights of Accomplishments and Results: The Administration of George W. Bush, 2001–2009* (Washington: The White House, 2008).
4. Robert Bocock, *Hegemony* (Chichester: Ellis Horwood, 1986).
5. Karl Marx, *A Contribution to the Critique of Political Economy* (London: Lawrence and Wishart, 1971), pp. 20–21.

6. Antonio Gramsci, *Pre-Prison Writings*, edited by Richard Bellamy and translated by Virginia Cox (Cambridge: Cambridge University Press, 1994); Id., *Selections from the Prison Notebooks*, edited and translated by Quintin Hoare and Geoffrey Nowell Smith (London: Lawrence and Wishart, 1973).
7. Norberto Bobbio, 'Gramsci and the Concept of Civil Society,' in John Keane (ed.), *Civil Society and the State* (London: Verso, 1988), pp. 73–99.
8. Robert W. Cox, 'Gramsci, Hegemony and International Relations: An Essay in Method,' *Millennium*, Vol. 12, No. 2, 1983, pp. 162–175.
9. Robert W. Cox, *Production, Power, and World Order: Social Forces in the Making of History* (New York: Columbia University Press, 1987).
10. David Harvey, *A Brief History of Neoliberalism* (Oxford: Oxford University Press, 2005); on embedded liberalism see John Gerard Ruggie, 'International Regimes, Transactions, and Change: Embedded Liberalism in the Postwar Economic Order,' *International Organization*, Vol. 36, No. 2, 1982, pp. 417–455.
11. Susanne Soederberg, *Global Governance in Question: Empire, Class and the New Common Sense in Managing North-South Relations* (London: Pluto, 2006).
12. Rodney Bruce Hall, 'Explaining "Market Authority" and Liberal Stability: Toward a Sociological-Constructivist Synthesis,' *Global Society*, Vol. 21, No. 3, 2007, pp. 319–342.
13. Paul Cammack, 'The Matrix of All Governments: The World Bank's Matrix for Global Governance,' in Rorden Wilkinson and Steve Hughes (eds), *Global Governance: Critical Perspectives* (London and New York: Routledge, 2002), pp. 36–53.
14. Naomi Klein, *The Shock Doctrine: The Rise of Disaster Capitalism* (London: Allen Lane, 2007).
15. The Book of Daniel (Ch. 2) suggests that, from an eschatological viewpoint, there is nothing fundamentally wrong with such an attitude. But few radical scholars would be likely to accept they are holding eschatological views.
16. Michael Hardt and Antonio Negri, *Empire* (Cambridge, Mass.: Harvard University Press, 2000), pp. 412–413.
17. Daniel Green, 'Liberal Imperialism as Global-Governance Perspective,' in Alice D. Ba and Matthew J. Hoffmann (eds), *Contending Perspectives on Global Governance: Coherence, Contestation and World Order* (London and New York: Routledge, 2005), pp. 231–248.
18. National Intelligence Council, *Global Trends 2025: A Transformed World*, (Washington: US Government Printing Office, 2008).
19. Karl Polanyi, *The Great Transformation: The Political and Economic Origins of Our Time* (Boston: Beacon, 2001 [1944]).
20. Robert W. Cox, *Production, Power, and World Order: Social Forces in the Making of History* (New York: Columbia University Press, 1987); see also Robert O. Keohane, *After Hegemony: Cooperation and Discord in the World Political Economy* (Princeton, N.J.: Princeton University Press, 1984).
21. Edward Kolodyiej and Roger E. Kanet (eds), *From Superpower to Besieged Global Power: Restoring World Order after the Failure of the Bush Doctrine* (Athens, Georgia: University of Georgia Press, 2008); G. John Ikenberry, *Liberal Order and Imperial Ambition: Essays on American Power and World Politics* (Cambridge: Polity, 2006); Joseph S. Nye, *Soft Power: The Means to Success in World Politics* (New York: Public Affairs, 2004).

22. Ray Kiely, *Empire in the Age of Globalisation: US Hegemony and Neoliberal Disorder* (London: Pluto, 2005).
23. Mark Duffield, *Global Governance and the New Wars: The Merging of Development and Security* (London: Zed, 2002), pp. 257–265.
24. Justin Rosenberg, *The Empire of Civil Society: A Critique of the Realist Theory of International Relations* (London: Verso, 1994); Benno Teschke, *The Myth of 1648: Class, Geopolitics, and the Making of Modern International Relations* (London: Verso, 2003).
25. Susan Strange, *The Retreat of the State: The Diffusion of Power in the World Economy* (Cambridge: Cambridge University Press, 1996).
26. Frederick Powell, *The Politics of Civil Society: Neoliberalism or Social Left?* (Bristol: Policy, 2007).
27. Peter Wilkin, 'Against Global Governance? Tracing the Lineage of the Anti-Globalisation Movement,' in Feargal Cochrane, Rosaleen Duffy and Jan Selby (eds) *Global Governance, Conflict and Resistance* (Basingstoke: Palgrave Macmillan, 2003), pp. 78–95.
28. Polanyi, *The Great Transformation*; cf. Michael Burawoy, 'For a Sociological Marxism: The Complementary Convergence of Antonio Gramsci and Karl Polanyi,' *Politics and Society*, Vol. 31, No. 2, 2003, pp. 193–261.
29. Ronaldo Munck, *Globalization and Contestation: The New Great Counter-Movement* (London and New York: Routledge, 2007).
30. Robert W. Cox, *Approaches to World Order* (Cambridge: Cambridge University Press, 1996), p. 298.
31. *Contra* William K. Carroll, 'Hegemony and Counter-Hegemony in a Global Field,' *Studies in Social Justice*, Vol. 1, No. 1, 2007, pp. 36–66.
32. John Gerard Ruggie, 'Global Markets and Global Governance: The Prospects for Convergence,' in Steven Bernstein and Louis W. Pauly (eds), *Global Liberalism and Political Order: Toward a New Grand Compromise* (Albany, NY.: State University of New York Press, 2007), pp. 23–48.
33. Jason Beckfield, 'Inequality in the World Polity: The Structure of International Organization,' *American Sociological Review*, Vol. 68, No. 3, 2003, pp. 401–424.
34. Jörg Friedrichs 'Global Governance as the Hegemonic Project of Transatlantic Civil Society,' in Markus Lederer and Philipp S. Müller (eds), *Criticizing Global Governance* (Basingstoke: Palgrave Macmillan, 2005), pp. 45–68.

6
global governance as public policy networks and partnerships

julia steets

public policy networks and partnerships as a response to gaps in global governance

At the beginning of the twenty-first century, traditional political instruments and institutions are struggling to cope with important public policy problems. Faced with the twin forces of regional integration and decentralization, we are witnessing a 'hollowing out of the state'[1] and an erosion of the nation state's ability to fulfil its classical role. At the same time, with globalization a host of new political challenges are emerging that need to be tackled at the trans or international level. As a result, the traditional institutional architecture of international politics shows important governance gaps.[2]

One such gap is operational. Political and economic liberalization as well as accelerating technological change mean that public policy problems often span political borders and are increasingly complex. Conventional political actors such as nation states and intergovernmental organizations thus frequently lack the capacity to effectively address pressing problems ranging from climate change to international health crises.

Another crucial gap relates to the legitimacy of political institutions. First, the operational governance gap described above threatens the output-based legitimacy of traditional political actors.[3] Nation states and international organizations unable to tackle the world's most pressing problems quickly lose their credibility and the trust of citizens. Second, the input-based legitimacy of these institutions is also in question. Despite their growing power and political relevance, other transnational actors including NGOs and corporations are only represented to a very limited degree in the classical political architecture.

Multi-stakeholder networks and partnerships promise to help fill both these governance gaps. Public policy networks and partnerships can be defined as voluntary cooperative arrangements, involving public, private and/or civil society organizations that focus on a public policy problem.[4] Networks and partnerships can take a more or less institutionalized form. Some analysts prefer the term 'network' for more informal arrangements and 'partnership' for more strongly institutionalized forms of cooperation. The use of the concepts is, however, not consistent and while it was particularly popular to speak about 'networks' in the early stages of the debate, the current term of choice for analysts and practitioners seems to be 'partnerships'. Throughout this chapter, the two terms are therefore taken to be broadly synonymous.

What exactly are the potential contributions of networks and partnerships to global governance? Where can we find practical examples of policy-making through networks and partnerships? Have networks and partnerships managed to live up to the hopes invested in them? What are the major points of contention relating to networks and partnerships as an approach to global governance? The following paragraphs sketch out preliminary answers to these questions.

the promises and growing popularity of networks and partnerships

When the spotlight was first shone on networks and partnerships as a governance approach, analysts were enthusiastic about their potential. By encouraging cooperation across institutional and physical boundaries, networks and partnerships were hoped to achieve a long list of benefits, including among others:[5]

- *Creating greater operational capacity and effectiveness*. Different organizations bring different resources to the table. Governments, for example, have the unique advantage of possessing regulatory authority and can contribute democratic legitimacy to a governance process. Companies have access to financial resources and have technical expertise in their area of work. NGOs have also often acquired specific technical expertise and can often draw on good connections to local populations or other international players. By combining these complementary resources, networks and partnerships carry the potential of creating the operational capacity needed to address complex, cross-border policy problems. Moreover, the different actors involved can use networks and partnerships to coordinate their activities and thus avoid a duplication of efforts. Finally, the active involvement of different actors also increases their sense of ownership over the resulting policies. As a result, the developed problem-solving mechanisms are more likely to be sustainable in the long term.

- *Generating more flexibility and efficiency.* Traditional governance mechanisms employed by governments and international organizations have frequently been diagnosed as overly bureaucratic and therefore inefficient. Through their engagement in networks or partnerships, governmental organizations can escape some of their usual bureaucratic restrictions. This can allow them to react faster to emerging problems and to act more flexibly and therefore achieve results more efficiently.
- *Encouraging innovation.* The participating organizations contribute different resources, as well as different organizational cultures and work-styles to networks and partnerships. The combination of these alternative approaches can result in the development of genuinely new – and hopefully more effective and efficient – policies or problem-solving mechanisms.
- *Establishing a cooperative work culture in participating organizations.* Existing relationships between NGOs, corporations and governmental organizations are often characterized by conflict and a habit of blaming each other for policy failures. Successful cooperation in a problem-focused network or partnership can help global actors overcome that mutual blame culture and instead enables them to focus their energies on addressing problems.
- *Encouraging interorganizational learning.* By working together, different organizations can also learn from each other. This relates on the one hand to their substantive expertise in the relevant issue area. On the other hand, a confrontation with alternative work-styles and processes can help organizations improve the ways they are addressing problems. Thus, networks and partnerships can increase the capacity of their members.
- *Creating greater opportunities for participation and increasing the legitimacy of governance.* Finally, traditional instruments of global governance are mainly made up of or derive from national governments. Other players like civil society organizations or corporations are

> rarely represented. Both NGOs and trans or multinational corporations have, however, gained enormous influence and practical importance in the course of the twentieth century. Their sheer numbers, their presence on the ground and their financial scale have become hard to ignore. Networks and partnerships offer these as well as other institutions an opportunity to cooperate on an equal footing with national governments and international organizations. Networks and partnerships thus have access to relevant information from concerned parties and can design policies that are more responsive to their needs. By being more inclusive, networks and partnerships also promised to be seen as more legitimate than many traditional governance arrangements.

This early enthusiasm concerning the opportunities generated by networks and partnerships is mirrored in political practice. Over recent years, the United Nations (UN) as well as many bilateral development organizations have embraced the network approach to governance and have established different kinds of partnerships and partnership programmes.

The activities of the UN are particularly important in this respect. With strong support of Secretary-General Kofi Annan, it analysed the role of multi-stakeholder networks for the work of the UN in the run-up to the 2000 Millennium Summit.[6] The Millennium Declaration stresses the resolve of the Organization and its members to 'give greater opportunities to the private sector, non-governmental organizations and civil society, in general, to contribute to the realization of the Organization's goals and programmes'.[7]

The UN took another crucial step during the 2002 World Summit on Sustainable Development in Johannesburg. This giant conference aimed at devising effective ways to implement environmental policy goals. Many observers criticized the official consultations for their lack of progress and failure to break the political stalemate.[8] Next to the traditional political declarations and multilateral commitments, however, the UN recognized so-called type II outcomes as official Summit results. These are specific, voluntary commitments by various actors to contribute to and to reinforce the implementation of the outcomes of the intergovernmental negotiations through partnerships. During the Summit itself, around 220 such partnerships were announced. Subsequently, the Division for Sustainable Development of the UN's Department of Economic and Social Affairs established a database for collecting and sharing information on these initiatives. As of early 2008, the database listed 334 entries.[9]

Outside of the UN Commission on Sustainable Development, the UN Global Compact also embraced the network and partnership agenda. The Global Compact was established under the auspices of Secretary-General Annan and primarily addresses the private sector. It is a global corporate citizenship initiative for businesses committed to aligning their operations and strategies with ten universally accepted principles in the areas of human rights, labour, the environment and anti-corruption. To mainstream these ten principles in business activities throughout the world and to catalyse actions in support of broader UN goals, the Global Compact among others encourages cooperation in partnerships. Each UN Agency, Fund or Programme now has a designated Private Sector Focal Point to facilitate the cooperation with businesses and other private actors. Moreover, the UN has formulated basic guidelines for the selection of partner organizations and the design of partnerships and it has created a number of mechanisms for sharing lessons learned and training UN staff in matters related to partnerships.

The partnerships promoted and registered by the UN can not only involve UN institutions and other multilateral organizations or governments, but can also operate independently from governmental institutions. They are active in very different areas of work and fulfil different functions. Thus, networks and partnerships have been active in most areas relating to sustainable development. They are particularly prominent in promoting global health – with major initiatives like the Global Fund to Fight AIDS, Malaria and Tuberculosis or the Global Alliance for Vaccines and Immunization – and securing environmental protection, through partnerships such as the Forest Stewardship Council or the Marine Stewardship Council.

In terms of their functions, networks and partnerships contribute variously to the different stages of the policy cycle. Roll Back Malaria, for instance, strongly emphasizes advocacy and awareness-raising and works to concentrate donors' attention on fighting malaria. Other networks and partnerships are active in formulating policies and setting rules and regulations. The Global Reporting Initiative, for example, issues voluntary rules guiding the sustainability reporting practices of businesses and other organizations. The World Commission on Dams is well known for developing a set of rules for deciding on the construction of large dams. And the Extractive Industries Transparency Initiative has recently proposed transparency rules for governments and companies to reduce corruption in the extractive industries. A third group of networks and partnerships focus on policy implementation and serve as financing as well as coordination mechanisms. The large health partnerships mentioned above, for example, are investing billions of dollars in the fight against prominent diseases. A final set of networks and partnerships are concerned with monitoring policy implementation and verifying rule compliance. The Common Code for the Coffee Community, for example, has created a system for verifying the compliance of coffee producers with its code, and the Marine as well as the Forest Stewardship Councils are issuing product labels for companies complying with their production standards.

In addition to these stand-alone partnerships, many donor organizations have established specific programmes for engaging the business community in the pursuit of development goals. Thus, a recent study found that at least six out of 22 donors represented on the Development Assistance Committee of the OECD have established partnership programmes with the private sector, with another four just launching or developing similar schemes. Within the United Nations system and among the Bretton Woods institutions, analysts have counted almost another 20 such programmes.[10] Institutionalized partnership programmes vary significantly concerning their maturity, size and position within the donor institution. Moreover, they have adopted different approaches to involving the private sector. These can range from helping corporations explore new business opportunities and supporting investment activities with a promising development impact, to encouraging increased social engagement of companies.

One of the earliest such programmes is the Public–Private Partnership (PPP) programme of the German Development Ministry BMZ. Established in 1999, the programme only sponsors development-related projects that go beyond a company's core business activities. The PPP Facility focuses on small projects and invests a maximum of 200,000 Euros, amounting to no more than 50 per cent of the project costs. Between 1999 and 2006, the ministry channelled around 150,000,000 Euros through partnership programmes.

The Danish International Development Agency Danida runs a private sector development programme with two components. Its B2B programme aims at fostering partnerships between Danish companies and their counterparts in developing countries. With the goal of promoting the transfer of know-how and technology, Danida provides support for all steps leading up to commercial investment. The agency covers up to

90 per cent of project related costs, with a maximum contribution of 670,000 Euros. Alternatively, Danish companies, as well as other institutions including NGOs and public sector agencies, can apply to Danida's PPP programme. This provides similar amounts of funding for development-related activities outside an organization's core work area.

The UK's Department for International Development (DFID) has chosen another instrument in its cooperation with the private sector. It establishes so-called challenge funds that are typically administered by an external contractor. Each challenge fund runs for a limited period of time and focuses on a particular aspect of the private sector. Between 2002 and 2006, for instance, DFID allocated 16.6 million pounds through its Business Linkages Challenge Fund. With grants between 50,000 and 1 million pounds, the Fund promoted the establishment of partnerships between companies in industrialized and developing countries and supported the establishment of commercially viable business ventures.

The World Bank Development Grant Facility is a final example illustrating yet another approach to working in networks and partnerships. The Facility was established in 1997 and consolidates the Bank's various grant-making mechanisms under a common umbrella. Not only are grants directed at partnerships, but successful applications must also conform to the Bank's overall strategy and priorities. These include encouraging innovation, catalysing partnerships and broadening the scope of the Bank's services. As a result, a large proportion of approved proposals feature the participation of businesses and/or NGOs.

This sample of partnership initiatives and programmes goes to show that the focus on networked governance and partnerships is not just an intellectual fad. To the contrary, a large number of partnership initiatives have sprung up over recent years and donors have channelled an increasing amount of money through them. Although their total number and financial strength remain unknown, the diversity of approaches and high visibility of individual initiatives guarantee that networks and partnership will remain on the political agenda for some time to come.

operational challenges for networks and partnerships

New social partnerships are not a panacea. Nor are they easy. Even when they have the potential

> to solve a particular societal problem or set of problems, they often fail. Establishing and sustaining a mutually beneficial partnership is rarely simple, especially with non-traditional allies.[11]

During the early stages of the debate on networks and partnerships, the potential benefits of this approach to governance were highlighted. As a result, many policy-makers developed very high expectations for their new partnership programmes or initiatives. With growing experience, however, it became clear that networks and partnerships are not the panacea for the problems of global governance some had hoped for. Instead, a more realistic and differentiated picture of networks and partnerships is slowly emerging. Now, many do not see them as a magic bullet, but as a useful complement to the activities of other actors in certain situations and under specific circumstances.

Networks and partnerships as instruments of governance encounter problems on several levels. This section discusses the operational challenges inherent in partnership management. But concerns have arisen not only about the efficiency and effectiveness of networks and partnerships but also about their legitimacy and accountability. These normative concerns are subject of the next section.

The first major point of contention, then, is how effective and efficient networks and partnerships are in solving policy problems. While networks and partnerships have the potential to combine complementary resources, coordinate activities, generate more flexibility, harness different organizational cultures and create policy ownership among various actors, they can also create significant costs. Problematic features identified in the literature include[12]

- *High set-up costs*. In most cases, actors need to create the networks or partnerships they wish to use for exercising governance. Frequently, this is a time-consuming and costly effort. Instead of directly taking action to address a problem, governments, NGOs or businesses must first define the scope of the challenge, identify potential partners for tackling it, convince them to participate and agree on common goals, structures and processes. Creating a network or partnership is thus a significant investment for an organization and it can take many months to several years before they show any results.
- *High transaction costs*. Networks and partnerships do not automatically run on their own once they have been established. Rather, their

lead organizations must continuously nurture them and all partners must remain actively engaged. In practical terms, this means that somebody must feel responsible for managing and coordinating the network or partnership. In addition, participating organizations need to have the necessary staff time and resources for communication and travel. Where either of these elements is lacking, networks and partnerships are at a strong risk of turning into empty organizational shells or dead policy platforms.

- *Difficult decision-making procedures*. Networks and partnerships can adopt very different internal structures and processes. Yet, one of their defining features is that partners cooperate on an equal footing and eschew hierarchies. Important decisions do therefore usually require the consent of all core partner organizations. This can be a time-consuming process and hamper the network's or partnership's flexibility and ability to react rapidly to external events.
- *Divergence between goals and motivations*. A further managerial challenge stems from the fact that different partner organizations often have different motives for joining a network or partnership and pursue different goals through it. Governments and international organizations, for instance, can engage in partnerships to leverage additional resources, to explore more effective ways of addressing a problem or to feign activism and shirk their responsibilities. Business partners, by contrast, often see partnerships as a way to improve their reputation, as a mechanism to improve the enabling environment for investments or as a means to create new business opportunities. NGOs, in turn, may opt for partnerships to increase their access to resources or to gain a more active role in policy decisions. Upon joining a network or partnership, all participants sign up to the same mission statement. But when it comes to identifying activities and setting priorities, the divergences in interests and motivations can surface and make it difficult to reach an agreement.
- *Differences between organizational cultures and styles*. The practical difficulties of working with partners from several sectors are often aggravated by differences in style and organizational culture. At the risk of oversimplifying it can be said that governments and international organizations often focus on rules and bureaucratic procedures, whereas corporations are mainly interested in results and NGOs frequently place greater emphasis on inclusion and the representation of affected groups. Cooperation in networks and partnerships can encourage these organizations to learn from each other's strengths.

More often, however, the different attitudes and approaches clash and lead to frustration. To deal with these tensions, it is crucial to manage the expectations of participating organizations from the outset. Moreover, network and partnership managers need special skills to be able to mediate and foster mutual understanding. It can be very helpful, for instance, if these individuals have worked in different organizational contexts.

- *Limited contribution of resources.* Finally, many networks and partnerships have raised fewer new resources for global policy initiatives than initially hoped for. International organizations like the UN, as well as many government agencies, often entered partnerships with corporations expecting significant cash donations. In most cases, however, corporate engagement has focused on in-kind contributions or on financial support for limited, highly visible activities. Notable exceptions are global health partnerships like the Global Fund to Fight AIDS, Tuberculosis and Malaria, which receive the lion's share of their funds from private actors like the Bill and Melinda Gates Foundation.

In practical terms, then, networks and partnerships promise important benefits, but are also beset by a range of potential problems. The fundamental question therefore is whether or not networks and partnerships are on balance more efficient and effective in addressing global public policy problems than other governance instruments.

A small, but steadily increasing range of empirical studies addresses this question. Most studies, though, are based on small samples of case studies, making it difficult to extrapolate findings. They often rely on different concepts or definitions of 'networks' and 'partnerships', making their results hard to compare or aggregate. To date, researchers have therefore not come up with a conclusive answer. At the same time, it has become clear that the answer once it emerges will not be a categorical 'yes' or 'no'. Rather, networks and partnerships appear to be relatively effective in some, but not in other circumstances.

Hardly any systematic research exists analysing what determines network and partnership effectiveness. It is most likely, however, that several factors play a role.[13] First, the context in which networks and partnerships operate is important. What type of country do they work in? How do network or partnership participants relate to other relevant actors in the field? What degree of conflict is prevalent in the relevant issue area? Second, network or partnership composition and design play a role. Do networks or partnerships involve the most relevant actors? How large is the membership? What internal structures and processes have been adopted? Do networks or partnerships have strong leadership? Third, it is significant what sectors networks or partnerships address and which functions they exercise. Do networks and partnerships deal with a single issue like water, food or health (and if so, which?), or do they seek to address multifaceted problems? What is their core function – advocating policies and raising awareness, creating information and knowledge, setting rules and standards, implementing policies or verifying and evaluating policy implementation?

Even this quick overview suggests that the question of network and partnership effectiveness is a very complex one indeed. It will take researchers much additional time and effort to arrive at general conclusions. In the meantime, it is critical that policy-makers keep the potential downsides of a network or partnership approach to governance in mind and evaluate on a case-by-case basis whether partnerships are likely to create added value in an efficient way.

normative challenges for networks and partnerships

> As the UK and other states move from 'government' to 'governance' and place increasing emphasis on partnerships, the question of legitimacy and accountability is being blurred across the board. Other research that we have been engaged in suggests that in many of the new partnerships that are being introduced, accountability is unclear.[14]

As argued in the introduction, one of the promises held by networks and partnerships is that they help bridge the participatory gap in global governance. By involving ever more powerful private actors, so the argument goes, networks and partnerships can make global governance more inclusive and thereby more legitimate. Yet it is on this front that critics have raised the most significant principled objections against the network approach to governance.

Analysts have raised several different normative concerns with respect to networks and partnerships. First, critics have questioned whether the inclusion of private actors really renders global governance more representative and legitimate. They deny that multinational corporations or other business organizations are legitimate actors in global politics. In addition, they argue that NGOs, especially the large international kind, are also not truly representative.

Second, researchers have warned that networks and partnerships can undermine existing accountability arrangements and thus render global governance on the whole less accountable and less legitimate. Governments and international organizations, for example, can use networks or partnerships to feign activism while in reality shirking their responsibilities to address public policy problems. Moreover, by shifting policy decisions to partnerships, governments can circumvent control by their domestic constituencies and international institutions can weaken control by member states. Corporations for their part are accused of using partnerships to 'greenwash' or 'bluewash' their images. This means that they engage in partnerships to improve their reputation without significantly changing their management and operational practices. Networks and partnerships can thus help companies evade public pressure for moving towards more sustainable practices and can counteract the drive for binding regulations. Networks and partnerships can further reduce the accountability and legitimacy of the current system of global governance through their effect on NGOs. As NGOs participate in cooperative ventures, they risk being co-opted and losing their critical edge. Thus, networks and partnerships can reduce the capacity of civil society organizations to hold other global actors to account for their activities.

Finally, critics have found that many networks and partnerships do not have satisfactory accountability mechanisms for their own activities. Thus, networks and partnerships have variously been accused of being insufficiently transparent, failing to include all relevant parties, lacking in independence and not being able to demonstrate their impact.

These principled arguments amount to a very serious critique that has the potential to discredit the network or partnership approach to governance. To counter these objections, it is critical that networks and partnerships adopt appropriate accountability mechanisms in their structures, decision-making processes and activities. These mechanisms can help prevent the abuse of networks and partnerships by participating organizations and help ensure that their work is seen as relevant and legitimate.

What, though, does it mean for networks and partnerships to have 'appropriate' accountability arrangements? This is a very complex question and answers are only slowly forthcoming.[15] 'Accountability' is a political catchword and frequent use has obscured the meaning of the concept. It is only in the context of individual sectors that the term has been well defined and its practical consequences have been spelled out. Thus, an established tradition of thought and practice exists relating to corporate accountability as well as to political or democratic accountability. There is also an emerging and increasingly sophisticated discourse on the accountability of civil society organizations. These traditions, however, differ in the practical arrangements they deem appropriate. Thus, for example, the public sector usually focuses on rules and processes to create accountability, the corporate sector is more strongly driven by results and for NGOs independence is often seen as critical.

It is impossible to simply apply any one of these traditions and arrangements to networks and partnerships. First, networks and partnerships can have participants from all three sectors – government, business and civil society. Each member organization has to satisfy its own specific accountability requirements and justify its participation in a network or partnership in these terms. Second, networks and partnerships exercise different functions and are engaged in different kinds of activities. As mentioned above, networks and partnerships can operate among others as advocacy coalitions, as coordinating mechanisms, as rule or standard setting organizations, as financing and implementing tools or as knowledge generating institutions. Moreover, they can exercise these functions in a broad variety of policy arenas, ranging from global health and the protection of the environment to the regulation of technical issues.

An alternative approach is to devise pluralistic systems of accountability.[16] Proponents of this approach claim that it is unrealistic to expect fully fledged democratic accountability of global governance institutions. Rather, these organizations can draw on a variety of different accountability mechanisms. Networks and partnerships can, for example, be held accountable through the pressure of public reputation; market interactions; finances and fiscal rules; relevant laws and regulations; the unwritten codes of professional practice; or remaining elements of hierarchical control.

Yet, not all elements of accountability are equally necessary in all situations. Accountability arrangements have their downsides and can involve significant trade-offs. For example, transparency can be expensive to create and can divert resources away from other activities. Strongly inclusive and participatory governance arrangements can lead to slow decision-making processes. Adherence to strict and detailed rules and regulations can hamper flexibility and the capacity to innovate. A strong focus on process-oriented accountability can thus contradict attempts to create accountability for outcomes. Accountability, then, is not simply a question of 'the more, the better'. Rather, organizations have to choose carefully which accountability arrangements are appropriate for them.

For networks and partnerships, what is appropriate in any given situation strongly depends on their function. Networks and partnerships engaged in setting rules and regulations, for example, exercise a function that is usually reserved to national governments. The overwhelming normative consensus holds that governments ought to be democratic. The same reasoning suggests that rule-setting and regulation partnerships should emphasize democratic forms of accountability, including an inclusive or representative governance structure with clearly structured possibilities for participation and far-reaching transparency.

Policy-implementation networks or partnerships distinguish themselves from other forms of partnerships in that they are entrusted with significant resources. Those who provide these resources generally do so expecting that networks or partnerships will use them efficiently and effectively to address the policy problem in question. Implementation networks or partnerships should therefore espouse governance arrangements highlighting accountability for outcomes. To satisfy this requirement, networks and partnerships can conduct performance evaluations and introduce market elements in their work through outsourcing or the collection of beneficiary feedback.

Finally, there are networks and partnerships that are functionally similar to civil society organizations. These can, for instance, be mainly engaged in advocacy and awareness-raising. In that case, networks or partnerships do not assume any particular kind of authority. As a consequence, they only need to adhere to basic accountability arrangements that should be common to all forms of organizations, including basic financial accountability, compliance with legal and fiscal rules and accountability for working towards their mission. Another group of networks and partnerships in this category is concerned with generating information – either by creating knowledge or by evaluating the compliance of others with set norms or standards. For them, it is critical to be accountable for being independent and for adhering to high professional standards of work.

conclusion

Over the past decade, networks and partnerships have become a common feature in global governance arrangements. In the meantime, the initial enthusiasm of many policy-makers and analysts has waned and given way to a more realistic assessment of this governance instrument. Networks and partnerships are no panacea for the world's most pressing problems. Nor will they replace other governance institutions such as classical intergovernmental diplomacy and international organizations. But the fact remains that many important problems need a joint effort from governments, international organizations, international and local businesses and civil society to be tackled effectively.

Cooperative forms of governance are therefore sure to have a future. We are also in a position today to develop more targeted and better governed networks and partnerships. We can now draw on a wealth of practical experiences in setting up and managing networks and partnerships. Moreover, our theoretical and analytical understanding of these governance instruments, including the normative challenges they face, has been greatly improved. Carefully chosen and well designed, networks and partnerships can be an effective new tool for policy-makers. If used under the right circumstances, networks and partnerships are therefore in a very good position to extend the niche in international politics they have started to occupy.

notes

1. R.A.W. Rhodes, *Understanding Governance: Policy Networks, Governance, Reflexivity and Accountability* (Maidenhead: Open University Press, 1997).
2. For a detailed discussion of the operational and participatory gaps in global governance as a result of globalization, see W.H. Reinicke and F. Deng, *Critical Choices: The United Nations, Networks, and the Future of Global Governance* (Ottawa: International Development Research Centre, 2000).
3. The now widely accepted distinction between output and input legitimacy goes back to Fritz Scharpf. See F.W. Scharpf, *Demokratietheorie zwischen Utopie und Anpassung* (Konstanz: Universitätsverlag, 1970); F. W. Scharpf, *Regieren in Europa: Effektiv und Demokratisch?* (Frankfurt a.M.: Campus, 1999).
4. Similar definitions have been proposed, for example, in Reinicke and Deng, *Critical Choices*; T.A. Börzel and T. Risse, 'Public-Private Partnerships: Effective and Legitimate Tools of International Governance?' in E. Grande and L.W. Pauly (eds), *Complex Sovereignty: Reconstituting Political Authority in the Twenty-First Century*, (Toronto: University of Toronto Press, 2005), pp. 195–216; J. Steets, 'Developing a Framework: Concepts and Research Priorities for Partnership Accountability,' Global Public Policy Institute, Berlin.
5. Different benefits of the network or partnership approach to governance are highlighted, for example, by J. Nelson and S. Zadek, *Partnership Alchemy: New Social Partnerships in Europe* (Copenhagen: The Copenhagen Centre, 2000); J. Nelson, *Building Partnerships: Cooperation between the United Nations System and the Private Sector* (New York: United Nations, 2002); R. Tennyson,

The Partnering Toolbook (Geneva: International Business Leaders Forum, Global Alliance for Improved Nutrition, 2003); P. Vaillancourt Rosenau (ed.), *Public-Private Policy Partnerships*. Cambridge: MIT Press, 2000).

6. Reinicke and Deng, *Critical Choices*, forms the centrepiece of this analysis.
7. United Nations Millennium Declaration, 2000, available at http://www.un.org/millennium/declaration/ares552e.htm
8. For a detailed account of the emergence of partnerships as 'type II' outcomes of the Johannesburg Summit, see J.M. Witte, C. Streck and T. Benner (eds), *Progress or Peril? Partnerships and Networks in Global Environmental Governance. The Post-Johannesburg Agenda* (Washington: Global Public Policy Institute, 2003).
9. The database can be accessed at http://webapps01.un.org/dsd/partnerships/public/welcome.do
10. A. Binder, M. Palenberg and J. M. Witte, 'Engaging Business in Development: Results of an International Benchmarking Study,' Berlin: Global Public Policy Institute, 2007). The following conceptual distinctions and descriptions of individual partnership programmes draw heavily on that paper.
11. Nelson and Zadek, *Partnership Alchemy*, p. 18.
12. Ibid.; J. Nelson, *Building Partnerships*; Tennyson, *Partnering Toolbook*; Vaillancourt Rosenau, *Public-Private Policy Partnerships*.
13. F. Biermann, P. Pattberg, S. Chan and Ayşem Mert, 'Partnerships for Sustainable Development: An Appraisal Framework' (2007), produced by the Global Governance Project, Amsterdam, which has developed a range of hypotheses on factors influencing partnership effectiveness.
14. *M. Taylor* and D. *Warburton*, 'Legitimacy and the Role of UK Third Sector Organizations in the Policy Process,' *Voluntas*, Vol. 14, No. 3, *2003*, p. 336.
15. I have developed concrete accountability standards for different types of public policy partnerships elsewhere: J. Steets, *Partnership Accountability: Defining Accountability Standards for Public Policy Partnerships* (forthcoming).
16. The term has been coined by R. O. Keohane and J. S. Nye, Jr., 'Democracy, Accountability and Global Governance,' Politics Research group Working Paper, John F. Kennedy School of Government, Harvard University, 2001. The concept has been applied to networks and partnerships in Y. Benner, W.H. Reinicke and J.M. Witte, 'Multisector Networks in Global Governance: Towards a Pluralistic System of Accountability,' *Government and Opposition*, Vol. 39, 2004, pp. 191–210.

7
global governance as sector-specific management

jim whitman

introduction

As globalization has developed from being an emergent phenomenon to a pervasive condition, the global qualities of human relatedness have become inescapable and of routine importance. Increasingly, in matters as varied as human health, environmental quality and economic stability, national and even local concerns must take into active consideration world-encircling lines of causation. So when we attach the qualifier 'global' to an issue such as human health, it is on an understanding that global health is not merely a statistical abstraction, but a specific form of complex interrelatedness with a range of serious implications, not least in the form of epidemics and pandemics. To the extent that various actors – public and private, national and international, alone and in combination – seek to monitor and improve human health and to cure or prevent diseases worldwide, we can say that their combined activities amount to the global governance of health[1] (sometimes expressed as global health governance). This and related forms of global governance dedicated to specific arenas of activity or relations can best be termed sectoral. The other principal use of the term 'global governance' is summative – that is, global governance regarded as the totality of all governances, including but not limited to states and the international system.

Sectoral and summative global governance are meaningful abstractions rather than independent forms or levels of the regulation of human affairs. After all, the global governance of any form of human activity, or arena in which it takes place, depends upon a vast array of other orders, some quite distant from the sector under consideration. For this reason, the governances of what might fairly be said to comprise the infrastructure of globalization – air and sea transport, communications and finance – are only possible because of a summative global governance that enables myriad activities of such scale and complexity with a high degree of reliability. At the same time, the intensively globalized world we have created for ourselves is founded on but also requires global governance that cannot be merely local, spontaneous and additive – hence the analysis devoted to states and international organizations in devising, negotiating and maintaining the most prominent (and arguably the most important) forms of sectoral global governance. One might say that summative global governance and sectoral global governance are mutually constitutive, an understanding of which is captured in James Rosenau's characterization of 'governance without government' in which he sought to clear an analytical space for governance as a summative phenomenon related to, but not encompassed by, the governance activities of states:

> '[G]overnance without government' does not require the exclusion of national and sub-national governments from the analysis, [but] does necessitate inquiry that presumes the absence of some overarching governmental authority at the international level. Put differently, the concept of 'governance without government' is especially conducive to the study of world politics inasmuch as centralized authority is conspicuously absent from this domain of human affairs even though it is equally obvious that a modicum of order, of routinized arrangements, is normally present in the conduct of global life.[2]

Of course, quite extensive 'routinized arrangements' create planetary-level environmental crises, which require the most concerted forms of sectoral global governance negotiations (on climate change most notably); and so too do less crisis-driven concerns, such as world trade. From these two broad meanings of global governance – summative and sectoral – spring the many theoretical understandings and characterizations which comprise the largest part of the now extensive literature on the subject, including considerations of authority, legitimacy, agency and coordination.

There is a certain reassurance in the term 'global governance' and in the fact of regulatory oversight of activities that are generally taken to fall within any of its sector-specific forms. For example, the number and variety of organizations and mechanisms by which global finance is regulated are not only extensive but also command impressive resources – legal, political and capital. The governance of global finance also has a well-developed literature.[3] Of course, provisions for the regulation of global finance and its many sub-systems are considerably more than a matter of minor adjustments to a stable and equitable status quo. As with every other area over which we can say that global governance is exercised, political contention, the pursuit of national and/or private interests and systemic uncertainties are a large part of its *raison d'être* – as the regular reports of the World Bank, IMF and WTO as well as academic critiques of those organizations make plain.[4] And as with so many other forms of sectoral global governance, globalizing dynamics not only facilitate it but they also necessitate and/or exacerbate the conditions or issues it must contend with.

No form of sectoral global governance is proof against systemic shocks – that is, actions, events or configurations of circumstance which undermine the capacity of a governance regime to function adequately, or which challenge its fundamental assumptions. Indeed, crises can stand as important tests of the reach, inclusivesness and responsiveness of regulatory systems in highly dynamic, globalized circumstances. Certainly systemic disruption in global finance is nothing new – notable recent examples include the stock market collapse of 1987; the1994 Mexican Peso crisis; the Asian financial crisis of 1997; and the bail out of the hedge fund Long-Term Capital Management in 1998.[5] In order for the governance of global finance to have meaning, there must be a degree of preparedness and a demonstrable ability to cope with unforeseen events, unconsidered but pertinent dynamics or large-scale turbulence – and in each of the foregoing cases, order and stability were resumed after various kinds of intervention. But from a sectoral global governance perspective, what are we to make of global financial turmoil as it began in 2007 and unfolded throughout 2008? Certainly, the crisis is of a span and severity that frustrates both measurement and prediction. In April 2008, the International Monetary Fund (IMF) predicted losses on US loans and securitized assets at 945 billion US dollars; in September, this was revised upward to 1.3 trillion dollars; and a month later, to 1.4 trillion.[6] By the end of the year, the World Bank's *Global Economic Prospects 2009* summarized:

> The United States government introduced a $700 billion rescue package and has taken equity positions in nine major banks and several

> large regional banks.... At the same time, European governments have announced plans for equity purchases of bank assets worth some $460 billion, along with almost $2 trillion in guarantees of bank debt.... Virtually no country, developing or high-income, has escaped the impact of the widening crisis.[7]

Similarly, the IMF's year-end *World Economic Outlook* described the turmoil as 'the largest financial shock since the Great Depression':

> The subprime crisis that unfolded in 2007 has now morphed into a credit crisis that has caused major disruption to financial institutions in the United States and Europe. Intensifying solvency concerns about a number of the largest U.S.-based and European financial institutions have pushed the global financial system to the brink of systemic meltdown.[8]

Even without a reliable indicator of how much worse the situation might become, the looming possibility of a 'systemic meltdown' obliges us to ask hard questions about global governance and about this most extensive and politically supported form of sectoral global governance in particular. Certainly, there was no hiatus in governance initiatives or suspension of the activities of national and international institutions for this purpose. Indeed, as developments threaten to spiral out of control, we are more rather than less dependent on the institutions and mechanisms that were in place in the years before the current crisis. But it is also abundantly clear that the governance of global finance has been reduced to crisis management.

Yet perhaps the most compelling feature of the crisis is its extent. This is most succinctly expressed in the depiction of its impacts on the world beyond the esoteric particulars of derivatives, futures and credit default swaps – what quickly came to be referred to as the 'real economy'. On proposing an initiative by EU governments to combat the economic effects of global financial turbulence via a stimulus package of 200 billion euros, European Commission President Jose Manuel Barroso asserted that 'Exceptional times call for exceptional measures. The jobs and well-being of our citizens are at stake. Europe needs to extend to the real economy its unprecedented coordination over financial markets.'[9] Wherever one might have chosen to draw the sector boundaries of global finance, the meaning of 'systemic meltdown' soon came to be understood as a system of systems – that is, one not confined to the familiar substance of global finance such as international banking and currency exchange, but one that included a severe downturn in the housing and commercial real estate markets in several countries; rapidly escalating unemployment which carries with it a range of secondary impacts; rising public sector borrowing requirements, exacerbated emergency provisions and declining tax revenues; and large losses on investment portfolios affecting pension funds and a wide range of public and private institutions. The shock waves also quickly reached the developing world as Robert Zoellick, President of the World Bank Group made plain: 'In July [2008] at the G8 summit, I said that developing countries were facing a double jeopardy from the impact of high food and fuel prices. But what was then a double jeopardy is now a triple hit – food, fuel, and finance – threatening not just to knock the poorest people down, but to hold them down.'[10]

In these circumstances, it becomes difficult to maintain a clear separation between the sector-specific governance of global finance and the wider, summative global governance of which it is not only a key element, but with which it is also highly interactive. Once the unravelling of global finance had widened and gained pace, even historically unprecedented remedial action appeared to fall far short of the intended effect. US Treasury Secretary Henry M. Paulson's 700 billion dollar bailout of Wall Street was 'focused on buttressing U.S. financial institutions. But it was global markets that plunged [immediately afterwards] as investors sold off commodities in Brazil, currency in Mexico, bank stocks in Russia and the short-term debt of the state of California'.[11] One could argue that what was required was more effective, or perhaps more truly *global* governance initiatives, as expressed by the reaction of a currency trader in response to the Paulson bail out: 'Quite frankly, what the market is looking for is some kind of coordinated action from central banks around the world. [The Paulson plan is like a] Band-Aid for a problem that stretches way beyond the banking system now'[12] – and way beyond the wealthiest nations and peoples, too, as Robert Zoellick acknowledged:

> The events of September [2008] could be a tipping point for many developing countries. A drop in exports, as well as capital inflow, will trigger a fall off in investments. Deceleration of growth and deteriorating financing conditions, combined with monetary tightening, will trigger business failures and possibly banking emergencies. Some countries will slip toward balance of payments crises. As is always the case, the most poor are the most defenseless.[13]

It would appear that that metaphor beloved of advocates of economic globalization – that a 'rising tide lifts all boats', also applies in reverse.

Even allowing for the centrality of global finance to so many other systems, and for the severity of the crisis, the threat of a global financial meltdown was less the outcome of a 'perfect storm' than the dissolution of unsustainable positions and the practices that established them – all made possible either directly by governance initiatives (such as deregulation), by default[14] and/or by developments which outpaced our systems of governance.[15] As we struggle to contain the effects of the crisis and to find a rectificatory course that balances urgency against various social and political pressures, we might best reflect on the kinds of sector-specific global governance on which we rely to a considerable degree to ensure the fundamentals of stability and sustainability under globalized conditions.

sectoral global governance: thematic considerations

In outline terms, it is not difficult to identify a span of activities, relations or conditions which comprise a sphere of sectoral governance, either active or prospective. This is a practical necessity as well as an analytical convenience, since the effects of human activity are so profuse, wide-ranging and complex that they render impossible a single global governance which is both comprehensive and coherent. Globalizing dynamics ensure that the additive and cumulative consequences of human activity are felt ever more widely and quickly, and these prompt focused global governance undertakings not only in anticipatory modes (as in preparations for an avian flu pandemic), but also in ways that are both reactive and urgent, which certainly applies to our efforts to halt climate change.

Although we can register failure and inadequacy in our governance arrangements, 'success' is a more problematic concept because the business of governance is not the solution of problems but the adjustment of human ends and means to changing conditions. The essential aim of all forms of governance is the avoidance of severe and prolonged instability, as described by Geoffrey Vickers:

> I shall describe as unstable any state of affairs in which the nature and rate of change makes regulation impossible and thus defeats the creation of *any* order. I shall also include as unstable that state of

> affairs in which any order generates its own negation so quickly that none of them can effectively be realized. I shall further include as unstable those orders which are realized only at the cost of leaving the physical, the institutional or the cultural environment unfit to support a worthy successor. None of these definitions is precise, but they include all the states which ... would be generally recognized as unstable today.[16]

By the end of 2008, the failure of the governance of global finance had become the epicentre of wider and more generalized instability; climate change was the most serious and urgent of a range of environmental threats to ecosystem integrity; and the effects of an avian flu pandemic would be disastrous. The consequences of failed or failing sectoral global governances on this scale might (and should) concentrate minds, but it neither concentrates nor simplifies the conduct of governance, for the thematic reasons outlined below.

porous boundaries

Our world is messy, dynamic and complex – and in the twenty-first century it is all of these things on a global scale. Any form of sectoral global governance is neater in respect of what it manages *for* than in respect of the number and kinds of variables it must manage. Globalization has configured the world so that local or individual concerns cannot entirely be sheltered from global dynamics; and at the same time, large-scale and/or inclusive global issues can be created or exacerbated by the cumulative and sometimes synergistic outcomes of small-scale activities. What this means for the practical purposes of exercising governance is not only that a failing in sectoral global governance can have extensive, multiple impacts (as we have seen in the case of global finance), but also that a great many actors and dynamics that have a bearing on sector-specific governance originate outside of its purview – yet these need to be regulated and/or coordinated for the purpose of achieving systemic stability. For example, the calculation of emissions limits for atmospheric pollutants must eventually find expression across a span of human enterprises and activities that include mining, electricity generation, agriculture and transport; and it will impact national economic development and output as well as individual opportunities and choices.

The 'seamlessness' of our globalized world ensures that most forms of sectoral governance will need to be highly adaptable (the global governance of health cannot prevent the mutation of pathogens); to undertake monitoring in the absence of effective 'reach' (the World Health Organization's GOARN system[17] is a case in point); to frame goals that do not require oversight of every pertinent variable; and to accept that in some cases, the avoidance of the worst outcomes will not only be a *sine qua non*, but also the lowest common denominator amongst what have come to be known as 'stakeholders'.[18]

Indeed, the effects of sectoral global governances will by no means be limited to willed outcomes, much as, more generally, the attainment of larger goals usually entails unforeseen and/or unacknowledged risks and costs.[19] In addition, distinct sectoral governances also impact on each other in ways that have often proved highly contentious, such as between trade and environmental protection.

no hierarchy of governances

The arena of sectoral global governance is, like the arena of international relations, anarchic. There is no overarching global governance, and the aims of any one sectoral global governance are not conceived for, and do not aspire to, a larger, common global governance goal, or even to necessarily compatible outcomes. This is because there are no sectoral governances detached from sectoral interests – and these are frequently of a much narrower and self-interested cast than the claims of human security or planetary sustainability. The governance goals determined for any sector of activity (such as trade) or condition (such as the physical environment) need to be internally self-consistent, but there is no 'global' requirement that they do not conflict across sectors. However, there is some hope that although our sectoral governances are unlikely to become seamless, they could at least be made more congruent with each other.[20]

Although there are no hierarchies of governance *per se*, there are hierarchies of power. These find expression in the ends as well as the means of governance. In the following critique of governance and development, 'good governance' criteria (means) are linked to larger neo-liberal governance ends, via the Bretton Woods institutions and the interests of powerful states:

> A discussion over governance becomes important as it influences not only mechanisms but also strategies, each of which in turn responds to ideological presumptions about development and the means to attain greater economic democracy. Unfortunately the overly eager

> leadership of the World Bank in framing the good governance debate, as with the UNDP and World Bank partnership to implement the Millennium Development Goals, tends to narrow the possibilities for a critical examination of the World Bank's role in creating poverty and malgovernance through their structural adjustment programs and 'state modernization' schemes. Questioning the global trade and finance regime, and global political malgovernance, is clearly outside the hegemonic discussion parameters – to avoid approaching malgovernance, hunger and extreme poverty as political issues, preferring instead to leave them in the hands of highly-paid 'technical' experts.[21]

One need not adopt the position that sectoral global governances in sum comprise a hegemonic project[22] to discern that the powerful will use the means at their disposal, including the mechanisms of governance, to secure their interests. At the same time, governance arrangements that can truly said to be global will inevitably entail negotiation and compromise rather than imposition, since power is highly differentiated across sectors, and because systemic stability and the maintenance of a broadly favourable status quo is a key interest for the powerful. World trade is a cooperative endeavour, sustained by kinds and degrees of interdependence which require extensive and intricate governance arrangements; and although this governance is shaped by the needs and interests of the powerful, their own needs enmesh them in complex relationships that cannot be supplanted by the exercise of power alone.

there is no escape from politics

It is certainly the case that 'Governance theorists see the role of government in governance as a contextual phenomenon; the pursuit of the collective interest takes different forms in different political and institutional contexts and governments can be either the key, coordinating actor or simply one of several powerful players in the process.'[23] However, large-scale, *global* governance arrangements will almost certainly entail the participation of states, either directly or in the form of international organizations or regimes. The 'governance without government' phenomenon notwithstanding, the scale of the challenges presented by global issues generally require the mobilization of resources and the legitimacy and authority to enact or enforce agreements that only states possess. (Acting on their own, no coalition of NGOs and/or

sometimes with pernicious effect, as we have seen with the 'toxic debts' that originated in the sub-prime US housing market. These had been packaged into collateralized debt obligations (CDOs) which have now engulfed some of the world's largest banks and other financial institutions, with a scale of asset write-downs that were so difficult to estimate (or risky to reveal) that banking confidence was further undermined, thus exacerbating the credit squeeze and impacting economic performance more generally. Presently, the volume of foreign exchange exceeds three trillion dollars a day – and this is but one aspect of financial flows that are beginning to run beyond the kinds of comprehension necessary for ensuring systemic stability. But it is precisely those forms of deliberation that one experienced trader had in mind when he compared what he termed the 'old psyche' with the operation of the money markets in 2006:

> [The 'old psyche' meant that] when somebody said to 'take a few weeks' to execute a trade, you didn't have to be attuned to the market all the time. Now, you have to be on top of it all the time and there's so much more to watch.... Money used to flow via bank loans, which is an insignificant game now. If there has been a real major change it's that hedge funds have taken over the role of global financing, Where banks were methodical and slow, hedge funds are fast. Hedge funds don't get themselves invested with clients by doing weeks of credit work, committee meetings, cross-selling and so on. For them, it's just a question of in or out, then a push of the button.[27]

The additive risk-taking by banks and other financial institutions, as we now know, was of systemic proportions or, through high-speed interconnectedness between systems, it had systemic implications. Whatever the future of financial regulation within and between states, it is open to question whether the kinds of complexity and speed which both underpin and result from globalizing processes can be subjected to the kinds of deliberation that any full understanding of 'governance' implies.[28]

Global dynamics which present us with unanticipated and/or unwanted consequences of the complex interaction of human and natural systems have lately come to be recognized as an integral and probably inescapable feature of globalization. With cheap international air travel comes the facilitated spread of infectious diseases;[29] mundane, carbon-emitting behaviours such as car driving now have planetary implications (reflected in the 'carbon footprint' concept applied to individuals no less than to nations); and global warming has a secondary impact, thawing arctic tundra releases methane, which further debilitates the ozone layer.[30]

In an intensely globalized world, the room for 'disregarded externalities' is quickly disappearing; but by the same token, our ability to conceive and implement adequate systems of governance even on a sectoral level is coming under strain, particularly if one regards 'adequate' as including a comprehensive understanding of causal pathways and the capacity to collect and analyze data in a timely fashion. At the global level, further difficulties include insufficient or inconclusive data; inadequate conceptual grasp of systems and systems behaviour; scientific uncertainty; and the problem of prediction under sensitive-dependent conditions (the so-called butterfly effect) – the capacity of small, initial factors to affect outcomes in non-linear natural and human systems.

Although in general we can assign more or less weight to each of the four thematic particulars above, in practice, they are often configured together, in ways which can present formidable challenges to summative as well as sectoral forms of global governance. Climate change, for example, traverses all four: there can be few significant forms of sectoral governance that will be able to shelter from its direct and indirect effects; there is no prioritization of governances such as would secure the future of the planet more urgent than it has been to date; our attempts to address it are intensely political; and as the consequences of changing climate begin to be felt more immediately and sharply, few will doubt the importance of the complex interaction of human and natural systems. All of these considerations can seem quite distant from a developed world perspective, from which the benefits of globalization and the kinds of governance it both requires and supports appear generally effective and broadly beneficent. But tensions, inequities and unsustainable practices are part of our governance arrangements no less than in other forms of social and political organization, and they become visible on an examination of any form of sectoral global governance, two of which are briefly considered below.

sectoral global governance in practice: human health and food

The global governance of health is well established and extensive and includes the World Health Organization (WHO), national health authorities, regional bodies, specialist establishments (such as the US Centers for Disease Control and the Pasteur Institute), international organizations with remits concerned with or related to health (such as UNDP) and a vibrant epistemic community linking epidemiologists, medical practitioners and vaccine researchers.[31] There are some advantages to the global governance of health as a network rather than as a formal structure, but national, political, cultural and other divides dictated the form, rather than considerations of effectiveness.

The global governance of food is more diffuse, and the network of governance systems is much more closely attuned to powerful sectoral interests. The remits of the UN World Food Program (WFP) and the Food and Agriculture Organization (FAO) are less extensive than their titles suggest; and national political considerations keep them constrained in the scope of their non-emergency operations. Yet there are also numerous sub-sector governances covering aspects of agriculture and agricultural trade, food security, food safety and nutrition, to list but a few. This work is strengthened and sometimes critiqued by private, voluntary and humanitarian organizations in both developmental and emergency modes.

For both the health and food sectors, there are separate but related enterprises which have a practical bearing on them but which largely operate 'across' rather than from within the generally acknowledged boundaries of both. In the case of food, for example, the governance of trade has a powerful, sometimes determining effect on nations' food security, their balance of payments, import and export needs and the availability and nature of employment. Agriculture that is geared to export entails questions of ownership of land, access to water, use of pesticides and fertilizers, and in some cases, the introduction of genetically modified crops – all of which have extensive, secondary effects beyond the immediate compass of food needs and production.[32] In the case of health, nearly all of the world's larger systems of governance have strong and often multiple impacts on individual and community health, beginning with our halting efforts to address climate change.[33] To this, one can add the mortality and morbidity statistics that parallel inequalities of every kind between the developed and developing worlds. War and other forms of political violence and their aftermaths further add to this burden.[34]

In short, although both food and health can be meaningfully abstracted as arenas for dedicated attention and practical governance initiatives, the sources of much of what is amiss in both are located in other arenas, shaped by different (if not altogether conflicting) interests and subject to their own forms of governance. For example, in the following, a WTO technical note describes the provisions of the Trade-Related Aspects of Intellectual Property Rights (the TRIPS Agreement) as a tensioned balance between what are deemed 'short-term interests' – that is, access to cheaply produced pharmaceuticals by people in the developing world – and the need to provide 'incentives' for continuing research and development:

> Finding a balance in the protection of intellectual property between the short-term interests in maximizing access and the long-term interests in promoting creativity and innovation is not always easy. Doing so at the international level is even more difficult than at the national level. Perhaps nowhere do these issues excite stronger feelings than in regard to pharmaceutical patents, where tension between the need to provide incentives for research and development into new drugs and the need to make existing drugs as available as possible can be acute.[35]

On the matter of the availability of food, even in 2008, the United Nations Human Rights Council was unable to achieve a unanimous vote in favour of there being a human right to food – a logical necessity in view of the long-accepted human right to life.[36]

The boundaries of sectoral governances are not all permeable to the same degree; and those which have human security as either an explicit goal or an implicit remit – such as food and health – are most likely to be impinged upon by others. This is due in no small measure to the porosity of all sectoral governances and because of the number of variables that need to be secured in order for all human beings to enjoy adequate nutrition and at least basic standards of health care. Of course, hard interests, both material and political, also feature. Also, global governance of food or of health considered as a dedication to global inclusion would, in addition to unprecedented degrees of political consensus, require regulatory coherence that does not exist in any other area of governance. As a consequence of these factors, both food and health as sectoral global governances are themselves functionally 'sectorized' – that is, the arenas are global but the governances are confined to place-specific and/or subject specific initiatives which are at their most effective when the practical and political interests of powerful constituencies are engaged (as in the prevention of an avian flu pandemic), or when costs to them are sited within manageable bounds. Any inclusive and equitable global governance of food could hardly coexist with the level of agricultural subsidies currently in place in the developed world; instead, we have the sum of many sub-sectoral governances of food, neither entirely consistent nor necessarily global in compass or outlook. More striking is that the indirect effects of pressures from within other sectoral governances can push the governance of food and health further away from regulatory and normative matters towards emergency provision. So as governments slash their aid budgets in the wake of financial turmoil, the WFP revealed that it would be hard pressed to provide food for 49 million people in the world's worst hunger-stricken countries. Yet '... one per cent of the money being used to fund financial bail-outs in Europe and the US could entirely fund the WFP's operations'.[37]

Explicit political considerations not only determine the lager contours of sectoral global governance but they can also drive instrumental uses (or abuses) of governance systems.[38] And political responses also arise in response to quite specific occurrences or grievances, even when they can obstruct the attainment of much larger governance goals:

> Indonesia sent a chill through the World Health Organization recently when it refused to supply any more samples of the avian flu virus that has killed scores of its people. The move, which seemed aimed at gaining access to vaccines at an affordable price, threatens the global effort to track the virus and develop vaccines. But Indonesia has raised a valid point that needs to be addressed: if a pandemic should strike, poor countries would be left without protection. ... The WHO relies on a global network of laboratories to provide virus samples so experts can determine which are most likely to spread. ... Indonesia decided to act after a foreign company announced work on a vaccine that would be based on its samples. Indonesia stopped cooperating with the WHO and started negotiations to send future samples to another vaccine maker in return for technology that would allow Indonesia to make its own vaccine. That may be good for Indonesia but could be harmful to global health – especially if other countries follow. Clearly Indonesia, which is in discussion with WHO officials, needs to rejoin the global network. Unfortunately, the organization has no good answer to the inequities Indonesia has spotlighted.[39]

The global governance of food is rooted in the complex interaction of human and natural systems through agriculture; and as agriculture extends to transnational agribusiness and world trade, food becomes enmeshed in these dynamics on a global scale. The most recent global food crisis of 2008 is particularly wide-ranging in the number of its pertinent contributing elements and quite dramatic in its effects and implications. However, it can also be read as indicative of the difficulties confronting the global governance of any sector of activity. According to FAO, the factors that led to the crisis (which has given rise to food riots and some countries banning the export of rice) included 'weather-related production shortfalls; reduction of stock levels; increasing fuel costs; the surge in demand for biofuels and agricultural commodities; the changing structure of demand; operations of the financial markets; and short-term policy actions and exchange rate swings'.[40] Added to this, food aid declined to a 50-year low even before the worst of the 2008 financial turbulence manifested itself.[41] At the same time, the speed and responsiveness of another set of human systems ensured that there were winners as well as losers: the emergency food summit in Rome in June 2006 failed to reach an agreement to ensure that demand for bio-fuel crops did not worsen the food shortages, but 'corn prices rose on the world markets throughout the last hours of the summit'.[42]

Within the arena of global health, local human susceptibility to pathogens is now greatly amplified by the ease and speed of global travel, which is how HIV/AIDS quickly became a pandemic. Our many failings and inconsistencies in meeting the challenges of this pandemic mean that it has now become a global dynamic itself,[43] undermining the balances of and between human and natural systems, within Africa most strikingly, but also beyond its shores. More broadly, indices of human health are a particularly sensitive measure of the interchange between global dynamics and local contingencies and of what Paul Farmer has termed 'the biological consequences of social inequalities'.[44]

conclusion

None of the foregoing diminishes the importance of sectoral global governance; and it is important to bear in mind what can be accomplished given sufficient interest or incentive. The outbreak of SARS and the international response which so quickly halted it was far from perfect in all its particulars, but remains an impressive example of the marshalling of health governance actors and mechanisms and the swift use of other well-governed scientific, political and social resources. What is perhaps more impressive was the elimination of smallpox in the 1970s, driven by those least susceptible to the disease; and currently, there is no shortage of goodwill and concerted efforts are devoted to eliminating a number of other diseases, several of them most severe in, or particular to, the developing world.[45] But the global governance of health and of food persists alongside more than 800 million malnourished people. Some aspects of both forms of governance struggle against this and other injustices (or are obliged to mitigate their consequences); but other aspects are contributory factors.

There are clearly serious disjunctions in our organizations of political community. We are capable of creating and maintaining intricate and complex forms of sectoral and intersectoral governance sufficient to maintain the routine functioning of bewilderingly fast and complex human systems, yet find ourselves unable to find a modicum of political consensus necessary to ensure planetary sustainability, let alone human security for those currently disenfranchised. There are innumerable inefficiencies and dysfunctions within sectoral governances, but as the fundamentals of the human condition are increasingly shaped by global dynamics of many kinds, these functional matters are less immediately important than the 'global' quality of the oversight we bring to our various forms of governance – and to their coordination. It appears to be the case that the least global aspect of our globalized world is the governance systems in place to regulate and stabilize it. Nor is it difficult to discern sectoral interests (particularly at state level) which have been sharpened by globalizing processes and secured by governance mechanisms at the expense of any truly *global* governance. So while there is no doubting the importance of the performance of sectoral global governances for purposes and constituencies of varying inclusiveness, true global governance remains a daunting task – all the more because we are very unlikely to be able to undertake it at a leisurely pace.

notes

1. Keley Lee (ed.), *Health Impacts of Globalization: Towards Global Governance* (Basingstoke: Palgrave, 2002); Andrew F. Cooper, John J. Kirton and Ted Schrecker (eds), *Governing Global Health: Challenge, Response, Innovation* (Aldershot: Ashgate, 2007).
2. James N. Rosenau, 'Governance, Order and Change in World Politics,' in James N. Rosenau and Ernst-Otto Czempiel (eds), *Governance Without Government: Order and Change in World Politics* (Cambridge: Cambridge University Press, 1992), p. 7.

3. Horst Siebert (ed.), *Global Governance: An Architecture for the World Economy* (New York: Springer, 2003); Kern Alexander, Rahul Dhumale and John Eatwell, *Global Governance of Financial Systems: The International Regulation of Systemic Risk* (Oxford: Oxford University Press, 2005); Rodney Bruce Hall, *Central Banking as Global Governance: Constructing Financial Credibility* (Cambridge: Cambridge University Press, 2008).
4. Robert O'Brien, Anne Marie Goetz, Jan Aart Scholte and Marc Williams, *Contesting Global Governance: Multilateral Economic Institutions and Global Social Movements* (Cambridge: Cambridge University Press, 2000).
5. For a brief chronology of international monetary, securities and banking crises, see John Braithwaite and Peter Drahos, *Global Business Regulation* (Cambridge: Cambridge University Press, 2000), table 8.2, p. 135.
6. 'IMF predicts $1.4 trillion in losses from crisis,' *International Herald Tribune*, 7 October 2008.
7. World Bank, *Global Economic Prospects 2009*, available at http://web.worldbank.org/WBSITE/EXTERNAL/EXTDEC/EXTDECPROSPECTS/GEPEXT/EXTGEP2009/0,,contentMDK:21959964~pagePK:64167702~piPK:64167676~theSitePK:5530498,00.html
8. International Monetary Fund, 'World Economic Outlook: Financial Stress, Downturns, and Recoveries,' October 2008, available at http://www.imf.org/external/pubs/ft/weo/2008/02/index.htm
9. 'EC pushes $256 Billion in spending to battle crunch,' 26 November 2008. Available at http://www.700billiondollarbailoutplan.com/category/eu-economy/
10. The World Bank, News and Broadcast, available at http://web.worldbank.org/WBSITE/EXTERNAL/NEWS/0,,contentMDK:21933764~menuPK:51416187~pagePK:64257043~piPK:437376~theSitePK:4607,00.html
11. David Cho and Binyamin Appelbaum, 'Unfolding Worldwide Turmoil Could Reverse Years of Prosperity,' *Washington Post*, 7 October 2008, page A01.
12. Ibid.
13. Robert B. Zoellick, 'Modernizing Multilateralism and Markets,' Prepared remarks at the Peterson Institute for International Economics, 6 October 2008, available at http://www.petersoninstitute.org/publications/papers/paper.cfm?ResearchID=1012
14. Edmund L. Andrews, 'Greenspan Concedes Error on Regulation,' *New York Times*, 24 October 2008.
15. One analyst commented 'If this is the death of Wall Street as we know it, the tombstone will read: killed by complexity.' Nils Pratley, 'The day the ticking time bombs went off,' *The Guardian*, Tuesday 16 September 2008, in which he quotes the investor Warren Buffett, writing a decade before the crisis: 'The derivatives genie is now well out of the bottle, and these instruments will almost certainly multiply in variety and number until some event makes their toxicity clear. Central banks and governments have so far found no effective way to control, or even monitor, the risks posed by these contracts.'
16. Geoffrey Vickers, *Freedom in a Rocking Boat: Changing Values in an Unstable Society* (London: Allen Lane/Penguin, 1970), p. 127. Italics original.
17. The World Health Organization's Global Outbreak Alert and response network, available at http://www.who.int/csr/outbreaknetwork/en/

18. Mikael Wigell, 'Multi-Stakeholder Cooperation in Global Governance,' The Finnish Institute of International Affairs, June 2008.
19. See Bent Flyvbjerg, Nils Bruzelius and Werner Rothengatter, *Megaprojects and Risk: An Anatomy of Ambition* (Cambridge: Cambridge University Press, 2003).
20. Margaret Lay, 'Can Trade Policy Support the Next Global Climate Agreement? Analyzing the International Trade and Environment Regimes,' Carnegie Papers, Number 96, September 2008; Aseem Prakash and Matthew Potoski, 'Racing to the Bottom? Trade, Environmental Governance, and ISO 14001,' *American Journal of Political Science*, Vol. 50, No. 2, April 2006, pp. 350–364.
21. Alejandro Bendaña, '"Good Governance" and the MDGs: Contradictory or Complementary?' paper presented at the IGNIS-Conference 'Whose Governance? Obstacles to the MDGs' at Mastemyr (Oslo) 20–21 September 2004, available at http://www.rorg.no/Artikler/740.html
22. Jörg Friedrichs, 'Global Governance as the Hegemonic Project of Transatlantic Civil Society,' in Markus Lederer and Philipp S. Müller (eds), *Criticizing Global Governance* (Basingstoke: Palgrave, 2005), pp. 45–68; Mark Duffield, *Global Governance and the New Wars: The Merging of Development and Security* (London: Zed Books, 2001).
23. Jon Pierre, 'Conclusions: Governance beyond State Strength,' in Jon Pierre (ed.), *Debating Governance* (Oxford: Oxford University Press, 2000), p. 241.
24. Rodney Bruce Hall and Thomas J. Biersteker (eds), *The Emergence of Private Authority in Global Governance* (Cambridge: Cambridge University Press, 2002; see also Braithwaite and Drahos, *Global Business Regulation*.
25. Peter Baker, 'Russia Backs Kyoto to Get on Path to Join WTO,' *Washington Post*, 22 May 2004, available at http://www.washingtonpost.com/wp-dyn/articles/A46416-2004May21.html
26. Bhagirath Lal Das, 'Strengthening Developing Countries in the WTO,' Third World Network (Trade and Development Series No. 8), available at http://www.twnside.org.sg/title/td8.htm
27. Interview with Yra Harris, Chicago Mercantile Exchange, in Steven Dronby, *Inside the House of Money: Top Hedge Fund Traders on Profiting in the Global Markets* (Hoboken: Joseph Wiley & Sons, 2006), p. 204.
28. See Jim Whitman, *The Limits of Global Governance* (Abingdon: Routledge, 2005).
29. David P. Fidler, *SARS, Governance and the Globalization of Disease* (Basingstoke: Palgrave, 2004).
30. 'Siberia feels the heat: a frozen peat bog the size of France and Germany combined, contains billions of tonnes of greenhouse gas and, for the first time since the ice age, it is melting,' Ian Sample, 'Warming hits "tipping point",' *The Guardian*, 11 August 2005.
31. For a list of global health authorities and organizations, see http://www.pda.org/MainMenuCategory/QualityRegulatoryAffairs/LinkstoGlobalHealthAuthoritiesandOrganizations.aspx
32. For an introduction to the range of social, political, health and environmental factors involved in the global governance of food, see Peter Oosterveer, *Global Governance of Food Production and Consumption: Issues and Challenges* (Cheltenham: Edward Elgar Publishing Ltd, 2007); and Raj Patel, *Stuffed and*

Starved: From the Farm to the Fork, the Hidden Battle for the World Food System (London: Portobello Books, 2007).

33. World Health Organization, Report by the Secretariat, 'Climate Change and Health,' EXECUTIVE BOARD EB122/4, 122nd Session 16 January 2008, available at http://www.who.int/gb/ebwha/pdf_files/EB122/B122_4-en.pdf; UK Department of Health, *Health Effects of Climate Change* (2001/02), available at http://www.dh.gov.uk/en/Publicationsandstatistics/Publications/PublicationsPolicyAnd Guidance/DH_4007935
34. E.G. Krug, L.L. Dahlberg, J.A. Mercy, A.B. Zwi and R. Lozano, (eds), *World Report on Violence and Health* (Geneva: World Health Organization, 2002), available at http://www.who.int/violence_injury_prevention/violence/world_report/en/
35. World Trade Organization, 'Pharmaceutical patents and the TRIPS Agreement,' 21 September 2006, available at http://www.wto.org/english/tratop_e/TRIPS_e/pharma_ato186_e.htm
36. UN General Assembly, GA/SHC/3941 (Sixty-third General Assembly, Third Committee), 'Third Committee draft text endorses recommendations, future workplan of Human Rights Council's working group on right to development,' available at http://www.un.org/News/Press/docs/2008/gashc3941.doc.htm
37. Peter Beaumont, 'UN aid agencies facing hunger funding crisis,' *The Guardian*, 17 December 2008.
38. Peter Wallensteen, 'Scarce Goods as Political Weapons: The Case of Food,' *Journal of Peace Research*, Vol. 13, No. 4 (1976), pp. 277–298; Robert L. Paarlberg, 'Food as an Instrument of Foreign Policy,' *Proceedings of the Academy of Political Science*, Vol. 34, No. 3 (1982), pp. 25–39.
39. International Herald Tribune (Opinion), 'Indonesia's avian flu holdout,' 16 February 2007.
40. UN Food and Agriculture Organization, 'Soaring Food Prices: Facts, Perspectives, Impacts and Actions Required,' April 2008, p. 4, available at http://www.fao.org/fileadmin/user_upload/foodclimate/HLCdocs/HLC08-inf-1-E.pdf
41. Javier Blas, 'Food aid declines to near 50-year low,' *Financial Times*, 9 June 2008, available at http://www.ft.com/cms/s/0/06e5b31a-3645-11dd-8bb8-0000779fd2ac.html
42. Julian Borger, 'Food summit fails to agree on biofuels,' *The Guardian*, 6 June 2008; see also Geoffrey Lean, 'Multinationals make billions in profit out of growing global food crisis,' *The Independent*, 4 May 2008.
43. Robert L. Ostergard, Jr, *HIV/AIDS and the Threat to National and International Security* (Basingstoke: Palgrave, 2007); Nana K. Poku, Alan Whiteside and Bjorg Sandkjaer (eds), *AIDS and Governance* (Aldershot: Ashgate, 2007).
44. Paul Farmer, *Infections and Inequalities: The Modern Plagues* (Berkeley: University of California Press, 1999). See also Laurie Garrett, *Betrayal of Trust: The Collapse of Global Public Health* (Oxford: Oxford University Press, 2001).
45. See the *New York Times* 2006 series of articles, 'Disease on the Brink,' available at http://www.nytimes.com/ref/health/2006_BRINK_SERIES.html

8
global governance as a summative phenomenon

w. andy knight

> Global order is conceived ... [as] a single set of arrangements even though these are not causally linked into a single coherent array of patterns. The organic whole that comprises the present or future global order is organic only in the sense that its diverse actors are all claimants upon the same earthbound resources and all of them must cope with the same environmental conditions, noxious and polluted as these may be.[1]

introduction

The post-Cold War period, marked by the intensification of globalization and a new world disorder, has triggered an intense and growing interest in governance at all levels. The interest in what can be called 'summative global governance' is held by scholars and practitioners, by state and non-state actors, by public and private institutions and by licit and even illicit groups. This chapter is concerned with global governance as a summative phenomenon and the extent to which globalizing dynamics are forcing us to reconceptualize the governance of the globe.

I argue here that this holistic conceptualization of global governance is in part linked to the recognition that international governance institutions are no longer adequate to address contemporary transnational issues and problems and that 'summative' global governance (the sum total of all governance processes and institutions that seek to address transnational issues affecting our planet) represents, in effect, a definite shift in paradigm – from 'international' to 'global' politics – and an evolution in multilateralism, as top-down and bottom-up multilateral activities and institutions intersect. In the absence of world government, the patchwork concoction that we call 'global governance' may in fact be our best hope for bringing stability, equity, justice and sustainability to our present new world disorder.

The chapter is divided along the following lines. It first examines the characteristics of the new world disorder and the effects this environment of turbulence, flux, fragmentation, disequilibrium and uncertainty is having on established forms of governance. Since this is only one part of the puzzle, the next section highlights the integrative and fragmentary forces that stem from complex interdependence and the intensification of globalization and argues that these forces challenge traditional notions of multilateralism and the Westphalian form of governance at the international level. Those challenges have raised the prospects for the establishment other forms of governance to deal with transnational issues and problems. The next section decribes the evolution of the concept and practice of global governance, distinguishing it from international governance by suggesting that in the case of the former there is a decreased salience of states and increased salience of non-state actors in the processes of norm-building, rule-setting and compliance-monitoring that occur at the global level. It also shows that global governance can operate at many levels – local/sub-national, national, regional, trans-regional and global. What follows is a discussion of the contemporary interest in global governance as a summative phenomenon. That interest stems from various scholarly attempts to align the re-conceptualization of governance with what is actually happening on the ground. Clearly, global governance has not replaced international governance. Rather, both forms of governance currently operate alongside each other, at times complementing one another but at other times clashing with each other. Finally, the conclusion sums up the chapter and explains that the patchwork of what we call 'summative global governance' is actually a response to globalizing dynamics which has resulted in a messy entanglement of state-centric and multi-centric institutions and processes at multiple levels, both formal and informal, top-down and bottom-up, which strive to address the transnational issues arising from the new world disorder.

characteristics of the new world disorder

So far, global politics in the early part of the twenty-first century has been shaken by rampant terrorism, multilateral and unilateral military reprisals, global economic downturns and mounting civil strife. These turbulent times reveal cracks, if not a total breakdown, in the prevailing global order and have led to ever-louder demands for the establishment of new institutions of global governance to replace, or at least complement, existing 'international' institutions. This is not the first time in world history when prevailing systems of governance have been challenged by pronounced structural change. In past centuries, there have been repeated attempts at reforming existing institutions or creating new ones to tame the conflicts and disorders of those periods.[2]

During the immediate post-Cold War period we witnessed the removal of some of the structural and ideological underpinnings of superpower conflict that characterized the last half of the previous century. Apart from relaxing global tensions, this changed structural condition ostensibly reduced the major security threat that the world faced during the Cold War, notably the threat of nuclear war between two heavily armed military camps (Mutual Assured Destruction – MAD). But the end of the precarious balance of power between the two superpowers (the US and the USSR) created a climate of uncertainty with a rise in the number of civil conflicts and the spread of internecine violence in places like Afghanistan, the Democratic Republic of the Congo (DRC), Rwanda, Somalia, Sudan and the Former Yugoslavia. In the aftermath of the collapse of the Soviet Union, there have been approximately 93 conflicts around the world in which 5.5 million people were killed – 75 per cent being civilians.[3] Almost all of these were intra-state conflicts, thus explaining the disproportionate number of civilian casualties.

This immediate post-Cold War period was also characterized by an exponential increase in transnational challenges. Some of these challenges included the horizontal proliferation of weapons of mass destruction (WMD); the spread of hate material, pornography and computer viruses via the Internet; an increase in drug trafficking, trafficking in women and children and illicit trade in small arms and light weapons (SALW); an increase in mass migration and the number of internally displaced persons due to civil conflicts; a rise in the phenomena of sex slavery, forced labour and other organized criminal activity; financial and market collapses; piracy on the high seas (especially in the Malacca straits and off the coasts of Somalia and Nigeria); the circumvention of national regulatory policies and taxes and so on. Clearly, '... the national institutions that are supposed to express people's preferences in these matters are increasingly ineffective in coping with them'.[4] The post-World War II institutions that were designed to address interstate issues were all of a sudden showing signs, at the end of the Cold War era, not only of ineffectiveness but also of irrelevance. This raised the alert amongst scholars and practitioners of the need for a new global governance architecture which would deal effectively with transnational issues.

The debacle in Somalia, the Rwandan genocide, the at times indiscriminate but politically motivated slaughter in the DRC, Sierra Leone, Liberia, Mozambique, Cote D'Ivoire, and the continued violence in other places such as the Middle East, Asia, Chechnya and Latin America all indicated a persistent adherence to a culture of violence as hyper-nationalism and long-suppressed ethnic conflicts reared their ugly heads in the latter part of the twentieth century. Other human tragedies and gross human rights violations occurred in so-called failed states where the degeneration or total absence of national governance structures meant that civilians were particularly vulnerable to futile violence. Millions of innocent people fleeing the violence became refugees and displaced persons – and thousands of children have been, and continue to be, recruited as child soldiers by both government and rebel forces. The destruction of national infrastructures and of governmental and societal institutions worth billions was due at times to internecine violence but also at other times to natural and man-made disasters during this immediate post-Cold War period. Again, national governments found it difficult to address the spillover problems associated with internal conflicts and humanitarian disasters. Similarly, international governmental organizations, like the UN system, and regional intergovernmental bodies, like the African Union, were also struggling to cope with the increasingly transnational nature of these problems.

In general, the above narrative paints of picture of a new world disorder – an environment of turbulence, flux, fragmentation, disequilibrium and uncertainty which cries out for the establishment of novel forms of governance activity and institutions, since existing forms seem ineffectual. But this picture is only one part of the puzzle. There are certain integrative/fragmentary forces at work which are also putting pressure on existing international governance.

complex interdependence and globalization

James Rosenau has alerted us to some of the ways in which the advent of dynamic technologies has resulted in a decline of distances in the modern world (what he calls 'distant proximities'). Technological advances in communications and transportation have resulted in an increase in the level of complex interdependence.[5] Modern communications (in the form of television, radio, newspapers, telephones, fax machines, computers, the Internet, electronic mail and so on), appear to be producing contradictory outcomes: uniting and fragmenting audiences; exacerbating social cleavages as well as bringing formerly disparate groups together; heightening existing antagonisms as well as providing a means through which such friction can be resolved; eroding national boundaries as well as propelling ultra-nationalist fervour; increasing political cynicism as well as raising the level of civil society's political consciousness. Individual citizens have also been empowered as a result of the media's influence. At the same time, because of their adeptness with the utilization of communication systems, state leaders have also been empowered vis-à-vis civil society. Modern transportation has allowed people of formerly distant societies to interact more frequently. It acts as a conduit for bringing individuals from different countries with similar interests together. But it has also served to facilitate transnational criminal activities.

The overall effect of the above has been shrinkage in social, political, economic and cultural distances. As a consequence of this phenomenon, formerly dense and opaque frontiers are being dissolved, thus breaking down the Westphalian notion of 'inside versus outside'. National boundaries are no longer able to divide friend from foe. Indeed, the technological revolution has the potential of creating in the minds of people around the world a sense of global citizenship which could result eventually in the transfer of individuals' loyalties from 'sovereignty-bound' to 'sovereignty-free' governance bodies. 'The changing relationship between the public and private spheres and the virtual collapse of the dividing line separating the domestic from the external environment suggest a fluid but closely integrated global system substantially at odds with the notion of a fragmented system of nationally delineated sovereign states.'[6] However, it does not yet mean that a global civil society has been formed, although one could argue that such an entity is in the process of being established, as will be shown later.

Aided by the technological revolution, globalization has contributed to global space and time shrinkage. The globalization of trade, production and finance has resulted in a marked decline in some governments' ability to control these sectors and has challenged the traditional concept of state sovereignty.[7] It has also expanded the number of players that can be involved in multilateral processes. The globalization movement and the seemingly paradoxical adherence to territorialism are two concepts of world order that stand in conflict but are also interrelated. The globalization of economic processes 'requires the backing of territorially-based state power to enforce its rules'.[8] But post-fordism, the new pattern of social organization of production that is congruent with the globalization phenomenon, implicitly contradicts the lingering territorial principle that has long been identified with fordism.

The results of post-fordist production have been, *inter alia*, the dismantling of the welfare state and the diminishing of the strength of organized labour. But it also has had the effect of increasingly fragmenting power in the world system, providing fodder for 'the possibility of culturally diverse alternatives to global homogenization'.[9] If Cox is right, we can see how this dialectical 'double movement' of the globalization process can alter the relationship people have established with the political arena and how it can eventually cause a reaction leading to what Rosenau terms 'explosive sub-groupism',[10] as seen below in examples of anti-globalization protests. This sub-groupism has already spurred the revival of what can be called civilizational studies that are further unearthing anti-globalization movements and ideas, and a bottom-up form of governance.

There are other ways in which globalization is facilitating the dissolution of formerly dense and opaque boundaries. For instance, economic globalization has resulted in a global division of labour that hardly respects state boundaries and sovereignty. It has to a large extent been responsible for the feminization of work, particularly in the developing world, which penetrates traditional gender boundaries. The international movement of capital via electronic transfers has also had a major effect on the relocation of authority and power structures.[11] Similarly, media globalization – via satellite news networks like CNN, the BBC, al Jazeera and the Internet superhighway – has contributed to the diffusion of power. Its impact raises the possibility of the development of a truly global civil society; something that could again transform the nature of multilateralism and the way we view governance.

Finally, another challenge to the traditional notion of multilateralism and international governance has to do with transnational issues: for example, environmental pollution, global warming, currency crises, the

drug trade, human rights degradation, terrorism, the AIDS epidemic, refugee flows, gender inequality and so on. These issues, by their very nature, all impel cooperation on a transnational scale, since in the majority of cases they cannot be resolved by individual states acting alone or bilaterally. Multi-centric actors have pushed many of these issues onto the global agenda.[12] The impact of the multiplication of transnational issues is that the state-centric multilateral intergovernmental institutions have had to find ways of acknolwedging, if not embracing, the input of NGOs and other civil society actors who formerly would not have been considered important players on the international stage. The alternative of not embracing these entities could very well be the establishment of parallel multilateral arrangements that by-pass existing state-centric multilateral bodies or compete with them.

As James Rosenau reminds us, we live in a messy world, a world that seems in disarray due to high levels of poverty, division, ethnic and cultural conflicts, terrorism, over population, pollution and other forms of environmental degradation.[13] Our world is a postmodern one of extraordinary complexity and uncertainty as contradictory forces are unleashed by the intensification of globalization. It is a world in which integrative forces coexist alongside fragmentary ones, and homogeneization is being challenged by civilizational diversity.[14] What is clear from the above overview is that complex interdependence and globalization phenomena have challenged international governance and raised the possibility of developing other forms of governance at the global level that can adequately address transnational issues and problems.

evolving governance at the global level

While the term 'global governance' is relatively new, the word 'governance' has a long tradition.[15] Etymological searches reveal that the term can be traced back to classical Latin and Greek words for the 'steering of boats'. Originally, the word governance, therefore, referred to the action or way of managing or coordinating interdependent activities. Throughout history there have been attempts to manage the interactions of people, clans, tribes, city-states and states to ensure harmonious relations or deal with common problems. One can find examples of various forms of governance over the course of history including empires/imperialism, balance of power, plurilateralism, formal and informal limited purpose intergovernmental organzations, formal and informal multipurpose international organizations, regional intergovernmental organizations, transnational international non-governmental organizations (INGOs) and embryonic global governance institutions.

The form of governance labelled as empires has a long asssociation with imperialism. This form of governance has recurred at different points in history and in many different regions of the globe. Imperialism provides the ideology underpinning this form of governance. Imperial powers exercise dominance and control over the subjugated regions they conquer. As a result, they develop a form of governance that is based on power asymmetries, coercion and attempts to enforce homogeneity. One can find evidence of governance by empires when the Greek city-state of Athens was a dominant power. But this form of governance has reappeared at different junctures in history, including during our contemporary period.[16] And each time it has appeared, it manages to provoke resistance among those subjugated to this form of governance. Imperial powers have usually declined due in large part to military, economic and imperial overstretch.[17]

Another prominent form of governance has been the balance of power system. This form of governance emerged after the peace of Westphalia in 1648 and the creation of the modern states system. It became the principle mechanism for maintaining international order in Europe. Underpinning the balance of power system were the notions of self-preservation, particularly for those states that were predominant, and the preservation of the status quo. To accomplish those two things, the great powers of the day would use this balance of power mechanism of governance to prevent the emergence of a hegemonic or imperial power and prevent upstart powers from advancing in position up the hierarchical power ladder. Although diplomacy was utilized to manage the relations between states participating in the Euro-centric balance of power system, at other times balance of power governance utilized violent conflict to maintain equilibrium in the international system. War, or the threat of war, was used as a means of preserving equilibrium within the international system. Realists have described the balance of power system well as one in which independent 'rational actor' states have little interaction beyond their borders, and one that emphasized order and stability.

By the nineteenth century, the balance of power form of governance gave way to a series of ad hoc and plurilateral conferences and congresses.[18] While this form of governance was generally limited to the European states system and controlled by the great powers of the time (member states of the Concert of Europe), eventually it broadened to include states in Latin America and Asia – thus expanding the scope of plurilateral multilateralism. However, because the conferences and congresses were intermittent, this form of governance stopped short of establishing formal intergovernmental institutions. In fact, by the mid-nineteenth century, the Concert of Europe became the first attempt at formalizing intergovernmental organization to govern interstate relations as contact between states increased.[19] Out of this interaction, state leaders became increasingly aware of the common problems they faced and of the need for formal institutional devises and systematic methods for regulating their behaviour and relationships. This governance via formal intergovernmental organizations and regimes was steered by the great powers directorship of the Concert and included such activity as regulating traffic on the great rivers of Europe, adjusting relations between belligerent and neutral states, redivision of the Balkans and the carving up of the African continent.

However, while the great powers of the nineteenth century proved relatively successful in governing the subordinate states in the international system, problems arose when the dominant powers clashed among themselves. Since there was no higher power to mediate great power conflicts and those conflicts open the door for rising powers to challenge the great powers, the Concert of Europe and the intermittent conference/congress system soon became ineffective and largely irrelevant. As Murphy recalls, in the late nineteenth century there were also other challenges coming to this form of governance from civil society organizations which began to establish a presence on the global stage. Such organizations included the anti-slavery movement and financial and corporate interests, as well as private associations.[20] This 'parallel' non-state system of governance, combined with emerging powers beyond Europe and a dramatic increase in the volume and scope of international activity, caused some major strains on the ad hoc conference/congress governance system. As Claude puts it: 'When all is said and done, the political conference system contributed more to awareness of the problems of international collaboration than to their solution and more to opening up the possibilities of multilateral diplomacy than to realizing them.'[21] But the conference/congress system did make a significant contribution to the institutionalization of modern-day multilateral/intergovernmental organization because it got European governments into the habit of meeting together to discuss and iron out problems of common concern.[22]

As the start of the twentieth century, great efforts were made to establish more formal institutions of governance at the international level.

International public unions began to regulate telecommunications and postal systems. Between 1860 and 1914 about two dozen organizations were created to govern interstate and transnational activity. Many of them were designed to foster industry and commerce, but most were focused on meeting social and economic needs as well as on managing a variety of conflicts stemming from the effects of the second industrial revolution and the increased volume and scale of interactions between states.[23] But note that there was a persistence of non-state organizations, like the International Committee of the Red Cross (ICRC) – founded in 1919, that operated in parallel with state-centric organizations on the world stage.

It took World War I to actualize the formal institutionalization of intergovernmental governance with the founding of organizations like the Permanent Court of International Justice and the League of Nations. Liberals have argued that the underlying cause of the war was the balance of power's failure to maintain stability, order and ultimately peace. For this reason, Woodrow Wilson and other liberals sought to replace balance of power politics, with its ad hoc methods and reliance on military power and alliance politics, with a formal institutionalized system of law and conflict prevention mechanisms, including the collective security provisions outlined in the Covenant of the League of Nations.

The League of Nations itself was an attempt to create an institutional framework to control war by eliminating or reducing states' concerns about security. The principle of collective security was seen as a remedy for the security dilemma that confronted states. A collective security system is based on a number of critical assumptions. It assumes that wars are principally the result of acts of aggression conducted by one state against another. It also assumes that such wars could be deterred if potential aggressors knew that their actions would be met with the combined force of all of the other states in the system either in the form of harmful sanctions or, ultimately, with armed force. This brings into play other assumptions including, most importantly, the willingness of other states to respond collectively in the face of aggression. Collective security rests on the premise of shared vulnerability among states. Yet, in practice, few states were willing to leave their security in the hands of the collective security instrument devised at the League of Nations. This was especially true for those states – Japan, Italy and Germany – which were dissatisfied with the prevailing international order. As they sought their own solutions to interwar security issues, other states took notice and felt threatened.

So this governance system via a multipurpose intergovernmental organization, the League of Nations, did not last long. The League's inability to overcome the security dilemma has been seen by many as one of the greatest failures of the interwar period, leading to the outbreak of war on the European continent in 1939. Of course, the League was not an entity unto itself, but rather it merely represented the collective will of its member governments. The United States, one of the world's pre-eminent powers never took up membership and, by the late 1930s, most of the disaffected powers – Germany, Japan, Russia – had left this intergovernmental organization. Those major powers that remained, principally Great Britain and France, were unwilling for a variety of domestic and foreign policy considerations to provide the League with the support it needed to respond to the political and military challenges that developed in the international system during the 1930s. Beginning with Japan's attack on Manchuria, through to Italy's annexation of Abyssinia and on to the German anschluss against Czechoslovakia in 1939, the League and its member governments shamefully stood by and did nothing. Yet it would be somewhat misleading to lay the blame for World War II solely at the door of the League.

For some historians, the war that began in 1939 was the continuation of a European-wide war that had not ended in 1919, but merely paused as the combatants regained strength and armour. World War I had failed to resolve the pressing balance of power issues that had plagued the continent since the late nineteenth century. States such as Germany and Italy remained dissatisfied with their place in the European power structure. Germany, especially, suffered from the punitive measures imposed on it as part of the Treaty of Versailles. From the Germans' vantage point, there was much ground to recover. Added to all of these factors was, of course, the emergence of fascist regimes in Germany and Italy led respectively by Hitler and Mussolini. Hitler's ambitious expansionist plans posed a direct and significant challenge to European and international order and to the fledgling intergovernmental governance. In light of these factors war became more a matter of when, not if.

The demise of the League of Nations once World War II began clearly indicated that the system of governance via intergovernmental organizations needed to be reformed, at least.

In August 1941, just months before the United States (the emerging great power) entered that war, American President Franklin D. Roosevelt joined with British Prime Minister Winston Churchill to establish what became known as the Atlantic Charter. That charter formed the basis for the Declaration of the United Nations, which was signed on 1 January 1942 in San Francisco by some 26 governments. In essence, the declaration was an attempt to introduce a permanent governance system for ensuring general global security once the war was over.[24] The victorious Allied countries were envisioned to be at the centre of this new system which, in effect, was expected to constitute the institutionalization of the immediate post-1945 world order. In San Francisco, on 25 April 1945, two weeks before Roosevelt's death, the UN system was ushered into existence on the promise that it would not be a house of cards, like its ill-fated predecessor, but rather a stable and authoritative base for global tranquillity and a mechanism for preserving international peace and security. The UN was supposed to be a much more powerful intergovernmental governance organization than was the League of Nations. Whereas the Covenant of the League made no provision for that organization to be involved in direct military action, the UN Charter envisioned a military staff committee to oversee military enforcement of UN Security Council resolutions. While the Covenant had contemplated decision by unanimity, the Charter pictured a majority capable of binding all UN members, and in some cases non-members, to its determinations.

But there were many features of this governance form that were worth keeping. The permanent institutional mechanism developed with the establishment of the League was preserved with the founding of the UN at the tail end of World War II. So too was the multipurpose infrastructure. Indeed, the institutionalization of the UN system was much more extensive that that of the League, with six main organs, a permanent secretariat and subsidiary bodies, as well as a large number of specialized agencies, functional commissions, regional commissions, committees, programmes, funds, research and training institutes and related and affiliated bodies.

The UN Charter listed some key governance goals for this multipurpose intergovernmental organization that went beyond the maintenance of international peace and security. These were as follows: developing friendly relations among nations based on respect for the principle of equal rights and self-determination of peoples; achieving international cooperation in solving global socio-economic, cultural and humanitarian problems; encouraging and promoting respect for human rights and for fundamental freedoms for all; and, becoming the centre for harmonizing the actions of nations to attain the above common ends.[25] Over the years since 1945, the UN grew in size and mandate. Its Charter goals were extended to include protecting the global commons and encouraging democratization across the globe. One could add to these the recent goal of countering terrorism that is reflected in the UN Security Council's resolution 1373, passed on the 28 September 2001 in response to the 11 September 2001 attacks on the United States.[26]

While the main purpose of international governance under the UN system was to 'save succeeding generations from the scourge of war', this intergovernmental organization is mandated to address a variety of other issues,[27] for example, economic development (UN Development Program), health (World Health Organization), communications (International Telecommunications Union), human rights (Office of the UN High Commissioner for Refugees), refugees (UN High Commissioner for Refugees), women (UN Development Fund for Women) and children (UN Children's Fund). The UN retains its support for state sovereignty as exemplified in its membership and its resistance (until recently) to intervention. It is for this reason that Rosenau considers it a 'sovereignty-bound' organization. It has been the principal forum in which newly independent states seek recognition and confirmation of their independence and sovereignty. At the same time, it has been pursued by human rights advocates as the organization through which the rights of individuals against the state are to be advanced and ultimately protected; and by civil society organizations to gain their own recognition and opportunities for participation in the process of global governance. So, in essence, the UN – a sovereignty-bound organization – has had to find ways of accommodating non-state actors that pursue some of the same goals it shares with them. Elsewhere I speak of this evolving multilateralism as the intersection of bottom-up and top-down global governance.[28]

It is clear, however, that this universal, intergovernmental organization has not always been successful in addressing many of the different representational concerns of member governments. This explains the proliferation in the establishment of regional and sub-regional intergovernmental organizations (some multi-purpose and others single-purpose) as well as the attempts to construct alternative institutional frameworks (hybrid global governance bodies) to meet diverse sets of interests. In some cases, these bodies are viewed as alternatives of a complementary sort, but some of them can also be seen as alternatives that challenge the legitimacy, credibility and relevance of the UN. If the contemporary global agenda seems crowded by the number and scope of activities that occur in so many different sectors, the response in governance terms is equally staggering. While the total number of governance mechanisms is seemingly countless, the variety is clearly evident. At the interstate level alone, there are numerous formal groupings: G3, G8, G20, G21, G25, G77, G90. There are also now the seemingly ubiquitous 'coalitions of the willing'.[29]

This considerable variety of intergovernmental bodies forms only one element of global governance. Tanja Brühl and Volker Rittberger make a conceptual distinction between 'international' and 'global' governance. They suggest that international governance consists of the 'output of a non-hierarchical network of interlocking international (mostly, but not exclusively, governmental) institutions which regulate the behaviour of states and other international actors in different issue areas of world politics'. For them, global governance is 'the output of a non-hierarchical network of international and transnational institutions: not only IGOs and international regimes but also transnational regimes are regulating actors' behaviour'. In other words, they differentiate global governance from international governance by suggesting that in the case of the former there is a decreased salience of states and increased salience of non-state actors in the processes of norm-building, rule-setting and compliance-monitoring that occur at the global level.[30] They also equate global governance with multi-level governance involving the management of the above processes at sub-national, national, regional trans-regional and global levels.

contemporary interest in summative global governance

The recent interest in multi-level global governance stems, in large part, from a recognition of the scale of global change: the shrinkage of time and space witnessed over the past 64 years or so; the emergence of a transnational civil society;[31] rising interdependence among actors (state and non-state) within international society; the rise in the number and complexity of transnational issues that cannot be addressed adequately by the UN intergovernmental system; and national governments' failure/inability not only to deal with these transnational issues but also to provide common goods and security guarantees for their citizens.

Particularly since the end of the World War II, we have witnessed at least three different challenges to traditional Westphalian international governance as represented in institutions like the UN system. First, the technological revolution (particularly with regard to information, communications, computing and transportation) has made it possible for many other actors besides states to enter the world stage and demand a role in decision-making that affects them directly. Second, the intensification of globalization has altered the relationship between citizens, the state and intergovernmental organizations (IGOs). Globalization has facilitated greater participation of non-state actors in governance processes normally reserved for state actors. But because globalization is a double-edged sword, it has also made it easier for transnational criminal organizations and terrorist groups to command the attention of governance bodies at all levels. It has also widened the gap between rich and poor, thereby increasing the challenge to intergovernmental bodies. Third, the end of the Cold War can be seen as a historical turning point for intergovernmental institutions. It has resulted in an exponential expansion in the scope and agenda of IGOs, so much so that these organization are having to contract out certain services.[32] All three challenges have created new problems for governance, including the concept itself, and ensured that even more actors are involved in managing those problems. Apart from states and IGOs operating at multiple levels, today we have a plethora of non-state actors vying for attention on the world stage: transnational corporations, business associations, public–private consortia, bond-rating agencies, transnational social movements, transnational advocacy networks, epistemic communities, coalitions of non-governmental organizations, transnational criminal organizations, terrorist groups, security communities and so on.

Recently, there have been a plethora of critical works that have tried to stand outside the prevailing thought about multilateralism and global governance to give those concepts meaning in what is considered to be changed circumstances. The most influential of these works was initiated by Robert Cox through his 'Multlateralism and the United Nations System (MUNS)' research project that began in 1992. Because the MUNS programme focused on long-term structural change, it was cognizant of attempts by the less powerful in society to create space for themselves in multilateral activity and fora. Indeed, an explicit goal of the Fiesole symposium (1992) was the consideration of a future 'new multilateralism built from the bottom up on the foundations of a broadly participative global society'.[33] This bottom-up multilateralism is conceived as organic and network-based with discourse mechanisms as well as democratic structures to ensure accountability to the world's peoples. At the same time, MUNS researchers were cognizant of the constraints imposed by the more powerful on the attempts of the less powerful to play a greater role in global governance.

What emerged from the volumes of literature published by MUNS was an expanded and historically sensitive view of multilateralism obtained through careful empirical observation as well as through the questioning of conventional and traditional analyses of the phenomenon. Multilateralism in the MUNS' orientation is accorded a broad meaning that encompasses all those entities that may be (or may become) relevant in dealing with general or sector-specific areas of policy that have relevance for the globe, whether they are trans-regional, regional, interstate, state or sub-state. Thus, the units of analysis for the MUNS group not only included the state but also encompassed forces in civil society, above and below the state.[34]

Another realted paradigmatic shift in conceptualizing both governance and multilateralism is linked to a movement towards establishing a post-Cold War global agenda that has given rise to what Richard Falk calls a potential 'counter-project' to that of post-Cold War geo-politics.[35] At the base of this counter-project is a normative pre-occupation with strengthening the role of civil society (sovereignty-free actors) in matters of world affairs at local, regional and global locales to balance the influence of sovereignty-bound actors. This is now generally viewed as an essential 'bottom-up' counter-balance to the state-centric 'top-down' views of world order and global governance that are so deeply entrenched in much of neo-realist and liberal institutionalist thinking and scholarship.

In some respects, this conception of the counter-project has been borne out in the recent anti-globalization protests we have been witnessing. The end of the twentieth century and beginning of the twenty-first century proved to be a defining moment for bottom-up struggles against top-down governance at the global level – what some have called a 'Grotian Moment'. For many commentators, this defining moment began at the end of 1999 when the WTO's Third Ministerial meeting collapsed because of the anti-globalization/capitalism protests in Seattle, Washington. But the contestations between governmental and intergovernmental bodies versus non-state actors can be traced earlier than the end of the Cold War, the collapse of the Soviet bloc and the embrace of democratization in formerly authoritarian states. Mary Kaldor writes authoritatively about civil society movements that sprung up against authoritarian states and actually brought down some of those regimes.[36] The end of several authoritarian governments – most from Central and Eastern Europe – opened the door for the emergence of a number of social counter-movements. One should note as well that this wave coincided with the emergence of a transnational, militant Islamic movement as well as with the coalescing of a number of other social movements (environmentalists, feminists, human rights and indigenous peoples.)

However, the Seattle protests can be considered the 'turning point' in the clash between bottom-up and top-down forces in the struggle for how the global economy will be governed in the future.[37] That protest involved an estimated 50,000 people, as well as 'the rebellion of developing country delegates inside the Seattle Convention Center'. Although it may have been difficult to pinpoint the position of all of the protesters, what united them was 'their opposition to the expansion of a system that promoted corporate-led globalization at the expense of social goals like justice, community, national sovereignty, cultural diversity, and ecological sustainability'.[38] Note that this protest was met by a major assault on a largely peaceful gathering by Seattle police in full view of television cameras. Similar anti-globalization protests occurred during 2000 in Bangkok, in Washington, DC, in Chiang Mai, Thailand, in Melbourne, Australia and in Prague, Czech Republic. In 2001, despite the attempts by government leaders in the major industrial states to find ways to keep demonstrators away from major summit meetings, we witnessed major civil society demonstrations in Windsor, Ontario at the Summit of the Americas and in Genoa, Italy where a protester was killed and many injured. The lack of civil society's confidence in intergovernmental institutions was a sure sign that these top-down governance bodies were beginning to lose their legitimacy. These protests represented the clash between two worlds: a state-centric one and a multi-centric one.

Rosenau and Durfee note that 'alongside the traditional world of states, a complex multi-centric world of diverse actors has emerged, replete with structures, processes, and decision rules of its own'. These authors go on to label these two worlds in turn as 'state-centric' and 'multi-centric'. As these two sets of structures intersect, one should expect that multilateralism at that specific historical juncture would be different in character from the multilateralism that emerged out of the immediate post-World War II period. Certainly, the empirical evidence points to a changed socio-political environment within which multilateral institutions are forced to operate today. The global stage 'is dense with actors, large and small, formal and informal, economic and social, political and cultural, national and transnational, international and subnational, aggressive and peaceful, liberal and authoritarian, who collectively form a highly complex system of global governance'.[39] The large number and vast range of collectivities that clamber onto the global stage exhibit both organized and disorganized complexity.[40] Literally, thousands of factions, associations, organizations, movements and interest groups, along with states, now form a network pattern of interactions, which reminds one of Burton's 'cobweb' metaphor.[41] The advent of this bifurcated system of governance does not mean that states are in the process of disintegration. The interstate system will continue to be central to world affairs for decades to come.

This proliferation of sovereignty-bound and sovereignty-free actors suggests that existing international governance systems have failed to deal adequately with the new transnational problems or with new actors' aspirations. It would seem as though international governance has been reflexively adapting to these challenges in two ways: grafting new elements and transforming itself. But certainly, the concept of governance itself is undergoing change.

Governance can be distinguished from government in that the former is an umbrella concept while the latter constitutes the institutions and agents charged with governing. Government refers to 'formal institutions that are part of hierarchical norm- and rule-making, monitoring of compliance rules, and rule enforcement'.[42] It is basically what governments do. Governments have the power to make binding decisions and to enforce those decisions, and they have the authority to allocate values.[43] Indeed, at least over the past two decades, the term 'governance' has enjoyed a revival of sorts, linked to attempts by scholars to distinguish between 'governance' and 'government'.[44] And, since 1995, in particular, the term 'global governance' has become an integral part of the lexicon of scholars and practitioners globally, in large part because of the emergence of the academic journal, *Global Governance: A Review of Multilateralism and International Organizations* and the widely distributed report of the Commission on Global Governance titled *Our Global Neighbourhood*.[45]

Why has there been a revival of the concept of governance of late? The answer seems to lie in the paradigmatic crises that occurred in the social sciences during the late 1970s and early 1980s in response to the systemic challenges referred to above. As Bob Jessop puts it, the paradigmatic crises were 'the possibility of culturally diverse alternatives to global homogenization and the capacity of paradigms in use to describe and explain the "real world." '[46]

Finkelstein asserts that political scientists have been 'uncomfortable with traditional frameworks and terminologies associated with the idea of international relations in an interstate system' ever since the emergence of 'complex interdependence' and what James Rosenau aptly called 'the crazy-quilt nature of modern interdependence'.[47] It should not come as a surprise to learn that the use of the term 'global governance' has 'paralleled the advent of globalization'.[48]

We are all well aware that there is no overarching government at the international level that can handle all facets of the globalization phenomenon. Yet, there is a desire to control, steer and address all levels of human activity that have transnational repercussions. This desire to control, steer and deal with such activities is labelled 'global governance', and it can occur at many levels – global, trans-regional, regional, state and local. The purpose of global governance, therefore, is to steer and modify the behaviour of actors who operate on the global stage in such a manner as to avoid deadly conflicts and control intense socio-economic and political competition. In that sense of the term, global governance implies a purposive activity, in the absence of world government, that could involve a range of actors besides states. As Marie-Claude Smouts puts it: 'governance is order plus intentionality'.[49]

Global governance also refers to more than formal institutional processes. As shown later, this can involve the interactions of informal networks and regimes. Indeed, the value of thinking in terms of global governance these days is to recognize that the majority of cross-border transactions are managed not by formal institutions but by informal regimes (principles, norms, rules, practices and decision-making procedures).[50] One should note that during the 1980s the term 'governance' was used by international financial institutions to justify the political conditionalities imposed on developing countries. Used in that sense, global governance has developed ideological overtones.[51]

While national governments and the UN system are very much central to the activities of global governance, they are only a part of the overall picture. Indeed, at the end of the twentieth century, global governance was already being conceptualized as systems of rule at all levels of human activity. The Commission on Global Governance defined governance as 'the sum of the many ways in which individuals and institutions, both public and private, manage their common affairs'.[52] This definition was broad enough to allow for the participation of state and non-state actors in the art of global governing. The issues dealt with by global governance institutions are transnational ones – that is, they transcend national frontiers. Again, the work of the Commission on Global Governance is useful here. The Commission considered the tasks of global governance today to include the maintenance of peace and security; the control of expanding economic activity; dealing with environmental problems; combating trans-border diseases such as AIDS; preserving genetic diversity; saving endangered species; curbing horizontal and vertical proliferation of weapons; deterring terrorists; warding off famine; eradicating poverty; developing fair ways to share the earth's resources; halting drug trafficking and the trafficking of women and children and so on. No single government, on its own, can properly tackle these issues. Likewise, at the present time, neither the UN system nor regional, intergovernmental organizations can hope to perform the above tasks on their own. Thus, the work of global governance requires the actions of a plurality of actors, and not just the actions of a collection of nation states. As Forman and Segaar note,

> In addition to the multipication of countries seeking a voice in international fora, transnational movements of civil society, NGOs, multinational corporations and even wealthy individuals are influencing the ways in which international public policy is made and implemented. Through advocacy, lobbying and direct service provision (and now global terrorism), these non-state actors are changing perceptions and behavior in fields as diverse as international health, environmental management, peace and security, human rights, and trade.[53]

But there is more to the concept of global governance than the above indicates. As one peels away the skin of the concept, one finds a number of insinuated sub-texts. The concept of governance implies a measure of control, orderliness and manageability. It implies that intersubjective norms, principles and rules are in play. It implies functional administrative capacities. There is also the implication that a governance regime ought to be accountable and responsive to those it serves. Connected to this is the notion that meaningful governance ought to be transparent. Smouts adds to the above four defining characteristics of governance that are worth mentioning. According to her: (1) governance is neither a rule system nor an activity but a process; (2) governance is not founded upon domination but upon accommodation; (3) governance involves public and private actors at the same time; and (4) governance is not a formal institution but is reliant on continual interaction. These characteristics 'share the extreme misgivings about the way in which global society functions: the increasing ungovernability of complex societies, and the need to manage externalities in a context of interdependence'.[54]

Mihaly Simai uses what he calls 'an unconventional systems theory framework' to show the complexity and multi-level nature of contemporary global governance. He conceives of the global system as encompassing the entirety of relationships among actors that influence processes and changes beyond nation-state frontiers. That system, he tells us, operates within a structure that has traditionally been dominated by states but has now made room for other important actors – non-governmental organizations (NGOs), transnational corporations and others – that have demonstrated an interest in managing destablizing forces and risks that could affect the entire globe. Furthermore, the global system, for Simai, is conceptualized as embedded within social, ideological and cultural structures as well – structures through which power may be concentrated, diffused and transformed. At the base of the system is a political subsystem consisting of the totality of the relations between states. At the next level, according to Simai, are those relations that are formed between states and non-state actors and conditioned by a number of forces such as domestic, political motivations. The next rung is a subsystem dominated by what the author calls the 'price makers' – a handful of leading economic powers – whose decisions result in a permanent condition of adjustment for the smaller states or the 'price takers'.[55]

Global governance can therefore mean (1) the centralization of authority at the global level; (2) authority that is limited to specific situations and issues; and (3) the sum of all diverse efforts of communities at every level to achieve specific goals while preserving coherence from one moment in time to the next. The last of these definitions describes global governance as a summative phenomenon. To quote Rosenau, global governance 'is a summarizing phrase for all sites in the world where efforts to exercize authority are undertaken'.[56] The concept of global governance is relatively new, but widely used. It is a concept that, while contested, reflects the growing unease with international governance. Global governance has not replaced international governance; instead, both forms of governance currently operate alongside each other, sometime complementing each other, sometimes clashing with each other.

conclusion

As we entered the new millennium, it was evident that intergovernmental organizations operated alongside a complex web of a multi-level governance structures. It was also obvious that ideological, socio-political and economic changes were putting pressure on the state-centric organizations to adjust to what some have called a 'post-modern era'. Even as international organizations have proliferated, expanded the range of their governance and increased the level of their influence, major questions remain about their efficiency, effectiveness and relevance. These questions intensified as the seeming 'new world disorder' unfolded. Yet more than ever, governance institutions are needed to address transnational problems and challenges that states are unable to deal with on their own. As Oran Young remarked at the end of the last century, 'The demand for governance in world affairs has never been greater.'[57] This explains the continued appeal of, growth in and dependence on, international organizations today.

However, this need for governance cannot be met solely by state-based international organizations. Furthermore, state-centric organizations have tended to 'act as a conservative force against radical change by conforming to the status-quo and by further institutionalizing the present international framework'.[58] For humankind to survive on this planet, in this global neighbourhood, a network of governance institutions that not only includes multipurpose and limited purpose international governmental organizations (IGOs) but also embraces international non-governmental organizations (INGOs), transnational corporate bodies and civil society organizations (CSOs), is emerging and giving new meaning to the concepts of multilateralism and global governance.[59]

Bob Jessop delineates three modes of governance. These are anarchic governance; organizational hierarchical governance; and heterarchic governance. The forms of governance as used in the latter sense 'include self-organizing interpersonal networks, negotiated inter-organizational co-ordination, and decentred, context-mediated inter-systemic steering'. Anarchic governance is not possible in a world that is as interdependent as ours is today. Organizational hierarchical governance served its purpose during the interwar and post-World War II period but has since been challenged by groups within civil society. As Jessop further explains, heterarchic governance is the type of governance that involves 'self-organized steering of multiple agencies, institutions, and systems which are operationally autonomous from one another yet structurally coupled due to their mutual interdependence'.[60] This form of governance has become especially important with the intensification of globalization processes, which has resulted in a marked shift in state–market–society relations. As a result of this shift, it is becoming evident that top-down state planning and market-mediated anarchy may not be able to manage the attendant socio-economic problems that have emerged. Even top-down multilateral mechanisms, such as the UN system, the International Monetary Fund (IMF), the International Bank for Reconstruction and Development (IBRD) and the WTO have been unable to address such problems adequately. Indeed, there is a multitude of calls for reforming the UN system and for remodelling or revamping the global economic architecture.

The current boom in the theory and practice of 'new' multilateralism is in obvious reaction to the changing global environment. The globalization of the economy and the internationalization of the state, the growing unfeasibility and illegitimacy of large-scale warfare between states and the growth of transnational problems can all be identified as contributing to the promotion of new forms of multilateral cooperation today. Early multilateral thinkers envisioned various schemes for addressing problems of interstate conflict and for regulating the relationship between states and their civil societies,[61] with the primary goals of eliminating war, improving societal welfare conditions and promoting such issues as justice and human rights. Their thinking influenced subsequent conceptualizations of multilateral organization and played a major role in shaping the character of the concrete expressions of multilateralism, that is international organizations, from the late eighteenth century until the present.

However, the state-centric view of multilateralism has been challenged recently by a number of scholars. This critical scholarship, rather than being driven by a policy-relevant orientation, is normatively driven like that of early multilateral thinkers in the direction of promoting such values as greater social equity, justice, enhanced diffusion of power, a non-violence ethic for dealing with conflicts, respect for cultural and civilizational diversity and the preservation and sustainability of the environment. Instead of being overly concerned with the problem-solving and short-term issues of international organization and institutional reform, this critical scholarship is self-conscious about placing emphasis on long-term structural change and the impact of such change on the nature of multilateralism as we go further into the twenty-first century.

What makes the critical school on multilateralism and global governance more appealing is its ability to stand back from the tedious details of current events and offer a more holistic and panoramic view of the landscape of global changes to existing ideas, material capabilities and institutions. This 'reflectivist turn' in the multilateral scholarship has pointed out at least five challenges to the Westphalian state system: the emergence of bifurcated structures operating at the global level; increased complex interdependence assisted by the advent of dynamic technologies; the globalization of economies which has taken economic and political decision-making power away from some states; the emergence and importance of transnational issues with which individual states cannot deal on their own; and the gendering of governance institutions and processes that operate on the global level.[62] In effect, each of these challenges indicates a focus on disjunctures and discontinuities. Understanding the impact of such changes on existing structures and processes of multilateralism is important for reconceptualizing the governance of the globe.

We no longer live with the rigidity that characterized the Cold War period. The structural changes that we are currently witnessing in this early part of the twenty-first century are producing a complex, multilevel pattern of forces that challenge us to discard the oversimplified state-centric vision of world order and to replace it with 'a modified version of reality'.[63] In this period of transformation, the governance system for the globe is clearly a bifurcated one. The interstate system of governance is still with us. But we have seen the emergence of a multicentric system of diverse types of collectivities. Combined, we call it summative global governance.

Our international system now has 'proliferating centres of authority'. These centres are represented on a global stage which, to quote Rosneau, is now 'dense with actors, large and small, formal and informal, economic and social, political and cultural, national and transnational, international and subnational, aggressive and peaceful, liberal and authoritarian, who collectively form a highly complex system of global governance'.[64] There are times when these two systems collide or overlap in their attempts to deal with transnational problems. At other times, we have witnessed the creation of hybrid networks of governance at the global level that combine sovereignty-free and sovereignty-bound institutional features, or hierarchical and non-hierarchical institutional features, or top-down and bottom-up institutional features. These 'hybrid' networks have contributed to the disaggregation of authority channels and the formation of new non-hierarchical collectivities. Clearly, such novel forms of governance are needed to deal with the contradictory 'fragmegration' tendencies of our contemporary period. For instance, in those cases where globalizing dynamics have produced local opposition as a reaction to those dynamics, conflict and fragmentation can be the result unless some form of governance is in place to address locally felt grievances.

For humans to survive on this planet, in this global neighbourhood, a network of governance institutions that not only includes international governmental organizations (IGOs) but also embraces international non-governmental organizations (INGOs), transnational corporations (TNCs) and civil society organizations (CSOs), has emerged and is providing us with the phenomenon we can call 'summative global governance'. This emerging system of global governance resembles a network that links many centres of authority at multiple levels (universal, continental, trans-regional, regional, trans-national, national and sub-national). Some authors also refer to this as 'multilevel governance' – a 'form of rule system in which authority is voluntarily and legally dispersed among various levels of community where problems are located and local needs require attention'.[65] Clearly, the rapid evolution of new forms of cooperation, particularly over the past 64 years or so, has resulted in multi-level governance that is increasingly more sophisticated and flexible than previous forms and has outflanked the activities of traditional intergovernmental institutions because those institutions are proving to be either defective, inefficient, ineffective or largely irrelevant.[66]

notes

1. James Rosenau, 'Governance, Order and Change in World Politics,' in James N. Rosenau and Ernst-Otto Czempiel (eds), *Governance Without Government: Order and Change in World Politics* (Cambridge: Cambridge University Press, 1992), pp. 13–14.
2. See W. Andy Knight, 'Global Governance and World (Dis)orders,' in Janine Brodie and Sandra Rein (eds), *Critical Concepts: An Introduction to Politics*, 3rd edition (Toronto: Pearson Education Canada, 2005), pp. 252–263.
3. Thomas Keating and W. Andy Knight (eds), *Building Sustainable Peace* (Edmonton: University of Alberta Press and Tokyo: United Nations University Press, 2004), pp. 1–4.

4. For a good discussion of these transnational development see Amitai Etzioni, 'Beyond Transnational Governance,' *International Journal* (Autumn 2001), pp. 595–610.
5. See Robert O. Keohane and Joseph S. Nye, *Power and Interdependence* (Boston: Little Brown, 1977), especially chapter 2.
6. Joseph A. Camilleri and Jim Falk, *The End of Sovereignty? The Politics of a Shrinking and Fragmenting World* (Aldershot: Edward Elgar, 1992), p. 88.
7. James Mittelman, 'Rethinking Innovation in International Studies: Global Transformation at the Turn of the Millennium,' in Stephen Gill and J. H. Mittelman (eds), *Innovation and Transformation in International Studies* (Cambridge: Cambridge University Press, 1997), pp. 248–263.
8. Robert W. Cox, *Approaches to World Order* (Cambridge: Cambridge University Press, 1996), p. 278.
9. Ibid., p. 155.
10. James Rosenau, *Distant Proximities: Dynamics Beyond Globalization* (New Jersey: Princeton University Press, 2003).
11. Susan Strange, *Casino Capitalism* (New York: St. Martin's Press, 1997).
12. The environment is a case in point. The Ottawa process to ban landmines and the Rome meeting that created the ICC are equally valid examples.
13. James Rosenau, 'Governance in a New Global Order,' in David Held and Anthony McGrew (eds), *Governing Globalization*, 2nd edition (Cambridge: Polity Press, 2003), p. 223.
14. W. Andy Knight, *Adapting the United Nations to a Post-Modern Era: Lessons Learned*, 2nd edition (Houndmills: Palgrave/Macmillan Press/St. Martin's Press, 2005).
15. Anthony Pagden, 'The Genesis of Governance and Enlightenment Conceptions of the Cosmopolitan World Order,' *International Social Science Journal*, Vol. 50, No. 1, 1998, pp. 7–15; and Craig Murphy, *International Organization and Industrial Change* (Cambridge: Polity Press, 1994).
16. See Michael W. Doyle, *Empires* (Ithaca, NY: Cornell University Press, 1986) and Niall Ferguson, *Empire* (London: Basic Books, 2002).
17. Paul Kennedy, *The Rise and Fall of the Great Powers* (New York: Fontana Press, 1989).
18. On plurilateralism see W. Andy Knight, 'Plurilateral Multilateralism: Canada's Emerging International Policy?' in Andrew F. Cooper and Dane Rowlands (eds), *Canada Among Nations, 2005: Split Images* (Ottawa: McGill/Queen's Press, 2005), pp. 93–114. Note the examples of the Congresses of Vienna, Paris and Berlin (1815, 1856 and 1878 respectively); the London Conferences (1871 and 1912–1913); the Hague Conferences (1899 and 1907); and the Algeciras Conference (1906).
19. Inis Claude, Jr., *Swords into Plowshares*, 4th edition (New York: Random House, 1971), p. 21.
20. Murphy, *International Organization and Industrial Change*, pp. 56–57.
21. Inis Claude, Jr., *Swords into Plowshares*, p. 28.
22. Murphy, *International Organization and Industrial Change*, p. 56.
23. Ibid., pp. 32–37.
24. Thomas Weiss, David Forsythe and Roger Coate, *The United Nations and Changing World Politics* (Boulder, CO: Westview Press, 1994), p. 24.

25. See Article 1 of the UN Charter.
26. Resolution 1373 also established a Counter-Terrorism Committee (the CTC) that is made up of all 15 members of the UN Security Council. The CTC monitors the implementation of resolution 1373 by all States and promises to improve the capability of States to fight terrorism.
27. Jim Whitman notes that 'governance extends well beyond a monopoly of violence' and that it includes maintaining a variety of relationships and the functioning of a number of varied agencies (e.g. health, infrastructure, defence, and so on). Jim Whitman, *The Limits of Global Governance* (London: Routledge, 2005).
28. W. Andy Knight, 'Engineering Space in Global Governance: The Emergence of Civil Society in Evolving Multilateralism,' in Michael Schechter (ed.), *Future Multilateralism: The Political and Social Foundations* (London: Macmillan Press, 1997), pp. 255–291; and W. Andy Knight, 'Multilatéralisme ascendant et descendant: deux voies dans la quête d'une gouverne globale,' in Michel Fortmann, S. Neil MacFarlane and Stéphane Roussel (eds), *Tous pour un ou chacun pour soi: promesses et limites de la coopération régionale en matière de sécurité* (Québec: Institut Québécois des Hautes Études Internationales, Université Laval, 1996), pp. 43–69.
29. W. Andy Knight and Thomas Keating, *Global Politics, Globalization and Multilevel Governance Networks: Emerging trends and Challenges for the Third Millennium* (Toronto: Oxford University Press, forthcoming 2009).
30. Tanja Brühl and Volker Rittberger, 'From International to Global Governance: Actors, Collective Decision-making, and the United Nations in the World of the Twenty-first Century,' in Volke Rittberger (ed.), *Global Governance and the United Nations System* (New York: UN University Press, 2001), p. 2.
31. Note this term 'civil society' first appeared in the works of late eighteenth century and early nineteenth century social philosophers. Freidrich Hegel, for example, used the concept in reference to a middle point in the social structure between 'the state' at the macro level of society, and 'the family unit' at the micro level of society (see Adam B. Seligman, *The Idea of Civil Society* (New York: Free Press, 1992). Also see Ann M. Florini (ed.), *The Third Force: The Rise of Transnational Civil* Society (Washington, DC: Carnegie Endowment for International Peace, 2000).
32. See Thomas G. Weiss and Leon Gordenker (eds), *NGOs, the UN, and Global Governance* (Colorado: Lynne Rienner Publishers, 1996).
33. Robert W. Cox (ed.), *The New Realism: Perspectives on Multilateralism and World Order* (New York: St. Martin's Press/United Nations University Press, 1997), see Preface.
34. Keith Krause and W. Andy Knight (eds), *State, Society, and the UN System: Changing Perspectives on Multilateralism* (Tokyo: United Nations University Press, 1995), p. 261.
35. Richard Falk, 'From Geopolitics to Geogovernance: WOMP and Contemporary Political Discourse,' *Alternatives*, Vol. 19, No. 2, pp. 145–154.
36. Mary Kaldor, *Global Civil Society: An Answer to War* (Cambridge: Polity Press, 2003).

37. Walden Bello, '2000: The Year of Global Protest against Globalization,' *Canadian Dimension*, Vol. 35, No.2 (2001), p. 24.
38. Ibid., p. 24.
39. Rosenau, 'Governance in a New Global Order,' p. 225.
40. James N. Rosenau and Mary Durfee, *Thinking Theory Thoroughly: Coherent Approaches to an Incoherent World* (Boulder: Westview Press, 1999), p. 40.
41. John W. Burton, *World Society* (Cambridge: Cambridge University Press, 1972).
42. Brühl and Rittberger, 'From International to Global Governance', p. 5.
43. Gerry Stoker, 'Governance as Theory: Five Propositions,' *International Social Science Journal*, Vol. 50, No. 155, 1998, pp. 17–28.
44. Rosenau and Czempiel, *Governance without Government.*
45. The Commission on Global Governance, *Our Global Neighbourhood* (Oxford: Oxford University Press, 1995).
46. B. Jessop, 'The Rise of Governance and the Risks of Failure: The Case of Economic Development,' *International Social Science Journal*, No. 155, 1998, p. 31.
47. Lawrence S. Finkelstein, 'What is Global Governance?' *Global Governance*, Vol. 1, 1995, p. 367.
48. Rosenau, 'Governance in a New Global Order,' p. 224.
49. Marie-Claude Smouts, 'The Proper Use of Governance in International Relations,' *International Social Science Journal* 155, March 1998, p. 82.
50. See Knight and Keating, *Global Politics, Globalization and Multilevel Governance Networks.*
51. Smouts, 'The Proper Use of Governance in International Relations', p. 81.
52. The Commission on Global Governance, *Our Global Neighbourhood*, p. 2.
53. Shepard Forman and Derek Segaar, 'New Coalitions for Global Governance: The Changing Dynamics of Multilateralism,' Centre on International Cooperation, New York University, 2004, p. 1.
54. Smouts, 'The Proper Use of Governance in International Relations', p. 86.
55. See Mihály Simai, *The Future of Global Governance: Managing Risk and Change in the International System* (Washington, DC: United States Institute of Peace, 1994).
56. Rosenau, 'Governance in a New Global Order,' p. 224.
57. Oran R. Young, *Governance in World Affairs* (Ithaca, New York: Cornell University Press, 1999), p. 1.
58. A. Leroy Bennett and James K. Oliver, *International Organizations: Principles and Issues*, 7th edition (New Jersey: Prentice Hall, 2002), p. 449.
59. Like Joseph Camilleri, I distinguish between NGOs and CSOs. I see NGOs as a narrower term and a subset of CSOs – the broader, umbrella concept.
60. Jessop, 'The Rise of Governance and the Risks of Failure', p. 29.
61. Examples included Plato (427–347 BC), Aristotle (384–322 BC), St. Augustine (354–430), Thomas Aquinas (1225–74), Confucius (551–479 BC), Mo Ti (5th Century BC), Pierre Dubois (1250–1322), Dante (1265–1321), Erasmus (1466–1536), Grotius (1583–1645) and Channing (1780–1842), to name a few.

62. On the latter, see Shirin M. Rai, 'Gendering Global Governance,' *International Feminist Journal of Politics*, Vol. 6, No. 4, December 2004, pp. 579–601.
63. Robert W. Cox (ed.), *The New Realism: Perspectives on Multilateralism and World Order* (New York: St. Martins Press/United Nations University Press, 1997), p. xvii.
64. Rosenau, 'Governance in a New Global Order,' p. 225.
65. Ibid., p. 230.
66. On this point see, Rosemary Righter, *Utopia Lost: The United Nations and World Order* (New York: Twentieth Century Fund Press, 1995).

9
conclusion: the global governance prospect

jim whitman

Introduction

As we approach the end of the first decade of the twenty-first century, it is instructive to re-examine the territory sketched out by James Rosenau in his seminal article (reprinted in this volume as Chapter 1). At the time of its first publication in 1995, few would have contested that the myriad dynamics that made possible the benefits of globalization were also sources of disorder and boundary-traversing dynamics that offered profound challenges to world order as much as to international relations. But was nascent global politics also producing or facilitating commensurate forms of global governance? The uncertainties, paradoxes and ambiguities highlighted as inescapable features of intellectual engagement with global governance are with us still, but so too are Rosenau's insights into the actors and dynamics that continue to shape world order and to inform investigations into global governance in all its forms. These include the relocation of authority not only 'outward' from states toward forms of transnational control mechanisms, including state/non-state configurations, but also 'downward' to sub-national groupings and even to individuals[1] (sometimes in forms that are not necessarily either inclusive or beneficent). The actors and issues quickly change, but the themes persist, not least because globalization has quickened, spread and intensified. For this reason, the very considerable global governance literature that has now been produced in the years since 'Governance in the Twenty-first Century' has not diminished the degree to which trying to discern, create, adjust or sustain global governance is an intellectual adventure.

Does it remain the case today that 'too much remains murky to project beyond the immediate present and anticipate long-term trajectories'? It is undoubtedly easier to project the outcome of worrying trends and possibilities (the uncertainties of pandemics, climate change and financial turbulence notwithstanding), than to foresee how worldwide patterns of governance between all levels and arenas of human activity might combine in ways that are broadly to the human good. It is worth bearing in mind that if global governance is a 'catch-all' term, then the business of adequately comprehending what global governance we have, let alone calculating what we might be able to create, is a never-ending 'catch-up'. As one analyst describes it, 'Recognizing and recording... changing circumstances, global governance is the catch-all term used to acknowledge the fact and to pattern the complex results of all those strategies, tactics, processes, procedures or programmes coming from a wide variety of interacting interdependent, public and private, individual and collective agents as they try to control, shape, regulate, manage and eventually master whatever is happening on this new terrain.'[2] It is therefore difficult to believe that, important though they are, broadly accepted thematic approaches to understanding the sources and shifting patterns of established and emergent forms of governance will suffice to give us a clear view of world order even in the near future. Indeed, as the chapters of this book illustrate, there is no single, encompassing understanding of global governance as either the province of specific sets of actors or as a regulated condition. It would certainly appear that the actors and conditions that comprise governance are too numerous, varied and dynamic to make a convergence of governances any more likely than world government. Perhaps the best we can say is that the future of world order is less a matter of the 'paths to governance' than the paths that governances create. After all, it takes a great deal of governance of many kinds to support the mainstays of globalization, but not all of its outcomes are either willed or desirable. And default positions and governance failures are also hugely formative – witness the politics of climate change.

In addition to the emphasis on new actors and actor configurations, Rosenau's article also emphasizes the significance of all forms and levels of order for a larger, truly global governance. Instead of asking how global dynamics could be regulated by existing actors and mechanisms (especially international ones), the question is tuned on its head: what effect has globalization had on governance? It is a question that confronts us still, as our world becomes seamless in important ways – that is, any locale or sphere of activity is not merely subject to a large number of transnational forces but is altogether more extensively and immediately permeable than at any time in history. The observation that global dynamics are not only ubiquitous but also multi-directional provides (and in fact, necessitates) a richer understanding of the sources, kinds and means of creating and maintaining the order of the world; it provides an appreciation of the importance of sub-national actors operating within and between established hierarchical structures; and it serves as the foundation of the 'governance without government' phenomenon, given expression three years earlier:

> [G]overnance refers to activities backed by shared goals that may or may not derive from legal and formally prescribed responsibilities and that do not necessarily rely on police powers to overcome defiance and obtain compliance. Governance ... is a more encompassing phenomenon than governments. It embraces government institutions, but it also subsumes informal, non-governmental mechanisms ... Governance is thus a system of rule that is dependent on intersubjective meanings as on formally sanctioned constitutions and charters.[3]

This insight does not dissolve the distinction between state and non-state actors, or between the international and domestic arenas, but it does site all actors in the unfolding drama of the overall order of the world – summative global governance. As developed in 'Global Governance in the Twenty-first Century', it is in the shifting balances between actors of various kinds and at different levels that global governance has its work cut out.

But it remains open to question whether the sum of innumerable governances comprising many novel arrays of significant actors will make overall global governance more stable and resilient, less subject to dominance by one or more powerful actors and more truly inclusive – or, indeed, sufficiently global at a time when planetary sustainability is of immediate, practical importance. The same forces that make new modes of governance and global governance possible are at the same time reconfiguring the landscape of opportunity for more self-interested and even malign actors; creating highly complex tangles of interests and issues which cannot easily be separated and dealt with sequentially; and accelerating political, economic and social change in ways that challenge our deliberative systems.[4]

Chapter 1 began with the observation that 'To anticipate the prospects for global governance in the decades ahead is to discern powerful tensions, profound contradictions, and perplexing paradoxes.' The arrangements of myriad governance actors and the contours of world order buffeted by global dynamics and newly empowered groups and individuals ensure that these relations are still in place. However, it remains important to consider the global governance prospect, with a view to addressing whether, to what degree and by what means we might best mitigate those inevitable tensions and contradictions. At the same time, our essential engagement with the actors and dynamics of rapidly changing world order must leave room for the quality of the orders being produced. Whatever one's attitude towards the normative tenor of international relations and global order more generally, as globalization intensifies, measures of inclusiveness, equity and sustainability are unlikely to be epiphenomenal to global governance. In that spirit, there follow three propositions and three questions.

three propositions

global governance is at least as much a condition of relatedness as it is a distinct form of activity

Globalization greatly increases the number, variety and intensity of nearly all forms of human relatedness – interpersonal, commercial and cultural, to list but a few. To these we need to add 'environmental', since ecosystem degradation is a failure to adjust our behaviours in accord with known or observed ecosystem resilience. As human numbers increase and more nations adopt industrial and consumerist ways of life, the distinction between 'acting in' and 'acting on' our physical environment has begun to dissolve. At the same time, the integrity of the global environment has assumed practical and political significance – for individuals, for enterprises and for the security concerns of nations alike.[5] Because the global arena has assumed practical dimensions that are both pervasive and continuous, the 'interdependence' of IR theory has become a subset of much deeper and more extensive nets of interrelatedness. Of course, globalization has hardly made the world borderless, and nor have 'top-down' and 'bottom-up' become meaningless descriptors. But international relations have gradually become enmeshed in the remarkably varied and complex dynamics of an encompassing global politics, with the effect that states continue to act, powerfully and authoritatively, but they are also acted upon. What this means is that 'governance without governance' has not only a non-state actor dimension, but also incorporates more oblique forms of governance – activities that from a global perspective are effectively undeliberated but which nevertheless arise from, react to and/or impact on the higher-order governances that make them possible. The dense and intricate connectedness of the orders of the world is considerably in excess of the degree to which they are coordinated – and in some cases, fully comprehended – before the emergence of a crisis. The global financial turbulence from 2007 provides countless examples.

An emphasis on the relational over the 'command' aspects of governance bears some similarity with the Marxist view that to fully comprehend the meaning of capital, one must regard it not as a thing but as a social relation. But while for Marxists, capital drives the division of labour and social stratification, governance is an outcome of extensive and varied relations, and many of its formally elaborated expressions are designed to adjust and/or regulate relations of various kinds, world trade most notably.

These arrangements make generous provision for the interests of the powerful, but they are hardly determinist; and there is even the view that 'While ... sizable areas of global life rest on a form of governance that lacks democratic accountability, ... the dispersal of authority in globalized space is so widespread that severe violations of democratic values cannot be readily concentrated in hegemonic hands.'[6]

Many of the orders that comprise summative global governance are not global in character – that is, in terms of their compass or reach – but only by dint of their relationship to the aggregate of all governances. Global governance, particularly in its summative form, does not signify one or more shared goals so much as highly diffuse and bewilderingly complex nets of relationships. These can be both highly tensioned and remarkably extensive (as in the case of climate change), but they can also extend considerably beyond the ordering impulses of interested actors, in ways that bring globalization as a condition remarkably close to summative global governance, but without the latter's reassuring resonances. For example, soaring copper prices and keen demand from China has brought about a steep rise in thefts from railway lines, water facilities and electricity stations in a number of European countries, occasioning serious delays and dangers.[7]

A good deal of attention in global governance studies has been devoted to the empowerment of non-state actors and new actor configurations, with a particular bias towards the possibilities for progressive politics.[8] Beyond the acknowledged facilitation of transnational crime syndicates and terrorist networks, some excellent research has been conducted on the meanings of private authority in global governance.[9] But in the wake of the global financial turbulence from 2007, there are some important research lines to be opened up which investigate private actor networks – with the networks considered less as now-familiar actor linkages and state/organizational configurations[10] than as electronically mediated, high-speed forms of interconnectedness. The disruptive possibilities and the limitations of our existing forms of governance are already apparent in the speed, extent and seriousness of global financial turmoil. The governance implications, both specific and thematic, are important areas for future research.

global governance in any form will not necessarily ensure coherence or sustainability

One of the legacies of the global governance literature as it has developed to date is that it has helped to 'fill in the gaps' of IR theory between hierarchically ordered levels and types of actors. In other words, global governance embraces and attempts to site actors and dynamics that many another theoretical construct would relegate to insignificance – and in the process, it outlines the many important ways in which state power is variously complemented, supplemented, challenged and subverted. There is little doubt that our concurrent attempts to comprehend the complexities of globalization and its nets of causal relations have also advanced and strengthened this perspective. Characterizations of international order such as the following are now unexceptional: '[T]he international world is governed. The domain outside and between nation states is neither an anarchic political space beyond the reach of law, nor a domain of market freedom immune from regulation. Our international world is the product of an intense and ongoing project of regulation and management.'[11]

Yet there is no quality common to human social orders that will necessarily make them compatible, or ensure that in combination they will produce a larger order that is at least the sum of the parts – or one that is coherent. It is for this reason that definitions of governance inclusive of state/non-state, public/private and high/low only sketch the territory, rather than indicate a positive trajectory: 'Given a perspective that allows for governance occurring apart from what governments do, ... governance is conceived as systems of rule, as the purposive activities of any collectivity that sustain mechanisms designed to ensure its safety, prosperity, coherence, stability, and continuance.'[12]

'Purposive activities' include criminal and pernicious endeavours, the largest of which also requires systems of rule. But the problem of ensuring that innumerable governances cohere – that is, they serve a consistent, global purpose – extends far beyond invalidating and countering parasitic or destructive organizational forms. Concerns for the prosperity, stability and continuance of any social group or enterprise are universal, but their formulation is, at least in the first instance, particular. As matter of course, they are not formulated with a global constituency or planetary considerations in mind. We can speak easily and meaningfully about both sectoral or summative global governance, but the depiction of either can obscure as much as it reveals.

> Occasionally, of course, we do get a glimpse of these background vocabularies, rules and conditions – as in the trade struggles over 'normal' levels of background regulation. It is difficult to think about the ebb and flow of military violence in a place like Congo without thinking about the norms and institutional practices responsible for trade in diamonds and other materials. Just as it is difficult to think about a global health crisis like AIDS by focusing only on the United Nations, the World Bank or World Health Organization, while ignoring intellectual property law and big pharmaceutical companies.[13]

Governances clash with the frequency that any group perceives (and pursues) its interests in an exclusive, or short-term fashion, abstracted from other constituencies and dynamics. This is perhaps clear enough in the case of state interests and the global governance of the environment, but the background to state recalcitrance in climate change negotiations throughout the developed world is popular unease about the costs and impacts of necessary carbon emission reductions on patterns of energy consumption and mobility that are deeply embedded in ways of life down to the local and individual levels. This pattern repeats itself elsewhere in the world, albeit in conditions considerably less cushioned against shocks. For example, mass culls of poultry are an effective means of preventing the spread of avian flu outbreaks, but in parts of Asia where small-scale animal husbandry is a hedge against destitution, the demands of global health governance can have terrible repercussions at the local level, as the World Bank acknowledges:

> The livelihoods of the rural poor are particularly threatened. The Asian region is home to two thirds of the world's poor, with the great

beneficial behaviours – norms. But there is little effective enforcement provision for international laws; and global governance has no 'command' authority. This means that even for a specific issue, a large part of effective global governance – that portion which relies on state cooperation and furtherance – can be dependent on normative expression at two levels: a critical mass of citizen willingness; and state adherence to formal agreements with other states. One might suppose that at minimum, looming crises and clearly drawn lines of self interest or negotiable trade-offs would concentrate minds, but norms have a good deal of inertia, which even planet-threatening climate change has been slow to alter. If law enforcement is not an option in this and other cases, and if directive, norm-contravening action by states, either unilaterally or in concert with others is unlikely, the importance of norms – and of normative change – is thrown into sharp relief.

There is an established literature on the role of norms in international politics;[18] and on the role of 'norm entrepreneurs',[19] particularly as a subset of the literature on transnational NGOs.[20] But what is the prospect of normative change on the likely scale required to reverse the most threatening and/or debilitating global conditions and dynamics? As evidence of what is possible, one might point to the 60-year history of human rights which has created a widely and deeply held conviction in the hearts of peoples everywhere and has become a determining force in national and international politics. But normative change of such magnitude is historically unique; it is by no means clear that globalized conditions make something on the same scale more likely, or that it can be brought about on a timescale set by pressing developments; or that it will have the purchase and resilience to withstand violations or the sort that the human rights regime has endured.[21] To date, the attention in the global governance literature devoted to norms has largely focused on new actor configurations and the ways/extent to which norm entrepreneurship and advocacy has had an impact in the national and international realms, most often with an emphasis on the shifting patterns of authority, allegiance and legitimacy as transnational dynamics have begun to make themselves felt. But the prospects for norm transformation of a kind and on a scale that might well be required to enable action to address global issues in a concerted manner are much less clear. As a global governance thematic consideration, this should move centre-stage, incorporating the insights and investigative lines of several disciplines.

three questions

governance of, by and for whom?

What is common to all forms of governance is a desire to create and sustain order, but the crucial 'of, by and for whom?' questions mean that a substantial portion of the energies devoted to governance will find expression as contention, as opportunistic manoeuvring or as exercises in power. Governance and global governance are not technocratic exercises, or detached from self-serving interests; and there is nothing in the *fact* of any particular form of governance that promises equity, comprehensiveness or even legitimacy and accountability – deficiencies in the latter two is a risk implicit in at least some forms of 'governance without government'. Similarly, there is no issue so large, encompassing or threatening (climate change again) that it dissolves more exclusive or localized interests, or obviates the need for hard negotiation; and questions of justice and equity underpin more calculable considerations of cost and/or burden-sharing. At the same time, however, sectoral interests can be powerful advocates for much wider global public goods, as is the case with the reinsurance industry's stance on climate change.[22]

But 'of, by and for whom?' global governance questions cannot be fully addressed by considerations of actor types, exclusive (and sometimes countervailing) interests and well-defined issues. Although global governance as an activity is most obvious when international organizations or the international system as a whole responds to an urgent need (such as the global financial turbulence that ensued from 2007), summative global governance – those often less visible but determining sources of world order – has in recent years come under closer scrutiny for the patterns of domination, exclusion and disenfranchisement which appear integral to, rather than an unintended outcome of, the maintenance of peace and prosperity for the privileged.[23] Seen in this way, the answer to many 'of by, and for whom?' global governance questions can be seen to have an underside; and the 'global' quality of global governance can be considerably more qualified than the word suggests.

In any event, as globalization makes local conditions and individual prospects ever more subject to dynamics and decision-making distant both physically and politically, it is going to become more difficult to reconcile the needs of systemic stability against the lives of individuals and communities.

is governance global or just all over the map?

What would effective, summative global governance comprise? How might it come about in the absence of a 'governance of governances' (in short, a world government) and with an international system which is now as likely to be acted upon as act, that the sum of innumerable governances might suffice for something more than a set-of-all-sets category; something more than the sum of innumerable parts? Can globalization be governed by the globalization of regulation, or by an accumulation of uncoordinated but nevertheless complementary sectoral global governances? For any stated purpose, what would an adequate global governance be the governance *of*?

can global governance keep pace?

The distinct possibility of runaway climate change,[24] even in the face of protracted international negotiations and global governance arrangements, obliges us to confront this question. And in posing it, we implicitly accept that we are capable of creating an ungovernable world – that cumulatively and inadvertently, the outcomes of our ways of life can supplant, outrun or overwhelm our systems of governance and global governance. Confronting this as a foreseeable prospect rather than as a logical possibility underpins the considerable literature advocating immediate and far-reaching initiatives to reverse climate change, but it is not yet reflected in the more general global governance literature. This is partly an outcome of the very considerable implications which the emergence of the 'global governance' concept has held for IR, IPE and the study of international organizations; and the importance of recognizing and understanding new actor configurations and modes of operation as part of the changes wrought by globalizing processes of many kinds. And because there is hardly a shortage of what have come to be regarded as global issues, there has been a concentration on functionalist and/or problem-solving approaches to the study of global governance, both as practice and potential.

But undesirable forms of complexity of the sort we are now capable of producing both by accident and design are not always or easily amenable to the application of complex 'solutions', as scholars in other fields have argued for some years, drawing attention to the kinds of assumptions that routinely feature in global governance. For example, Joseph Tainter has argued that 'Complexity is a long-term paradox of problem-solving. It facilitates the resolution of problems in the short run while undermining the ability to solve them in the long term. Maintaining a society or other kind of institution requires that the problem-solving system itself become sustainable.'[25] Yet the familiar logic which informs both national interests and 'solutions' to the problems they inevitably bring in their wake, is with us still – as in the following, a report sponsored by the US Department of Commerce and the US National Science Foundation, advocating a national effort to advance the convergence of nanotechnology, biotechnology, robotics, information technology and cognitive science: 'Science and technology will increasingly dominate the world, as population, resource exploitation, and potential social conflict grow. Therefore, the success of this convergent technologies priority area is essential for the future of humanity';[26] and 'Unification of science based on unity in nature and its holistic investigation will lead to technological convergence and a more efficient societal structure for reaching human goals.'[27] Of course, there are few human goals that are uncontestable; and many that are unsustainable, or which will add further complexities to the already considerable burdens of governance. Even if we were able to count on unprecedented political consensus, we might do well to consider whether the logic of 'more of the same, but better' will suffice for our governance arrangements any more than for the satisfaction of our interests and appetites on a global scale.

Fifty years ago, Geoffrey Vickers argued '[I]n the social as in the individual field the key to well-being lies more in the design of our aspirations than in the devising of means to satisfy them and ... any approach which takes as a given the particular design of the moment, especially today, is bound to miss what most needs to be scrutinized.'[28] Perhaps we need to begin a consideration of the global governance prospect with a humility appropriate to the circumstances we have already created for ourselves and others.

notes

1. James N. Rosenau, *People Count! Networked Individuals in Global Politics* (Boulder: Paradigm Publishers, 2007).
2. Jean-François Thibault, 'As if the world were a virtual global polity: the political philosophy of global governance,' available at *First Press*, http://www.theglobalsite.ac.uk/press/108thibault.htm#The%20Politics%20of%20Global%20Governance
3. James N. Rosenau, 'Governance, Order and Change in World Politics,' in James N. Rosenau and Ernst-Otto Czempiel (eds), *Governance without Government: Order and Change in World Politics* (Cambridge: Cambridge University Press, 1992), p. 4.

4. Jim Whitman, 'The Challenge to Deliberative Systems of Technological Systems Convergence,' *Innovation: The European Journal of Social Sciences*, Vol. 20, No. 4, December 2007, pp. 329–342.
5. US Center for Naval Analyses, 'National Security and the Threat of Climate Change,' April 2007, available at http://securityandclimate.cna.org/report/
6. James N. Rosenau, 'Change, Complexity and Governance in a Globalizing Space,' in Jon Pierre (ed.), *Debating Governance* (Oxford: Oxford University Press, 2000), p. 193.
7. David Willey, 'Copper theft stalls Italy trains,' *BBC News*, 13 November 2006, available at: http://news.bbc.co.uk/2/hi/europe/6144464.stm; Dan Milmo and Mark Milner, 'Copper thieves cause havoc for commuters,' *The Guardian*, 28 May 2007, available at http://www.guardian.co.uk/uk/2007/may/28/transport.topstories3
8. See, for example, Margaret E. Keck and Kathryn Sikkink, *Activists beyond Borders: Advocacy Networks in International Politics* (Ithaca: Cornell University Press, 1998); Helen Yanacopulos, 'Patterns of Governance: The Rise of Transnational Coalitions of NGOs,' *Global* Society, Vol. 19, No. 3 (2005), pp. 247–266; Helmut Anheier a.o., *Global Civil Society Yearbook 2009* (London: Sage, 2009).
9. Rodney Bruce Hall and Thomas J. Beirsteker (eds), *The Emergence of Private Authority in Global Governance* (Cambridge: Cambridge University Press, 2002).
10. James Rosenau has observed that '…hierarchies are being supplemented and not replaced by networks'. James Rosenau, *Distant Proximities: Dynamics beyond Globalization* (Princeton: Princeton University Press, 2003), p. 266. See also Anne-Marie Slaughter, *A* New *World Order* (Princeton: Princeton University Press, 2004).
11. David Kennedy, 'Challenging Expert Rule: The Politics of Global Governance,' *Sydney Law Review*, Vol. 27, No. 5 (March 2005), p. 6.
12. Rosenau, 'Change, Complexity and Governance in a Globalizing Space,' p. 171.
13. Kennedy, 'Challenging Expert Rule,' p. 14.
14. World Bank, 'Program Framework Document for Proposed Loans/Credits/Grants in the Amount of US$500 Million Equivalent for a Global Program for Avian Influenza Control and Human Pandemic Preparedness and Response,' (Report 34386), p. 3.
15. Brian R. Copeland and M. Scott Taylor, *Trade and the Environment: Theory and Evidence* (Princeton: Princeton University Press, 2005).
16. John Keane, *Global Civil Society?* (Cambridge: Cambridge University Press, 2003).
17. David Kennedy, 'Challenging Expert Rule,' p. 16.
18. See, for example, Ethan A. Nadelmann, 'Global Prohibition Regimes: The Evolution of Norms in International Society,' *International Organization*, Vol. 44, No. 4, Autumn 1990; Martha Finnemore and Kathryn Sikkink, 'International Norm Dynamics and Political Change,' *International Organization*, Vol. 52, No. 4, Autumn 1998, p. 916.
19. Cass R. Sunstein, 'Social Norms and Social Roles,' *Columbia Law Review*, Vol. 96, No. 4, 1996, pp. 929–930.

20. Margaret E. Keck and Kathryn Sikkink, *Activists Beyond Borders*; Ann Marie Clark, *Diplomacy of Conscience: Amnesty International and Changing Human Rights Norms* (Princeton: Princeton University Press, 2001).
21. Jim Whitman, *The Fundamentals of Global Governance* (Basingstoke: Palgrave, 2009), chapter 10, 'The Human Rights regimes as Global Governance.'
22. See the position adopted by Swiss re, available at http://www.swissre.com/pws/about%20us/knowledge_expertise/top%20topics/our%20position%20and%20objectives.html?contentIDR=c21767004561734fb900fb2ee2bd2155&useDefaultText=0&useDefaultDesc=0
23. Jörg Friedrichs, 'Global Governance as the Hegemonic Project of Transatlantic Civil Society,' in Markus Lederer and Philipp S. Müller (eds), *Criticizing Global Governance* (Basingstoke: Palgrave, 2005), pp. 47, 53–54; Mark Duffield, *Global Governance and the New* Wars: *The Merging of Development and Security* (London: Zed Books, 2001).
24. Paul Brown, 'How close is runaway climate change?' *The Guardian*, 18 October 2006.
25. Joseph A. Tainter, 'Problem Solving: Complexity, History, Sustainability,' *Population and Environment*, Vol. 22, No. 1, September 2000, p. 36; see also, T.F.H. Allen, Joseph A. Tainter and Thomas W. Hoekstra, *Supply-Side Sustainability* (New York: Columbia University Press, 2003).
26. M. C. Roco and W. S. Bainbridge, 'Executive Summary,' in NSF/DOC-sponsored report, Converging *Technologies for Improving Human Performance: Nanotechnology, Biotechnology, Information Technology and Cognitive Science* (Arlington, Virginia, 2002), available at http://www.wtec.org/ConvergingTechnologies/Report/NBIC_report.pdf, p. xiii.
27. Ibid., p. 1.
28. Geoffrey Vickers, *The Undirected Society, Essays on the Human Implications of Industrialization in Canada* (Toronto: University of Toronto Press, 1959), p. 55.

index